The Prevention of Crime

Social and Situational Strategies

CONTEMPORARY ISSUES IN CRIME AND JUSTICE SERIES
Todd Clear, *Series Editor*

The Prevention of Crime

Social and Situational Strategies

DENNIS P. ROSENBAUM

UNIVERSITY OF ILLINOIS AT CHICAGO

ARTHUR J. LURIGIO

LOYOLA UNIVERSITY OF CHICAGO

ROBERT C. DAVIS

VICTIM SERVICES, NEW YORK

WADSWORTH
CENGAGE Learning

Australia • Brazil • Japan • Korea • Mexico • Singapore • Spain • United Kingdom • United States

WADSWORTH
CENGAGE Learning

The Prevention of Crime: Social and Situational Strategies
Dennis P. Rosenbaum, Arthur J. Lurigio, Robert C. Davis

Criminal Justice Editor: Sabra Horne

Development Editor: Dan Alpert

Production Developmental Editor: Claire Masson

Editorial Assistant: Cherie Hackelberg

Marketing Manager: Mike Dew

Senior Project Editor: Debby Kramer

Print Buyer: Karen Hunt

Permissions Editor: Bob Kauser

Production: Robin Gold/Forbes Mill Press

Copy Editor: Robin Gold

Cover Designer: Sandra Kelch

Compositor: Forbes Mill Press

For product information and technology assistance, contact us at **Cengage Learning Customer & Sales Support, 1-800-354-9706**

For permission to use material from this text or product, submit all requests online at **cengage.com/permissions** Further permissions questions can be emailed to **permissionrequest@cengage.com**

Library of Congress Control Number: 98-14883

ISBN-13: 978-0-534-50760-2

ISBN-10: 0-534-50760-3

Wadsworth
10 Davis Drive,
Belmont, CA 94002-3098
USA

Cengage Learning is a leading provider of customized learning solutions with office locations around the globe, including Singapore, the United Kingdom, Australia, Mexico, Brazil, and Japan. Locate your local office at: **international.cengage.com/region**

Cengage Learning products are represented in Canada by Nelson Education, Ltd.

For your course and learning solutions, visit **academic.cengage.com**

Purchase any of our products at your local college store or at our preferred online store **www.ichapters.com**

Printed in the United States of America
6 7 8 9 10   15 14 13 12 11
FD361

Contents

p.viii = blank

Foreword

Surely there can be no more important question confronting today's students of crime than how to prevent it. We accept, of course, that "doing justice" is the central responsibility of the criminal justice system; yet we yearn for a society that is more just for all its citizens, not merely those who are accused of crimes. We recognize that in preventing crimes, we help construct a society that is more safe and a world that is better for us all.

The criminal justice system is constructed, in part, to prevent crime by deterring potential offenders and incapacitating actual ones. To this end, the American justice system has grown in unprecedented ways since the late 1960s—more than a 1,000 percent increase in the budget enables the system to handle a 500 percent increase in offenders since that time. Aside from computers, no other occupation has grown at this pace in our lifetimes.

The irony, of course, is that we are not that much safer today than when this stupendous growth first began. Crime is down in recent years, but today's decrease is part of a cycle: It follows periods of dramatic increases in crime that themselves succeeded drops in crime. We do not want to belittle the current reduction in crime, for this is a welcome change in our society. But after the enormous increases in the criminal justice system in the last 30 years, it turns out that the overall level of safety is just about the same—a statistical wash. For these reasons criminologists have begun investigating crime prevention programs that do not emphasize the accusing-convicting-punishing aspects of the criminal justice system but, rather, give central concern to analyzing the sources of criminal activity and eliminating them. Programs that take this approach are known as crime prevention programs.

Although there is a great deal of this kind of "crime prevention" activity underway all over the world, very little has been written to describe and analyze these approaches. That is why I am so pleased to introduce *The Prevention of Crime: Social and Situational Strategies,* by Dennis P. Rosenbaum, Arthur J. Lurigio, and Robert C. Davis, as the newest addition to The Wadsworth Contemporary Issues on Crime and Justice Series. This series provides readers with in-depth analyses of important and emerging topics in crime and justice—topics that might receive scant attention in typical textbooks but about which sophisticated students of crime and justice need to be informed. I am particularly delighted to welcome this text to the series, as it provides the most comprehensive, current, and well-organized analysis of crime prevention programs available today.

This book provides everything a person needs to know about crime prevention. After describing the historical basis for today's crime prevention movement, the authors provide an authoritative summary of several main crime prevention orientations, including self-protection, situational crime prevention, and community organization. Self-protection strategies—the steps people take to feel safer by acting against those who might victimize them—are not especially new, but they have often seemed to be a kind of idiosyncratic, marginal crime prevention. This book shows how a growing collection of studies support certain forms of self-protective action.

Situational crime prevention strategies are based on the well-established notion that crimes occur most often in particular places, at particular times, and under particular circumstances. To prevent crimes in these situations requires a strategy—sometimes very simple in design and execution—built on a foundation of understanding the situational components of these criminal events. Community organizing involves broader and stronger roles for citizens in preventing crime. This orientation has a long history and is very popular, but it also proves to be a very difficult approach with which to achieve success.

The authors introduce us to these orientations and provide a thorough review of what is now known about them. Many of the studies of crime prevention are very recent, so this book can also be used as an up-to-date review of what we know about how to make society safer. On a topic to which much bombast is often devoted, this book adds a grounding in research findings and actual results that makes it as valuable as it is unique.

In the end, we all know that successful crime prevention is a critical priority. Preventing crimes not only improves the quality of everyday life, but it also avoids the enormous financial and emotional costs crime imposes on its victims. In today's political rhetoric, people often express the problem of justice as though it is a contest between concerns about offenders and caring about their victims. If we really care about victims but also are concerned about offenders, there can be no more effective strategy for achieving both ends then to prevent crimes in the first place.

I commend this book to you, the reader. It is the first comprehensive treatment of a topic that will grow in popularity and importance in coming years, and because it is such a good book, it sets a standard other authors will find difficult to match.

Todd R. Clear, Series Editor
Florida State University

DEDICATION

In memory of Rose

Dennis P. Rosenbaum

For Michael, Caitlin, and Brianna

Arthur J. Lurigio

For Caitlin and Jennifer

Robert C. Davis

Preface

Since 1965 the United States has been deeply engaged in a domestic "war on crime." Despite the changing face of this war (violence, gang activity, drug abuse), the primary question has always been this: "How can we improve the efficiency and effectiveness of the criminal justice system—the law enforcement, judicial, and correctional institutions?" We wrote this book to turn the spotlight away from criminal justice procedures and policies to ask the question, "What is the role of ordinary citizens, neighborhood organizations, and noncriminal justice resources in the fight against crime?" This book is about the prevention of crime through social and situational strategies.

For students interested in crime prevention strategies, this book covers nearly three decades of research and practice as we review and evaluate hundreds of research studies and demonstration programs. Using the best available data, we describe the nature, extent, and effectiveness of community and situational crime prevention activities. The theory behind these initiatives is also articulated so that students will have a framework to help understand and interpret the research findings and conclusions.

For the ordinary citizen or community group, this book contains practical information about how best to prevent crime. For those interested in reducing their chances of being a crime victim, we review strategies for avoiding crime and describe effective self-defense techniques when facing a confrontational offender. For persons interested in protecting their property and loved ones, we examine the effectiveness of household and neighborhood crime prevention measures. For community organizers and police officers interested in creating and sustaining citizen patrols, neighborhood watches, and other community anticrime strategies, we review what is currently known about the advantages and disadvantages of these initiatives. For public planners and policy makers, this book provides an in-depth look at strategies for modifying the physical environment so that opportunities for crime can be significantly reduced. We also assess media strategies for educating the general public about crime prevention measures. For police administrators, this book examines the cutting edge of organizational reform efforts designed to create partnerships with, and enhance the contribution of, the community in the fight against crime and drug abuse. We explore the upside and downside of community policing and problem-oriented policing in detail as they pertain to the effective mobilization of resources outside the police organization.

For policy makers, professionals, and community leaders, this book is intended as a status report on what works and what does not work in the field of crime prevention. Drawing on our experience as evaluation researchers for nearly three decades, we feel qualified to help policy analysts and administrators distinguish between research findings that are worthy of serious attention and those that are based on poor research methods.

Yet this book is more than a status report on what works in this field—we believe it will stimulate the reader (as it did us) to think twice about how our society should approach crime prevention policies in the future. On the one hand, our review of the literature highlights some promising programs and strategies that seem to be effective in lowering neighborhood crime, disorder, and fear of crime. On the other hand, we also identify some rarely discussed drawbacks of community and situational crime prevention strategies. Many crime prevention measures are designed to protect individual property and persons, but these private-minded tactics can have adverse affects on the larger community. Also, various social and situational crime prevention strategies run the risk of violating privacy rights, enhancing fear of crime, encouraging vigilantism, and displacing criminal activity to other locations. Consequently, throughout this book the reader is reminded of the delicate balance between individual rights and community values.

These potential drawbacks of crime prevention strategies raise serious concerns but are dwarfed by a larger problem, namely, that our society's most effective community crime prevention programs are designed to *continually increase* the number of youths who have contact with the criminal justice system. We discuss the profound implications of this de facto policy and encourage policymakers to support a new goal of *reducing* the number of youths who have contact with the criminal justice system.

As we explore the benefits *and* costs to society of traditional crime prevention strategies, we encourage our readers to think about alternative pathways for building a safer society. We argue that enforcement strategies should continue, but should be supplemented with greater attention to programs that focus on early intervention in the lives of at-risk youths, delinquent youths,

and their families. We also believe that more attention should be given to opportunity reduction strategies that seek to deter or prevent criminal activity *before* contact with the criminal justice system (for example, situational crime
prevention measures) as long as these approaches do not jeopardize other cher-
ished community values. Finally, our analysis of crime prevention policy underscores the inherent limitations of individual and neighborhood-level
strategies—however promising they appear to be in the short run—and argues
for a more comprehensive approach to preventing crime. This conclusion is
based on the observation that the quality of community life is influenced by
macrolevel forces (economic and political decisions) that are outside the community and beyond the control of ordinary citizens. These forces, and the resources they represent, must be included in any new crime prevention equation
if we ever expect to see long-lasting improvements.

Writing this book was not an easy task for us because of the many com-
mitments we have to other people and other projects. We simply want to
thank our families for being supportive and tolerant of this work. Our
spouses—Susan, Colleen, and Pat—deserve special thanks. Maureen Allen,
Leanne Brecklin, Sandra Kaminska-Costello, Kathleen O'Connell, Garrett
O'Keefe, and Sarah Ullman also deserve thanks for reviewing various chapters. We also thank Sabra Horne at Wadsworth for keeping us on a reasonable
schedule and Robin Gold for her superb editing. Thank you also to the re-
viewers of this book: Stan Shernock, Norwich University; Roger D. Thomp-
son, University of Tennessee at Chattanooga; Marcus Felson, Rutgers
University; Daniel Baker, University of South Carolina

Dennis
Art
Rob

PART I

The Problem of Crime Control and Prevention

p.2 = blank

1

❖

A Thirty-Year War
on Crime

Finding a Place for
"Crime Prevention"

From the revolutionary war to the present, violence has been a defining feature of our nation. Although moral outrage against violence has been expressed at various times in American history, not until we reached the
turbulent 1960s—characterized by assassinations, civil disobedience, and
urban riots (all captured on national television)—did crime become a national
problem that required "urgent" policy attention. These sensational events co-
incided with large increases in more ordinary crimes against persons and property, which helped ensure that the "crime problem" remains a hot political
issue. Indeed, in recent years, national opinion polls have found that violent
crime is frequently considered the single "most important problem facing this
country today"—ahead of the economy, unemployment, poverty, healthcare,
and other problems that are regularly on the minds of American adults (see
Maguire & Pastore, 1996, p. 128).

Our country has been engaged in a domestic "war on crime" for more than
three decades. During this time, much has been written about the role of the
criminal justice system in this "war," but little scholarly research and debate exists on the crime-fighting roles of individual citizens, neighborhood organizations, and other resources outside the system. Furthermore, there has been
considerable discussion about reactive strategies for fighting crime "after the
fact," but comparatively little about preventive strategies. We wrote this book
to address this imbalance and help fill the knowledge gap about community-
oriented efforts to prevent crime.

We look critically at a wide range of individual and collective efforts to prevent crime, disorder, and neighborhood drug sales and describe the nature, extent, and effectiveness of community crime prevention activities in the United States. Specific programs and general strategies are placed in their proper theoretical and policy context, and then we critically assess them using the best available scientific evidence. In this first chapter, we briefly analyze the personal, social, and political factors that have contributed to a growing interest in the concepts of crime prevention and citizen participation. This chapter also provides an overview of the book itself.

COST OF CRIME

In communities across America, the public's concern about crime reflects, in part, the incredible costs associated with high levels of criminal victimization. Being the victim of serious crime often results in medical bills, property losses, and lost work productivity and wages. For the taxpayer, more crime translates into higher taxes for emergency responses by police, fire, and victim services. In addition, individual victims and neighborhoods must face the less tangible (but very real and quantifiable) losses associated with pain, suffering, and reductions in quality of life. Detailed estimates by economists and criminal justice experts indicate that, in the United States, the financial impact of personal crime on victims is staggering—approximately $450 billion annually in direct and indirect costs (Miller, Cohen, & Wiersema, 1996). This conservative estimate does not include the cost of maintaining a massive criminal justice system—estimated at $93.7 billion in fiscal year 1992, including approximately $41 billion for police, $21 billion for the judiciary, and $31 billion for corrections (Maguire & Pastore, 1996, p. 4)—or the multibillion dollar cost of drug abuse (Office of National Drug Control Policy, 1997).

For the average citizen, the cost of crime (and the impetus for action) is measured not so much by public expenditures but, rather, by the impact of crime on their personal lives and their neighborhoods. In survey after survey, urban residents express their anger and fear about local drug markets and gangs, their concern for the safety of their children, and their frustration regarding growing signs of disorder and incivility (Skogan, 1990). Today, many inner-city neighborhoods are characterized by loud music, youths hanging out, graffiti, and garbage on the streets. In higher-crime areas, local residents feel overwhelmed by open-air drug markets, gang conflict, prostitution, armed robbery, and (more privately) domestic violence (see Kelling & Coles, 1996).

One of the more destructive by-products of public disorder and crime is the attendant escalation in fear of crime (Skogan, 1990). Although the nation as a whole is not as fearful as the media often contend, fear and perceptions of risk are substantial problems in their own right and contribute significantly to neighborhood decline in communities where the threat of crime is high (Lewis & Salem, 1986). From 1965 to 1993, between 30 percent and 45 percent of U.S. adults consistently reported being afraid to walk alone at night within a one-mile radius of their homes (Maguire & Pastore, 1996, p. 151). By itself, fear has a number of adverse consequences on individuals and neighborhoods, including increased avoidance and isolation behaviors, which weaken society's informal defenses against criminality (see Rosenbaum & Heath, 1990).

GOVERNMENT RESPONSES TO CRIME

The nation has struggled with the problem of crime and how to control it for more than 30 years. Our domestic war on crime was launched by President Johnson in 1965, and, by the end of that decade, numerous recommendations were offered by the President's Commission on Law Enforcement and the Administration of Justice (1966–1967), the National Advisory Commission on Civil Disorders (1967–1968), and the National Commission on the Causes and Prevention of Violence (1968–1969). Despite encouragement by these commissions to pay more attention to community factors that can help prevent crime, our national crime control policy during the past 30 years has retained an unwavering focus on strengthening and professionalizing the criminal justice system.

Government officials responded to crime by throwing large sums of money at the criminal justice system, which yielded a rapid growth in budgets and personnel over several decades (see Jacob & Lineberry, 1982). Notably, at the recommendation of the President's Commission, the Law Enforcement Assistance Administration (LEAA) was created in 1968 to help improve the efficiency and effectiveness of the system. Over the next three decades, the infusion of federal dollars and technical assistance and harsher criminal codes helped an expanding army of law enforcement officers, prosecutors, and judges pursue their enforcement objectives. In the final analysis, the system—with the full support of lawmakers—emerged as an effective machine for increasing the numbers of arrests, convictions, and longer sentences for a wide range of offenders.

During these 30 years, criminologists have repeatedly questioned this approach to criminal justice. In a nutshell, our nation has sought to control and prevent crime primarily by deterrence (using apprehension and prosecution to increase the cost of future offending), by incapacitation (locking up repeat offenders for long periods to keep them off the streets), and by rehabilitation (helping incarcerated offenders turn their lives around). Reports from the National Academy of Sciences have concluded that little evidence can be mustered to support these traditional approaches to crime control and prevention (Blumstein, Cohen, & Nagin, 1978; Blumstein, Cohen, Roth, & Visher, 1986; Sechrest, White, & Brown, 1979).[1]

As we near the end of the century, the results of this reactive criminal-justice approach to crime control have become more apparent. Beefed-up enforcement of an expanding set of criminal codes has yielded massive jail and prison populations (Gilliard & Beck, 1996). As the cost of operating a multibillion-dollar criminal-justice system continues to escalate, and as prisons look more like warehouses for young persons of color (Mauer & Huling, 1995; Tonry, 1995), there should be little doubt that our current approach to crime control is neither cost effective nor just. Since the early 1980s, a substantial number of criminal justice scholars and leading professionals have argued that the criminal justice system cannot, by itself, solve the nation's crime and drug problems (for example, Lavrakas, 1985). Help is desperately needed from outside the walls of these bureaucracies, and new ways of thinking about crime control and prevention are urgently needed from inside the system as well. Fortunately, some clear "thinkers" and talented "doers" are beginning to chart a new course.

COMMUNITY RESPONSES TO CRIME

If traditional crime control measures are not cost-effective, what are the alternatives? Several national commissions have recommended expanding the role of ordinary citizens, as well as those of agencies and institutions outside the criminal justice system. The comprehensive and thoughtful report of the President's Commission (1967), *The Challenge of Crime in a Free Society*, cogently describes the alternative:

> While this report has concentrated on recommendations for action by governments, the Commission is convinced that governmental actions will not be enough. Crime is a social problem that is interwoven with almost every aspect of American life.. . . Controlling crime is the business of every American institution. Controlling crime is the business of every American. (p. xi)

The federal government should be credited with playing an important, albeit limited, role in promoting citizen involvement in civic life and crime control. Starting with the Kennedy administration and the civil rights movement, the government has encouraged citizens to get involved in decisions regarding community activism, health care, and the environment (Grant, 1981;

---

1. To be fair, deterrence and incapacitation have been tried extensively, but rehabilitation has never been fully tested. Our nation has never committed adequate resources to rehabilitate and reintegrate offenders into the community. Hence, the viability of this approach remains largely untested.

Kramer, 1969). During the 1960s, the United States witnessed a sizable growth in the number of grassroots community organizations (Bell & Held, 1969). Throughout the 1970s and 1980s, the Justice Department encouraged local law enforcement agencies to stimulate citizen participation in passive crime prevention programs such that citizens would serve as the "eyes and ears" of the police (Rosenbaum, 1987; 1988).

In the midst of all the rhetoric about community crime prevention, the federal government remained unwilling to provide direct financial support to community-based organizations until the late 1970s. Three programs—the Community Anti-Crime Program in 1977 (Krug, 1983), the Urban Crime Prevention Program in 1980 (Roehl & Cook, 1984), and the Community Responses to Drug Abuse Program in 1989 (Rosenbaum, Bennett, Lindsay, & Wilkinson, 1994)—are noteworthy because they involved small grants from the Justice Department to community groups for the purpose of encouraging citizen crime prevention actions at the neighborhood level. Although many of these early programs were poorly planned and weakly implemented, they represented an important breakthrough for community organizations and underscored the need for cooperative partnerships between law enforcement and the community.

Since 1994, the federal government has played a much more significant role in promoting community crime prevention activities. The Justice Department's Office of Justice Programs[2] and its Office for Community-Oriented Policing spent more than three billion dollars in fiscal year 1996 on local programs, and much of this funding supported community-oriented and prevention activities. Few of these initiatives directly funded local community organizations or agencies outside the criminal justice system. Nonetheless, many required law enforcement agencies to engage in partnerships with these groups and, thus, promoted a relatively new community-oriented, problem-solving approach to crime (see Goldstein, 1990; Kelling & Coles, 1996; Rosenbaum, 1994; Skogan & Hartnett, 1997).

The federal government's effort to stimulate local interest in new anti-crime strategies that emphasize community, prevention, and problem solving has been laudable, but there appears to be a growing awareness that crime is a local problem that must be solved by local means. Having toured a number of cities and neighborhoods across America, we believe that community leaders and city officials are feeling more efficacious and more creative in their own crime prevention strategies. Many communities continue to experience severe crime problems, but local leaders are cautiously optimistic that newly formed coalitions and partnerships will be effective at multiplying the resources available to fight crime and disorder (see Kelling, Rocheleau, Rosenbaum, Roth, Skogan, & Walsh, 1997).

---

2. The Office of Justice Programs includes the National Institute of Justice, Office of Juvenile Justice and Delinquency Prevention, Office for Victims of Crime, Bureau of Justice Statistics, and Bureau of Justice Assistance.

Ordinary citizens' motivation to join the fight against crime, either through individual or collective action, derives from a variety of sources, including their fear of crime, their sense of civic duty, and the perceived seriousness of the crime problem (Lavrakas, Normoyle, Skogan, Herz, Salem, & Lewis, 1981; Skogan & Maxfield, 1981). Although feelings of helplessness and despair are common in the toughest neighborhoods, many residents refuse to give up and, instead, have decided to fight back against violence and disorder (Davis & Lurigio, 1996). Some start or join a grassroots community organization as a way to improve local conditions, whereas others work with the police to organize citizen patrols, watches, and other surveillance programs. Some provide social services to meet the needs of at-risk populations, whereas others challenge city hall to deliver more services to the neighborhoods. In this book, we examine the nature, extent, and effectiveness of a wide range of crime prevention behaviors, programs, and policies.

CONCEPTUALIZING COMMUNITY AND SITUATIONAL CRIME PREVENTION

Our focus is on strategies and programs to prevent crime at the neighborhood level by modifying social behavior or the physical environment. More specifically, we evaluate the crime prevention behaviors of ordinary citizens, both individually and collectively, as well as programmatic efforts to reduce the opportunities for crime by redesigning the physical environment.

Many researchers have offered theoretical frameworks to classify crime prevention interventions and behaviors. One popular approach has been to apply the public health model—which distinguishes among primary, secondary, and tertiary prevention—to crime prevention (Brantingham & Faust, 1976; Lab, 1992; Lavrakas, 1995; Lavrakas & Bennett, 1988; van Dijk & de Waard, 1991). Essentially, primary strategies are intended to prevent crime from ever occurring; secondary strategies are intended to prevent crime among at-risk groups, and tertiary strategies reduce the cost of crime among those already affected by criminal activity. This approach has heuristic value. The problem is that applications of the public health model to crime prevention often differ in detail and are inconsistent with one another.[3]

Moving away from the public health model, Tonry and Farrington (1995) offer a framework that, to some extent, reflects existing currents of research in the field. They classify crime prevention strategies into four groups—

---

3. Lavrakas (1995), for example, proposes a 3 X 4 matrix, crossing the three (previously named) levels of prevention with four "operational realms"—individual, household, neighborhood, and societal. Van Dijk and de Waard (1991) propose a 3 X 3 matrix, crossing the three levels of prevention with three targets—offenders, situations, and victims.

developmental, community, situational, and criminal justice. Leaving aside the criminal justice approach, which is based on deterrence, incapacitation, and rehabilitation as defined earlier, developmental prevention refers to interventions that seek to prevent the emergence of "criminal potential in individuals" (see Tremblay & Craig, 1995, for a review), community prevention is defined as interventions that modify the "social conditions" that contribute to offending in residential communities (see Hope, 1995; Rosenbaum, 1988, for reviews), and situational prevention refers to interventions that reduce the opportunities and increase the risks associated with offending (see Clarke, 1995, for a review). Again, this scheme is helpful, but it includes categories that are overlapping and terms that have been used differently by other authors in the field (see Rosenbaum, 1988).

This book has been influenced by these attempts to classify crime prevention strategies. But in the final analysis, decisions about what to include in this volume and how to conceptualize them were driven largely by a "grounded theory" perspective—that is, we considered which crime prevention practices have received serious attention from policy makers, practitioners, and researchers and how these initiatives have been conceptualized in particular settings.

Although we cover all major types of crime prevention previously delineated, we concentrate on community and situational approaches. In addition, to the extent that community-based crime prevention strategies have received insufficient coverage by previous writers in this field, we have attempted to compensate for this shortcoming. Much of the work we review in this book would be classified, technically, as "situational crime prevention" by other theorists, but we have chosen to highlight interventions aimed at the *social influence* aspects of opportunity models. Specifically, we concentrate on strategies designed to enhance citizen participation in crime prevention practices at the individual and collective levels, wherein the goals are to both strengthen "community" and reduce opportunities for crime. This is not to suggest that we have ignored the classic "situational" crime prevention measures that involve changes to the physical environment. (To the contrary, we have devoted two full chapters to this important subject and have placed these interventions in their proper theoretical context.) Rather, we are attempting to remind the reader that neighborhoods respond to the threat of crime by engaging in a wide array of individual and social behaviors—some functional and others dysfunctional—for the protection of self, family, and community. In any event, these actions by local residents constitute the core of what we call "crime prevention" in urban and suburban neighborhoods. Hence, they will be critically reviewed in this volume.

Within the domain of community responses to crime, many attempts have been made to conceptualize community crime prevention activities. Notable conceptual distinctions include "avoidance" versus "mobilization" behaviors (Furstenberg, 1972), "individual" versus "collective" behaviors (Conklin, 1975), and "private-minded" versus "public-minded" behaviors (Schneider & Schneider, 1978). Alternatively, a model that has been empirically validated

(Lavrakas & Lewis, 1980; Lavrakas, Normoyle, Skogan, Herz, Salem, & Lewis, 1980) classifies community crime prevention behaviors into three categories: personal protection behaviors intended to defend oneself from victimization, household protection behaviors intended to protect one's property (and residents) by restricting access and opportunity for entry, and neighborhood protection behaviors intended to defend a specific geographic area, such as a block or larger neighborhood. Many classification schemes and theoretical constructs mentioned here are consistent with the presentation of programs and strategies in this book and, therefore, will become familiar to the reader.

CONTENT OF THE BOOK

At the heart of this "alternative" way of thinking about crime control is the basic notion that citizens can be mobilized and empowered to prevent crime in their neighborhoods. Hence, Part II focuses on the role of citizens in community-based crime prevention, including a review of strategies designed to enhance citizens' awareness of, and participation in, crime prevention activities. Chapter 2 articulates the basic philosophy and assumptions underlying federal initiatives to encourage citizen participation in formal "community crime prevention programs." Most important, Chapter 2 summarizes the scientific literature on the correlates of citizen participation in crime prevention: Who is likely to join a formal anticrime group or engage in specific crime prevention behaviors? We discuss the reasons that citizens will frequently refuse to participate or fail to rescue a person in need of emergency assistance. We also examine the demographic, psychological, and community factors that facilitate or inhibit citizen participation.

Chapter 3 provides a more in-depth look at the process of community mobilization and empowerment for the purpose of crime prevention. This chapter focuses on two of the most popular collective crime prevention strategies in the United States—Neighborhood Watch and citizen patrols. We assess these surveillance programs in the context of relevant theories of crime—social disorganization theory, social support theory, and opportunity theories, and we summarize relevant evaluation research. Finally, Chapter 4 covers media efforts to educate and persuade entire communities or the entire nation regarding appropriate crime prevention behaviors. In this chapter, we examine local and national programs aimed at increasing the public's knowledge, attitudes, and behaviors pertaining to community crime prevention. Included are the National Citizen's Crime Prevention Media Campaign, Crime Stoppers International, and local anticrime newsletters.

Part III continues our focus on citizens' preventive behaviors by discussing the many tactics that individuals and neighborhoods can employ to defend themselves against crime and drugs. Chapter 5 reviews the research literature on a wide range of *individual* protective actions that can be taken to protect oneself from confrontational crimes of sexual assault, domestic violence,

robbery, and stranger assault. From avoiding dangerous places to resisting attackers to carrying firearms, we examine the efficacy and price of commonly
used self-defense tactics. Chapter 6 highlights a decade of efforts by communities across the country to defend themselves against the onslaught of drug
markets. We describe the strategies adopted by community groups and individuals who have decided, in cooperation with law enforcement, to fight back
against local drug dealers.

Opportunity theories of crime provide the backbone of crime prevention
practices in the United States. For this reason, Part IV thoroughly reviews the
major strategies and programs designed to reduce criminal opportunities
through changes in the physical environment. Chapter 7 reviews the work
derived from the original environmental approaches to crime prevention—
Newman's (1972) "defensible space" model and Jeffrey's (1971) "crime prevention through environmental design" (CPTED) theory. In this chapter, we
explore the effectiveness of various attempts to modify the built environment,
including target hardening measures (for example, installation of alarms or security cameras), access control (for example, changes in street layout, accessibility), surveillance enhancement (for example, changes in street lighting,
security guards, building design), and land use. These pioneering models are
especially noteworthy because they consider the impact of physical changes
on the *social behavior* of persons using the environment, including natural surveillance, territoriality, or ownership of public space, fear of crime, attachment to the area, and social cohesion. These models also led to several
important demonstration-and-evaluation programs that included comprehensive, multifaceted interventions in both residential and commercial settings.

Chapter 8 provides a single theoretical framework—situational crime
prevention—to incorporate all environmental crime prevention strategies.
Although Clarke's (1992, 1995) situational crime prevention model fails to
address informal social control processes to the same degree as earlier environmental theories, he provides a comprehensive model of crime prevention
strategies that is supported by a wide range of small-scale studies. Moreover,
the situational crime prevention approach highlights how the immediate physical environment can be manipulated to change rates of offending. We review
the theoretical underpinnings of this model, including its connection to defensible space, CPTED, rational choice, and routine activity theories. We examine the 12 major situational crime prevention strategies and various
applications of these approaches to specific crimes and settings, including repeat victimizations. We also explore the limits of this approach for crime prevention practice, including community concerns about violations of privacy,
fear enhancement, and possible crime displacement.

Part V takes us outside our conventional way of thinking about crime prevention to explore the promise of mobilizing resources beyond the criminal
justice system and even beyond community volunteers. In Chapter 9, we describe the not-so-quiet revolution that is taking place in the world of policing,
commonly referred to as "community policing" or "problem-oriented policing." Given the long-standing tradition of allocating crime prevention funds

to law enforcement agencies (rather than the community), one could argue that the future of crime prevention will be heavily influenced by the capacity of the police to build partnerships with community-based agencies and organizations and to leverage resources that can be applied to persistent neighborhood problems. We also review the theory and research pertaining to community policing and problem solving and assess its promise, its documented successes, and its pitfalls. We emphasize partnership building because it refocuses attention on resources outside the police organization.

Chapter 10 completes our discussion of crime prevention by offering a distinct but complementary set of strategies and programs. In sharp contrast with previous chapters—which emphasize situational and community approaches to preventing crime and defending oneself and one's neighborhood against intruders—Chapter 10 focuses on the "social crime prevention" model, which encompasses early interventions in the lives of children to prevent criminality entirely, interventions to prevent at-risk kids from pursuing a delinquent lifestyle, and interventions to prevent juvenile recidivism. The approaches described in Chapter 10 cut across the classification systems described earlier—they include primary, secondary, and tertiary prevention strategies (compare Lavrakas, 1995), and both developmental and community crime prevention strategies (compare Tonry & Farrington, 1995). Their defining element is that they all focus on *youths and their families* and attempt to address the "root causes" of crime or factors that predispose individuals to be at risk of delinquency and criminality. We do not provide a comprehensive discussion of strategies in this rapidly expanding field; rather, we attempt to provide a few illustrative examples, extracted from the past four decades, of promising interventions in early family support, preschool education, community organizing, and youth employment. From the Perry Preschool Program in Ypsilanti, Michigan, to the Homebuilders Program in Tacoma, Washington, from the classic Chicago Area Project to the Eisenhower Foundation's Neighborhood Anti-Crime Self-Help Program, we attempt to describe innovations that promise to advance the dialogue about crime prevention. In this final chapter, we also review the efforts of youth service bureaus to divert kids from the criminal justice system.

Finally, a note about our methodology. From the start, we must confess to being data-driven social scientists. Therefore, we are inclined to take a hard and skeptical look at all programs, regardless of their popularity. Politicians, local government officials, and the media are more inclined to report anecdotal stories of crime prevention successes—especially programs that are labeled "community-oriented"—because such initiatives are often as politically appealing as "mother and apple pie." In contrast, our summaries and conclusions are based largely on empirical evidence—collected using accepted social science research methods—rather than on the beliefs, "guesstimates," and grateful testimonials of individual opinion leaders. This does not mean that we have limited our definition of "knowledge" to data collected in quantitative research studies, as has been the practice in the past. On the contrary, we report case studies and other findings that are based on good qualitative field research. Results from qualitative methods can yield insights that are simply not possible with structured, deductive methods of inquiry. Both approaches should play important and complementary roles in advancing knowledge about crime and crime prevention.

REFERENCES

Bell, D., & Held, V. (1969). The community revolution, *Public Interest*, 19, 142–177.

Blumstein, A., Cohen, J., & Nagin, D. (eds.) (1978). *Deterrence and incapacitation: Estimating the effects of criminal sanctions on crime rates*. Washington, DC: National Academy of Sciences.

Blumstein, A., Cohen, J., Roth, J, & Visher, C. (1986). *Criminal careers and "career criminals"* (Vol. 1). Washington, DC: National Academy of Sciences.

Brantingham, P. J., & Faust, F. L. (1976). A Conceptual Model of Crime Prevention." *Crime and Delinquency*, 22, 284–296.

Clarke, R. V. (ed.) (1992). *Situational crime prevention: Successful case studies*. Albany, NY: Harrow and Heston.

Clarke, R. V. (1995). Situational crime prevention. In M. Tonry & D. P. Farrington (eds.) *Building a safer society: Strategic approaches to crime prevention*. (Crime and Justice, Vol. 19). Chicago: University of Chicago Press.

Conklin, J. E. (1975). *The impact of crime*. New York: Macmillan.

Davis, R. C. & Lurigio, A. J. (1996) *Fighting back: Neighborhood antidrug strategies*. Thousand Oaks, CA: Sage.

Furstenberg, F. F. Jr. (1972). Fear of crime and its effects on citizen behavior. In A. Biderman (ed.) *Crime and justice: A symposium*. New York: Nailburg.

Gilliard, D. K., & Beck, A. J. (1996). Prison and jail inmates, 1995. *Bureau of Justice Statistics Bulletin*, August, NCJ-161132. Bureau of Justice Statistics. Washington, DC: U.S. Government Printing Office.

Goldstein, H. (1990). *Problem-oriented policing*. New York: McGraw-Hill.

Grant, J. A. (1981). *National policy, citizen participation and health system reform: The case of three health systems agencies in the San Francisco Bay Area*. Unpublished Ph.D. dissertation. Berkeley: University of California, Department of Sociology.

Hope, T. (1995). Community crime prevention. In M. Tonry & D. P. Farrington (eds.) *Building a safer society: Strategic approaches to crime prevention*. (Crime and Justice, Vol. 19). Chicago: University of Chicago Press.

Jacob, H., & Lineberry, R. L. (1982). *Government responses to crime*. Executive summary report to the National Institute of Justice. Evanston, IL: Northwestern University, Center for Urban Affairs and Policy Research.

Jeffrey, C. R. (1971). *Crime prevention through environmental design*. Beverly Hills, CA: Sage.

Johnson, L., O'Malley, P., & Bachman, J. (1995). Monitoring the future study. Press release #13.

Kelling, G. L, & Coles, C. M. (1996). *Fixing broken windows: Restoring order and reducing crime in our communities*. New York: Free Press.

Kelling, G. L., Rocheleau, A. M., Rosenbaum, D. P., Roth, J. A., Skogan, W. G., & Walsh, N. (1997). *Preliminary cross-site analysis of the Bureau of Justice Assistance Comprehensive Communities Program*. Cambridge, MA: BOTEC Analysis.

Kramer, R. J. (1969). *Participation and the poor: Comparative case studies in the war on poverty*. Englewood Cliffs, NJ: Prentice-Hall.

Krug, R. E. (1983). *Communities against crime: Two federal initiatives.* Washington, DC: U.S. Department of Justice, National Institute of Justice.

Lab, S. P. (1992). *Crime prevention: Approaches, practices, and evaluations.* Cincinnati: Anderson.

Lavrakas, P. J. (1985). Citizen self-help and neighborhood crime prevention policy. In L. A. Curtis (ed.), *American violence and public policy* (pp. 47–63). New Haven, CT: Yale University Press.

Lavrakas, P. J. (1995). Community-based crime prevention: Citizens, community organizations, and the police. In L. B. Joseph (ed.) *Crime, communities, and public policy.* Chicago: University of Chicago, Center for Urban Research and Policy Studies.

Lavrakas, P. J., & Bennett, S. (1988). Thinking about the implementation of citizen and community anticrime measures. In T. Hope & M. Shaw (eds.), *Communities and crime reduction.* London: Her Majesty's Stationery Office.

Lavrakas, P. J., & Lewis, D. A. (1980). The conceptualization and measurement of citizens crime prevention behaviors. *Journal of Research in Crime and Delinquency* 23, 254–272.

Lavrakas, P. J., Normoyle, J., Skogan, W. G., Herz, E. J., Salem, G., & Lewis, D. A. (1981). *Factors related to citizen involvement in personal, household, and neighborhood anticrime measures: An executive summary.* Washington, DC: U.S. Department of Justice, National Institute of Justice.

Lewis, D. A., and G. Salem (1986). *Fear of crime, incivility, and the production of a social problem.* New Brunswick, NJ: Transaction.

Maguire, K., & Pastore, A. L. (eds.) (1996). *Sourcebook of criminal justice statistics 1995.* U.S. Department of Justice, Bureau of Justice Statistics. Washington, DC: U.S. Government Printing Office.

Mauer, M., & Huling, T. (1995). *Young black Americans and the criminal justice system: Five years later.* Washington, DC: The Sentencing Project.

Miller, T. R., Cohen, M. A., & Wiersema, B. (1996). *Victim costs and consequences: A new look.* Department of Justice, National Institute of Justice. Washington, DC: U.S. Government Printing Office.

Newman, O. (1972). *Defensible space: Crime prevention through urban design.* New York: Macmillan.

Office of National Drug Control Policy (1997). *The national drug control strategy, 1997.* Washington, DC: Executive Office of the President.

The President's Commission on Law Enforcement and Administration of Justice (1967). *The challenge of crime in a free society.* Washington, DC: U.S. Government Printing Office.

Roehl, J. A., & Cook, R. F. (1984). *Evaluation of the urban crime prevention program.* Washington, DC: U.S. Department of Justice, National Institute of Justice.

Rosenbaum, D. P. (1987). The theory and research beyond Neighborhood Watch: Is it a sound fear and crime reduction strategy? *Crime and Delinquency, 33,* 103–134.

Rosenbaum, D. P. (1988). Community crime prevention: A review and synthesis of the literature. *Justice Quarterly, 5,* 323–395.

Rosenbaum D. P. (ed.) (1994), *The challenge of community policing: Testing the promises* (pp. 127–146). Thousand Oaks, CA: Sage.

Rosenbaum, D. P., Bennett, S., Lindsay, B., Wilkinson, D. (1994). *Community responses to drug abuse: A program evaluation.* Washington, DC: U.S. Department of Justice, National Institute of Justice.

Rosenbaum, D. P., & Heath. L. (1990). The "psycho-logic" of fear reduction and crime prevention programs. In J. Edwards, E. Posavac, S. Tindel, F. Bryant, & L. Heath (eds.) *Applied social psychology annual* (Vol. 9, pp. 221–247). New York: Plenum.

Schneider, A. L., & Schneider, P. R. (1978). *Private and public-minded citizen responses to a neighborhood-based crime prevention strategy.* Eugene, OR: Institute for Policy Analysis.

Sechrest, L. B., White, S. O., & Brown, E. D. (eds.) (1979). *The rehabilitation of criminal offenders: Problems and prospects.* Washington, DC: National Academy of Sciences.

Skogan, W. G. (1990). *Disorder and decline: Crime and the spiral of decay in American neighborhoods.* New York: Free Press.

Skogan, W. G., & Hartnett, S. M. (1997). *Community policing, Chicago style.* New York: Oxford University Press.

Skogan, W. G., & Maxfield, M. G. (1981). *Coping with crime: Individual and neighborhood reactions.* Beverly Hills, CA: Sage.

Tonry, M. (1995). *Malign neglect: Race, crime, and punishment in America.* New York: Oxford University Press.

Tonry, M., & Farrington, D. P. (1995). Strategic approaches to crime prevention. In M. Tonry & D. P. Farrington (eds.) *Building a safer society: Strategic approaches to crime prevention.* (*Crime and Justice,* Vol. 19). Chicago: University of Chicago Press.

Tremblay, R. E., & Craig, W. M. (1995). Developmental prevention of crime: From pre-birth to adolescence. In M. Tonry & D. P. Farrington (eds.), *Building a safer society: Strategic approaches to crime prevention.* (*Crime and Justice,* Vol. 19). Chicago: University of Chicago Press.

van Dijk, J. J. M., & de Waard, J. (1991). A two-dimensional typology of crime prevention projects. *Criminal Justice Abstracts,* 23, 483–503.

p.16 = blank

PART II

Community Awareness, Mobilization, and Participation

p.17 = blank

2

❂

Citizen Participation in
Crime Prevention

Who and Why?

There is a growing consensus among criminal justice professionals and re-searchers that citizen volunteers and local residents play a critical role in the prevention of crime (Heinzelmann, 1981; Lavrakas, 1985, 1992). Community crime prevention programs (CCPPs) were introduced in the mid-1970s as avenues for citizen participation in anticrime activities. These programs have assumed a variety of forms, usually operate under the authority of local police departments and community organizations, and are generally designed to mobilize citizens to prevent, detect, and report crime (Greenberg, Rohe, & Williams, 1982).

The fundamental philosophy of community crime prevention is that the most effective means of combating crime and improving the quality of neighborhood life involves individual residents in proactive efforts to reduce or preclude opportunities for crime (Lockhard, Duncan, & Brenner, 1978; Podolefsky & DuBow, 1981; Rosenbaum, 1988). In practice, this involvement is achieved through a wide range of undertakings, including resident patrols (Yin, Vogel, Lavrakas, & Green, 1977), Neighborhood Watch programs (Rosenbaum, Lewis, & Grant, 1985), home security surveys (International Training, Research, and Evaluation Council, 1977), property-marking projects (Heller, Stenzel, & Gill, 1975), police-community councils (Yin, 1979), and changes in the physical environment (Neuman, 1972).

Community crime prevention arose partly from a growing realization among citizens that the police and the rest of the criminal justice system were failing in their attempts to reduce crime and to restore and maintain social order (Silberman, 1978). Moreover, it had become increasingly clear that more police did not necessarily lead to less crime (Jacob & Lineberry, 1982; Wilson, 1975). In response, CCPPs emphasize that the success of law enforcement depends heavily on the participation and cooperation of neighborhood residents and that some crime prevention activities are better conducted by residents themselves (DuBow & Emmons, 1981).

In this chapter, we focus on questions that relate to individual participation in formal CCPPs: Who is likely to join an anticrime program? Why do citizens decline to become involved in collective crime prevention activities? How can community organizations encourage participation in such activities? We also focus on questions that relate to individual citizen's efforts to stop crime and to intervene in emergencies: Why are people hesitant to become involved in helping their neighbors? What circumstances are most conducive to citizen involvement? What implications does social psychological research have for CCPPs?

HISTORY AND FOUNDATIONS OF COMMUNITY CRIME PREVENTION PROGRAMS

Three national commissions have underscored the need for an active and involved citizenry that would engage in a variety of individual, household, and neighborhood activities to reduce crime in American communities (DuBow & Emmons, 1981; Curtis, 1985; Lavrakas & Bennett, 1988). In the language of the Omnibus Crime Control and Safe Streets Act of 1968, Congress espoused the view that "crime is essentially a local problem that must be dealt with by state and local governments if it is to be controlled effectively" (p. 3). This broad conception of community involvement acknowledged that law enforcement depends on citizen cooperation to successfully apprehend criminals and solve crimes.

The federal government's decision to fund CCPPs in the 1970s assumed that community organizations and local institutions play a critical role in creating and administering crime prevention efforts "through their ability to mobilize the voluntary potential of the local citizenry" (Lavrakas, 1992, p. 11). In theory, the police and indigenous community organizations, along with public and private sector agencies, provide both the impetus that starts neighborhood crime prevention efforts and the motivation that sustains them (Lavrakas, 1992).

Several years after the Law Enforcement Assistance Administration (LEAA) began to fund citizen anticrime projects, the Crime Control Act of 1976 established the Office of Community Anti-Crime Programs (CACP), which was authorized to "enable community and citizen groups to apply for grants to encourage community and citizen participation in crime prevention" (U.S.

Department of Justice, 1977, p. 14). The act also made 30 million dollars available for "crime prevention programs in which members of the community participate, and including but not limited to 'Block Watch' and similar programs" (p. 15). In interpreting the act, CACP was very clear in setting its funding agenda:

> Priority will be given to programs and activities that are public-minded in the sense that they are designed to promote a social or collective response to crime and the fear of crime at the neighborhood level in contrast to private-minded efforts that deal only with the actions of citizens as individuals or those that result from the provision of services that in themselves do not contribute to the organization of the neighborhood. (U.S. Department of Justice, 1977, pp. 58–63)

CACP guidelines stipulated that funded projects be designed to encourage neighborhood residents to join self-help organizations for the purpose of developing and conducting anticrime initiatives. CACP's goal was based on the notion that community residents must be willing to institute neighborhood-level social controls that are considered more essential for maintaining order than are the formal controls exerted by the criminal justice system. DuBow and Emmons (1981) characterized this strategy as the "community hypothesis," which posits a set of relationships among "community organizations, collective anticrime activities, neighborhood social integration, local social control, and crime or the fear of crime" (p. 171).

A key element in this model and in the entire field of community crime prevention is the assumption that community organizations can mobilize citizens to participate in collective crime prevention programs. Indeed, the success of CCPPs is predicated on the participation of individuals (Podolefsky & DuBow, 1981). Without the full cooperation of private citizens, the hypothesized benefits of anticrime efforts for individuals and the community as a whole will be diminished.

LEVEL AND NATURE OF INDIVIDUAL PARTICIPATION IN CCPPs

The assumption of citizen participation is problematic because most people simply do not volunteer for community organizations. Investigations conducted during the 1970s, in a variety of cities, showed that overall participation in local voluntary organizations ranged from 10 percent to 20 percent of the general population (see Greenberg, Rohe, & Williams, 1985). Belonging to a voluntary organization, however, does not necessarily indicate involvement in crime prevention. Skogan and Maxfield (1981) found that 13 percent of the respondents in Philadelphia, Chicago, and San Francisco reported involvement with CCPPs. Another study in Chicago (Lavrakas, Normoyle,

Skogan, Herz, Salem, & Lewis, 1980) and one in Atlanta (Greenberg, Rohe, & Williams, 1982) found participation rates of less than 10 percent.

CCPPs differ from other types of local voluntary organizations in three basic ways, which might account for differences among their respective participants (Rohe & Greenberg, 1982). First, CCPPs usually have a much more restricted focus and therefore may appeal to a narrower range of participants. Second, CCPPs often depart from the more traditional activities of other community organizations and can involve extreme kinds of activities, including occasional vigilantism. Third, the goals of CCPPs (that is, preventing crime), when achieved, are usually not as palpable as those of other local voluntary organizations (for example, cleaning up the neighborhood).

CORRELATES OF PARTICIPATION IN CCPPs

Research suggests that the participants of CCPPs are highly similar to the participants of other voluntary organizations (Greenberg, Rohe, & Williams, 1985). Several factors are correlated with participation in community organizations.

Knowledge

Knowledge of crime and awareness of crime prevention programs seems to provide a gateway for participation in prevention activities but does not explain fully why citizens participate in CCPPs. Podolefsky and DuBow (1980), who conducted a detailed qualitative analysis of participation in three major cities, reported that citizens who knew more about crime were more likely to participate in CCPPs. Using survey data in the same cities, Skogan and Maxfield (1981) found that participation in CCPPs averaged 34 percent for citizens with knowledge of CCPPs, in contrast with an average 13 percent participation rate in the general population. In North Carolina, Rohe and Greenberg (1982) found that 54 percent of the respondents in their study who were aware of local CCPPs were participants in those programs. In a major Chicago metropolitan study, Lavrakas and his associates (1980) reported the following participation rates among those persons who knew about various community crime prevention efforts: crime prevention meetings (44 percent), Whistle Stop programs (44 percent), Block Watch programs (36 percent), and citizen patrol or escort programs (20 percent). Together, these studies suggest that participation levels can be increased by just making citizens aware that CCPPs exist. However, knowledge is not enough. Across all the studies reported here, participation among citizens who were knowledgeable about crime and CCPPs was only about 40 percent.

Demographics

A substantial number of studies have shown that participants in voluntary community organizations tend to be middle to upper-middle income, married with children, home owners, highly educated, and residentially stable (Bell & Force, 1956; Bennett, 1989; Cook & Roehl, 1983; Curtis & Zurcher, 1971; Devereux, 1960; Fisher, 1989, 1993; Freeman, Novak, & Reeder, 1957; Greenberg, Rohe, & Williams, 1985; Hunter, 1974; Hyman & Wright, 1971; Lavrakas & Herz, 1982; Lavrakas et al., 1980; Podolefsky & DuBow, 1980; Roehl & Cook, 1984; Shernock, 1986; Skogan, 1988, 1989; Skogan & Maxfield, 1981; Smith, 1966; Tomeh, 1973; Wandersman, Jakubs, & Giamartino, 1981; Wright & Hyman, 1958). In addition, research on the organizations that sponsor anticrime programs also confirms the pattern of middle-class participation for a variety of crime prevention efforts (Lavrakas et al., 1980; Podolefsky & DuBow, 1981). Middle-class residents might be more likely to participate because they are more willing to join voluntary formal organizations or because they have a greater emotional or financial stake in the community, which are basic norms of middle-class culture (Greenberg, Rohe, & Williams, 1985).

Research regarding age, gender, and race has reported inconsistent results. Some investigations have found that participants in community organizations are more likely to be older (Lab, 1990; Menard & Covey, 1987; Shapland, 1988; Shernock, 1986; Skogan & Maxfield, 1981), whereas others have found them to be middle-aged (Brown, Flanagan, & McLeod, 1984; Fisher, 1993; Greenberg, Rohe, & Williams, 1985; Lavrakas & Herz, 1982) or younger (Smith & Lab, 1991). Some studies have found that males (Babchuk & Booth, 1960; Lavrakas et al., 1980; Palisi, 1965; Scott, 1957)—whereas others have found that females (Smith, 1972; Wandersman, Jakubs, & Giamartino 1981)— are more likely to participate in community organizations. Greenberg, Rohe, and Williams (1985) suggested that the apparent contradictory findings concerning gender can be attributed to the types of organization studied: "Women are more likely to be members of expressive groups (for example, those that emphasize socializing), while men are more likely to be members of instrumental groups (for example, those that emphasize goal achievement)" (p. 140).

Lavrakas et al.'s (1980) review of the literature on social participation demonstrated that before the 1960s, whites were consistently more likely to participate than were African-Americans, whereas after 1970 the opposite was true (for example, Ahlbrandt & Cunningham, 1979; Hunter, 1974; Lavrakas et al., 1980; Skogan & Maxfield, 1981). Rohe and Greenberg (1982) reported an interaction between race and income in their study of crime prevention programs: For whites, participation increased with income; for African-Americans, as income increased, participation decreased. Bennett (1989), however, found no racial differences in participation.

Psychological Factors

Several studies have examined the psychological correlates of participation in community organizations. Several factors have been identified, including communication skills, life satisfaction, happiness, sense of predictability in life, and locus of control (Beal, 1956; Bronfenbrenner, 1960; Gough, 1952; Hausknecht, 1962; Lavrakas et al., 1980; Phillips, 1967; Reddy, 1974; Rose, 1962; Smith, Reddy, & Baldwin, 1972). In all the investigations, participants were higher on these traits than were nonparticipants. Furthermore, research has found that participants report more favorable perceptions about the community and their neighbors (Ahlbrandt & Cunningham, 1979; Litwak, 1961; Smith, 1972; Wandersman & Giamartino, 1980), express more concern over local problems (Skogan & Maxfield, 1981; Wandersman, Jakubs, & Giamartino, 1981; White & Eidner, 1981), are more attached to the community (Riger & Lavrakas, 1980), and have more personal relationships in the neighborhood (Smith, 1972).

The influences of fear of crime and criminal victimization on participation are unclear. Some studies have found higher levels of fear among participants (DuBow, McCabe, & Kaplan, 1979), others have found lower levels (Podolefsky & DuBow, 1981; Skogan & Maxfield, 1981), and a few studies have failed to detect any relationship between fear and participation (Baumer & DuBow, 1977; Lavrakas, Herz, & Salem, 1981; Maxfield, 1987; Rohe & Greenberg, 1982). In an attempt to reconcile these inconsistent results, Skogan (1988) maintained that

> Impulses toward participation are maximal among those who are both aware of local crime problems and are moderately concerned about crime. High levels of fear are thought to be incapacitating, while people with no knowledge or concern about local crime are unmotivated. This is a complex hypothesis concerning nonlinear statistical interaction, and it has been suitably tested (and supported) only in England. (Hope, 1986, p. 54)

Community Characteristics

Several studies have indicated that community characteristics can partly explain participation in CCPPs (Skogan, 1988). Specifically, participation appears to be much more likely in homogenous, low-crime, middle-class neighborhoods than in heterogeneous, high-crime, lower-class neighborhoods. In the latter communities, residents generally feel less responsible for crime prevention, more suspicious of their neighbors, and more alienated from the police. Hence, they are less likely to form the relationships or to have the resources necessary to launch and sustain a CCPP (Bennett & Lavrakas, 1989; Greenberg, Rohe, & Williams, 1985; Henig, 1984; Lewis, Grant, & Rosenbaum, 1988; Skogan, 1988; Taub, Taylor, & Dunham, 1984).

However, Skogan (1989) reported a different pattern of results. He tested a model that described the relationships among measures of neighborhood crime, community resources, police services, and other important variables, which he examined across 60 neighborhoods in three metropolitan areas: Rochester, New York; Tampa–St. Petersburg, Florida; and St. Louis, Missouri. He found that more opportunities for participation existed in middle-class areas, but that more cohesive communities were less likely to rely on formal organizations; that is, "the more intensive the level of informal 'neighboring' in these areas, the less formally organized they were" (p. 449). He also reported that serious crime and the perceived inadequacy of the police stimulated organized anticrime activity; that is, "organized activity around crime issues was more visible in places where residents thought they were not getting good policing" (p. 450). Finally, organized anticrime activity was more "apparent in minority areas plagued by high levels of crime and a limited capacity for informal problem solving" (p. 454).

Problems with Correlate Studies

As noted thus far, findings on the correlates of individual participation in CCPPs have been quite diverse. Lab (1992) suggested that a few general characteristics of participation research make it difficult to compare results across investigations and can help explain the disparate findings. Specifically, researchers have studied a wide range of populations, including residents from urban, rural, and suburban areas. Researchers have also ignored the size and geographical coverage of a CCPP, which might be related to the characteristics of participants (Wandersman & Giamartino, 1980). Many studies have grouped together block, neighborhood, communitywide, and even national organizations (Greenberg, Rohe, & Williams, 1985). Moreover, investigators have defined key variables (for example, fear of crime, perceptions of risk, and neighborhood satisfaction) in a variety of ways. In particular, community crime prevention and participation have been variously defined and measured. According to Rosenbaum (1987), "Everything from youth recreation programs to architectural redesign is now subsumed under the title of 'community crime prevention'" (p. 104).

Few studies have distinguished among types (for example, workshops and seminars, Block Watch, and patrols) or levels of participation (for example, membership only versus weekly activities) (Fisher, 1993). Most investigators have employed a dichotomous (yes–no) variable to measure participation or have simply counted the number of organizations a person has joined. Therefore, researchers have virtually ignored more precise measures of participation such as frequency of meeting attendance, length of membership, and time spent on organizational activities (Greenberg, Rohe, & Williams, 1985). For example, Wandersman and Giamartino (1980) created a useful hierarchy of participation that distinguishes among nonparticipants and program members who only attend meetings, those who vote on program issues, those who join committees and do program-related work, and those who lead the program in defining its goals and tasks. In their review of research on social participation, Lavrakas and his associates (1980) stated that

> Distinctions between mere membership and active participation, and
> levels in between, are generally not made. Personal resources, specifically
> time and energy, undoubtedly distinguish active from passive group
> members, and are likely to play a role in long-term participation. Such
> factors may even change the previously hypothesized relationships

between simply joining groups and demographic characteristics. For example, although individuals with family ties are likely to join groups, they may be less likely to be active members due to conflicting obligations, than nonmarried people. Personality and attitudinal characteristics, which are expected to determine who will join formal voluntary organizations, may be more strongly pronounced among active and/or long-term members vs. members "in name only." (p. 3)

Motives for Participation

Aside from the known correlates of participation, several other variables can inhibit or facilitate participation in community organizations. For example, residents might not participate because they believe that their activities will not lead to any real benefits or changes in neighborhood conditions (Bar-Zohar & Nehare, 1978; Schmidt, Goldman, & Feimer, 1976). In addition, some residents might distrust formal organizations (Gans, 1962) or might be "freeriders" who realize that they can reap the benefits of a community organization (if they are area wide) without any participation in its programs (Goering, 1979; Rich, 1980; Salisbury, 1970).

When researchers directly ask individuals to explain their refusal to participate in community organizations, "lack of time" is the most frequent response given (Lavrakas et al., 1980; Rohe & Greenberg, 1982). Other obstacles to participation include "too many other obligations," "conflicting obligations," and "no desire to join groups" (Giamartino, Ferrell, & Wandersman, 1979). No study has found, however, that nonparticipation is the result of unfavorable attitudes toward CCPPs (Lavrakas et al., 1980; Rohe & Greenberg, 1982), that is, few people see them as ineffective or a waste of time (Greenberg, Rohe, & Williams, 1985).

Salisbury (1970) developed a typology for investigating incentives to participate in voluntary community organizations. According to his scheme, the potential benefits of participation can be categorized into three groups: (a) material, which includes the benefits of receiving tangible rewards such as goods or services; (b) purposive, which includes the benefits of expressing a value, interest, or ideology; and (c) solidarity, which includes the benefits of socializing and of achieving a sense of group identity and membership.

Most research on community organizations, including CCPPs, has shown that participants are primarily motivated by solidarity incentives (Babchuk & Edwards, 1965; Rich, 1980; Sharp, 1978). For example, Rohe and Greenberg (1982) asked residents why they participated in Neighborhood Watch programs. The most frequent response was "out of community responsibility" (37 percent), followed by "to prevent crime" (12 percent), "to feel safe" (7 percent), "to protect the home"(6 percent), and "to meet people" (1 percent). Rohe and Greenberg concluded that general civic-mindedness was an important determinant of participation. Other studies have also concluded that participation in collective crime prevention is driven by civic-minded attitudes more than by fear or other motives (Lavrakas et al., 1980; Podolefsky

& DuBow, 1980). The literature on Neighborhood Watch, however, does not fully agree, as researchers have suggested that the *initial motive for group formation* is often a threatening, fear-arousing crime or series of crimes in the neighborhood (Garofalo & McLeod, 1986; Rosenbaum, 1987). Social solidarity and civic mindedness are more likely to serve as incentives for *maintaining* (rather than stimulating) participation in these types of collective crime prevention programs.

INFORMAL INTERVENTIONS
TO STOP CRIME

Community involvement in crime prevention efforts can assume a variety of forms including participation in CCPPs and in unplanned or spontaneous activity based on the willingness of citizens to support each other or enforce a shared set of norms for appropriate public behavior. Crime prevention theorists refer to the enforcement of norms as informal social control (for a review of social control and social support theories, see Chapter 3). Studies of informal social control have mostly produced aggregate data on area crime rates, community ties, and perceptions of neighbors. As a consequence, this body of research has failed to carefully examine citizens' willingness to intervene or their specific behaviors when faced with an emergency or crime situation. Yet neighborhood anticrime behaviors constitute the key ingredient in efforts to regulate social behavior and prevent crime through informal means. Hence, in this section of the chapter, we discuss a body of research on informal action, known as the bystander intervention literature, to shed some light on crime prevention practice and theory.

This field was an outgrowth of an event that occurred thirty years ago: A young woman named Kitty Genovese was brutally murdered in a crowded residential neighborhood of New York City. At first, the crime was regarded as just another big-city homicide. But several weeks following the episode, the *New York Times* described a very disturbing aspect of the case: At least thirty-eight persons had witnessed the incident and not one of them came to the victim's aid or even called the police to report her murder (Rosenthal, 1964).

The Research Paradigm

Spurred by the Genovese homicide, Bibb Latané and John Darley (1968, 1969, 1970) conducted a series of seminal studies that examined helping responses in emergencies. Their work elicited a great deal of interest from the scientific community and stimulated much experimentation on the dynamics of bystander intervention (Latané & Nida, 1981). Latané and Darley (1970) developed a paradigm that has served as the prototype for the domain's research. A typical design consists of three elements: (a) a precipitating incident, that is, a contrived emergency (such as medical trauma, accident, or fire) staged in a laboratory or real-world field setting (for example, a subway or airport) and a perpetrator who causes the emergency or commits an antisocial act; (b) a victim in apparent danger or distress, that is, an individual in the throes of an emergency; and (c) a bystander, that is, a subject who witnesses an emergency either alone or in the presence of others.

The Decision to Intervene

Latané and Darley (1970) proposed a theoretical model that views intervention as the final stage in a decision-making process. In the initial stage, the bystander must notice that an event (that is, emergency) has occurred. The bystander must then interpret the event as an emergency or crime and must assume responsibility to intervene. Finally, if the bystander decides to intervene, he or she must choose an appropriate course of action.

Group Size and Helping

The most consistent finding of bystander research is that the presence of other people inhibits individuals from intervening in an emergency. This inhibitory effect is found across differences in the age, gender, and race of victims and bystanders; differences in the size of the bystander group; and differences in the location of the incident (for example, laboratory versus field).

Researchers have posited three social psychological processes to account for the effect of group size on the decision not to help. The first process, audience inhibition, inhibits helping because bystanders are afraid of ridicule if they misinterpret the situation. The more people around, the greater the risk of embarrassment. The second process, social influence, inhibits helping because bystanders look to other people to define the often ambiguous circumstances surrounding an emergency or crime. The inactivity of others stifles bystander responses. The third process, diffusion of responsibility, inhibits helping because bystanders shift the burden of responding onto other people; this shift in responsibility minimizes (for the bystander) the costs of nonintervention, which decrease as the number of other witnesses increases.

The Determinants of Helping

Apart from the group-size effect, research suggests that intervention in a criminal incident is more likely to occur when the following situational features are present: (a) a bystander believes that he or she is the sole witness to the crime; (b) it is clear that a crime has actually taken place (that is, the situation is low in ambiguity); (c) others are present who encourage the bystander to intervene; (d) the bystander feels some personal responsibility to intervene; (e) the bystander knows the surroundings, the other bystanders, or the victim; and (f) the costs of intervention are minimal relative to the benefits. Studies also indicate that persons who intervene are likely to be high in self-esteem, self-assurance, and empathy, previous victims of crime, and similar to the victims on one or more characteristics. Bystanders also feel competent to intervene because of their size, training, experience, or a combination thereof (Latané & Nida, 1981).

Implications for Informal Anticrime Activities

Research on bystander intervention suggests that greater familiarity with their neighbors and surroundings increases people's sense of security and responsibility (Latané & Darley, 1970). Hence, if the witnesses to a crime know one another or the victim, they are more likely to assist the victim directly or to call the police than are a group of strangers who witness the episode. Two studies support this conclusion. The first found that subjects were more likely to report that they would intervene in crimes that occurred closer to home and those that involved a victim they knew (Gillis & Hagan, 1982). The second found that residents of a multi-ethnic housing project who had intervened in crimes reported spending most of their leisure time in the project and regarded the project as the center of their social life (Merry, 1981). These results are consistent with literature that suggests that informal social control mechanisms and CCPPs are strongest in neighborhoods with stable residents and a lot of social networking (Greenberg, Rohe, & Williams, 1985).

Given these bystander studies, crime prevention education strategies should facilitate the decision-making process that leads to intervention. Specifically, citizens need the skills to recognize that a crime is occurring and to intervene directly, if that is the most appropriate (and safe) response to the incident. They also should be encouraged to communicate (if possible) with other bystanders or witnesses to a crime. These two measures could help dampen the effects of audience inhibition. Of course, communication can decrease the likelihood of helping if bystanders actively discourage intervention (for example, Staub, 1974). Furthermore, crime prevention education should reduce people's tendencies to diffuse responsibility when they are contemplating intervention (for example, "Don't hesitate to act just because you think someone else will do it").

Many complaints have been registered about the absence of informal social control and support processes in neighborhoods characterized by high levels of crime and disorder. The bystander intervention literature helps us understand some of the social processes that inhibit or encourage citizen intervention in crime and emergency situations. There is clearly room for experimental interventions designed to improve the exercise of informal social control in urban settings, but too much optimism would not be warranted given the complexity of high-crime environments. For example, citizens might recognize that a crime is occurring but they have learned to look the other way because the costs of intervening are too high (for example, being assaulted by gang members). However, efforts to increase familiarity among residents (for example, enhanced levels of social interaction) might be possible if the costs associated with such participation can be limited. The best and most effective applications of theories or research findings will occur when the persons involved have a full understanding of the social forces at work in the target setting.

REFERENCES

Ahlbrandt, R. S., & Cunningham, J. V. (1979). *A new public policy for neighborhood preservation.* New York: Praeger.

Babchuk, N., & Booth, A. (1960). Men and women in community agencies: A note on power and prestige. *American Sociological Review,* 25, 399–403.

Babchuk, N., & Edwards, J. N. (1965). Voluntary associations and the integration hypothesis. *Sociological Inquiry,* 35,149–162.

Bar-Zohar, Y., & Nehare, M. (1978). Conceptual structure of the multi-dimensionality of locus of control. *Psychological Reports,* 42, 363–396.

Baumer, T. L., & DuBow, F. (1977). *Fear of crime in the polls: What they do and do not tell us.* Paper presented at the American Association of Public Opinion Research, Bush Hills Falls, PA.

Beal, G. (1956). Additional hypotheses in participation research. *Rural Sociology,* 21, 246–256.

Bell, W., & Force, M. T. (1956). Urban neighborhood types and participation in formal associations. *American Sociological Review,* 21, 25–37.

Bennett, T. (1989). Factors related to participation in neighborhood watch schemes. *British Journal of Criminology,* 29, 207–218.

Bennett, S. F., & Lavrakas, P. J. (1989). The Eisenhower Foundation's Neighborhood Program. *Crime and Delinquency,* 35, 345–365.

Bronfenbrenner, V. (1960). Personality and participation: The case of the vanishing variables. *Journal of Social Issues,* 16, 54–63.

Brown, E. J., Flanagan, T. J., & McLeod, M. (1984). *Sourcebook of Criminal Justice Statistics.* Washington, DC: U.S. Government Printing Office.

Cook, R. F., & Roehl, J. A. (1983). *Preventing crime and arson: A review of community-based strategies.* Reston, VA: Institute for Social Analysis.

Curtis, L. A. (1985). Neighborhood, family, and employment: Toward a new public policy against violence. In L. A. Curtis (ed.), *American violence and public policy* (pp. 205–224). New Haven, CT: Yale University Press.

Curtis, R. L., & Zurcher, L. A. (1971). Voluntary associations and the social integration of the poor. *Social Problems,* 18, 339–357.

Devereux, E. C. (1960). Neighborhood and community participation. *Journal of Social Issues,* 16, 64–84.

DuBow, F., & Emmons, D. (1981). The community hypothesis. In D. A. Lewis (ed.), *Reactions to crime* (pp. 167–182). Beverly Hills, CA: Sage.

DuBow, F., McCabe, E., & Kaplan, G. (1979). *Reactions to crime: A critical review of the literature.* Washington, DC: National Institute of Justice.

Fisher, B. (1993). What works: Block Watch meetings or crime prevention seminars? *Journal of Crime and Justice,* 16, 1–27.

Fisher, B. S. (1989). *The "Community Hypothesis" revisited: The effects of participation after controlling for self-selection bias.* Paper presented at the American Society of Criminology Annual Meeting, Washington, DC.

Freeman, H. E., Novak, E., & Reeder, L. (1957). Correlates of membership in voluntary organizations. *American Sociological Review,* 22, 528–533.

Gans, H. J. (1962). *The urban villagers.* New York: Free Press.

Garofalo, J., & McLeod, M. (1986). *Improving the effectiveness and utilization of Neighborhood Watch programs.* Final report to the National Institute of Justice. Albany: State University of New York at Albany, Hindelang Criminal Justice Research Center.

Giamartino, G. A., Ferrell, M., & Wandersman, A. (1979). Who participates in block organizations and why: Some demographic considerations. In A. Seidel & S. Danford (eds.), *Environmental design: Research, theory and application* (pp. 73–97). Washington,

DC: Environmental Design Research Association.

Gillis, A. R., & Hagan, J. (1982). *Bystander apathy and the territorial imperative.* Toronto: University of Toronto, Centre for Urban and Community Studies.

Goering, J. M. (1979). The national neighborhood movement: A preliminary analysis and critique. *Journal of the American Planning Association, 45,* 506–514.

Gough, H. G. (1952). Predicting social participation. *Journal of Social Psychology, 35,* 277–333.

Greenberg, S. W., Rohe, W. M., & Williams, J. R. (1985). *Informal citizen action and crime prevention at the neighborhood level: Synthesis and assessment of the research.* Washington, DC: National Institute of Justice.

Greenberg, S., Rohe, W. M., & Williams, J. R. (1982). *Safe and secure neighborhoods: Physical characteristics and informal territorial control in high and low crime neighborhoods.* Washington, DC: National Institute of Justice.

Hausknecht, M. (1962). *The joiners.* New York: Bedminster.

Heinzelmann, F. (1981). Crime prevention and the physical environment. In D. Lewis (ed.), *Reactions to crime* (pp. 87–102). Beverly Hills, CA: Sage.

Heller, N. B., Stenzel, W. W., & Gill, A. (1975). *National evaluation program— Phase I summary report: Operation Identification Projects.* Washington, DC: National Institute of Justice.

Henig, J. (1984). *Citizens against crime: An assessment of the Neighborhood Watch program in Washington, DC.* Washington, DC: Center for Washington Area Studies, George Washington University.

Hunter, A. (1974). *Symbolic communities.* Chicago: University of Chicago Press.

Hyman, H. H., & Wright, C. R. (1971). Trends in voluntary association membership of American adults. *American Sociological Review, 36,* 191–206.

International Training, Research, and Evaluation Council. (1977). *National evaluation program—Phase I summary report: Crime prevention security surveys.* Washington, DC: National Institute of Justice.

Jacob, H., & Lineberry, R. L. (1982). *Government responses to crime: Executive summary.* Evanston, IL: Center for Urban Affairs and Policy Research, Northwestern University.

Lab, S. P. (1990). From "nothing works" to "the appropriate works": The latest stop in the search for the secular grail. *Criminology, 28,* 405–418.

Lab, S. P. (1992). *Crime prevention: Approaches, practices, and evaluations.* Cincinnati: Anderson.

Latané, B., & Darley, J. M. (1968). Group inhibition by bystander intervention. *Journal of Personality and Social Psychology, 10,* 215–221.

Latané, B., & Darley, J. M. (1969). Bystander apathy. *American Scientist, 57,* 244–268.

Latané, B., & Darley, J. M. (1970). *The unresponsive bystander: Why doesn't he help?* New York: Appleton-Century-Croft.

Latané, B., & Nida, S. (1981). Ten years of research on group size and helping. *Psychological Bulletin, 89,* 308–324.

Lavrakas, P. J. (1985). Citizen self-help and neighborhood crime prevention policy. In L. A. Curtis (ed.), *American violence and public policy* (pp. 87–116). New Haven, CT: Yale University Press.

Lavrakas, P. J. (1992). Community-based crime prevention: Citizens, community organizations, and the police. In L. B. Joseph (ed.), *Crime and community safety* (pp. 59–102). Chicago: Center for Urban Research and Policy Studies, University of Chicago.

Lavrakas, P. J., & Bennett, S. F. (1988). Thinking about the implementation of citizen and community anticrime measures. In T. Hope and M. Shaw (eds.), *Communities and crime reduction* (pp. 221–234). London: Her Majesty's Stationary Office.

Lavrakas, P. J., & Herz, E. J. (1982). Citizen participation in neighborhood crime prevention. *Criminology*, 20, 479–498.

Lavrakas, P. J., Herz, L., & Salem, G. (1981). *Community organization, citizen participation, and neighborhood crime prevention.* Paper presented at the Annual Meeting of the American Psychological Association, Los Angeles, CA.

Lavrakas, P. J., Normoyle, J., Skogan, W. G., Herz, E. J., Salem, G., & Lewis, D. A. (1980). *Factors related to citizen involvement in personal, household, and neighborhood anticrime measures.* Washington, DC: National Institute of Justice.

Lewis, D. A., Grant, J., Rosenbaum, D. P. (1988). *The social construction of reform.* New Brunswick, NJ: Transaction.

Litwak, E. (1961). Voluntary associations and neighborhood cohesion. *American Sociological Review*, 26, 258–271.

Lockhard, J. L., Duncan, J. T., & Brenner, R. N. (1978). *Directory of community crime prevention programs: National and state levels.* Washington, DC: Law Enforcement Assistance Administration.

Maxfield, M. G. (1987). *Explaining fear of crime: Evidence from the 1984 British Crime Survey.* London: Her Majesty's Stationery Office.

Menard, S., & Covey, H. C. (1987). Patterns of victimization, fear of crime, and crime precautions in non-metropolitan New Mexico. *Journal of Crime and Justice*, 10, 71–100.

Merry, S. E. (1981). *Urban danger: Life in a neighborhood of strangers.* Philadelphia: Temple University Press.

Newman, O. (1972). *Defensible space: Crime prevention through urban design.* New York: Macmillan.

O'Keefe, G. J., & Mendelsohn, H. (1984). *Taking a bite out of crime: The impact of a mass media crime prevention campaign.* Washington, DC: National Institute of Justice.

Omnibus Crime Control and Safe Streets Act of 1968. 8 R Stats. 197 (act of June 19, 1968).

Palisi, B. (1965). Ethnic generation and social participation. *Sociological Inquiry*, 35, 219–226.

Phillips, D. (1967). Social participation and happiness. *American Journal of Sociology*, 72, 479–488.

Podolefsky, A., & DuBow, F. (1980). *Strategies for community crime prevention: Collective responses to crime in urban America.* Evanston, IL: Center for Urban Affairs and Policy Research, Northwestern University.

Podolefsky, A., & DuBow, F. (1981). *Strategies for community crime prevention.* Springfield, IL: Charles C. Thomas.

Reddy, R. D. (1974). *Personal factors and individual participation in formal volunteer groups.* Unpublished doctoral dissertation, Boston College.

Rich, R. C. (1980). The dynamics of leadership in neighborhood organizations. *Social Science Quarterly*, 60, 570–587.

Riger, S., & Lavrakas, P. J. (1980). Community ties: Patterns of attachment and social interaction in urban neighborhoods. *American Journal of Community Psychology*, 8, 43–58.

Roehl, J. A., & Cook, R. F. (1984). *Evaluation of the Urban Crime Prevention Program: Executive summary.* Washington, DC: National Institute of Justice.

Rohe, W. M., & Greenberg, S. W. (1982). *Participation in community crime prevention programs.* Chapel Hill: University of North Carolina, Department of City and Regional Planning.

Rose, A. M. (1962). Attitudinal correlates of social participation. *Sociological Quarterly*, 3, 316–330.

Rosenbaum, D. P. (1986). The problem of crime control. In D. P. Rosenbaum (Ed.), *Community crime prevention: Does it work?* (pp. 11–18). Beverly Hills, CA: Sage.

Rosenbaum, D. P. (1987). The theory and research behind Neighborhood Watch: Is it a sound fear and crime reduction strategy? *Crime and Delinquency* 33, 103–134.

Rosenbaum, D. P. (1988). Community crime prevention: A review and synthesis of the literature. *Justice Quarterly*, 5, 323–395.

Rosenbaum, D. P., Lewis, D. A., & Grant, J. A. (1985). *The impact of community crime prevention programs in Chicago: Can neighborhood organizations make a difference?* Evanston, IL: Center for Urban Affairs and Policy Research, Northwestern University.

Rosenthal, A. M. (1964). *Thirty-eight witnesses.* New York: McGraw-Hill.

Salisbury, R. H. (1970). *Interest group politics in America.* New York: Harper & Row.

Schmidt, D. E., Goldman, R. D., & Feimer, N. R. (1976). Physical and psychological factors associated with perceptions of crowding: An analysis of subcultural differences. *Journal of Applied Psychology*, 61, 279–287.

Scott, J. C. (1957). Membership and participation in voluntary associations. *American Sociological Review*, 22, 315–326.

Shapland, J. (1988). Policing with the police? In T. Hope & M. Shaw (eds.), *Communities and crime reduction* (pp. 116–125). London: Her Majesty's Stationery Office.

Sharp, E. B. (1978). Citizen organizations in policing issues and crime prevention: Incentives for participation. *Journal of Voluntary Action Research*, 7, 45–58.

Shernock, S. K. (1986). A profile of the citizen crime prevention activist. *Journal of Criminal Justice*, 14, 211–28.

Silberman, C. E. (1978). *Criminal violence, criminal justice.* New York: Random House.

Skogan, W. G. (1988). Community organizations and crime. In M. Tonry & N. Morris (eds.), *Crime and Justice* (Vol. 10, pp. 39–78).Chicago: University of Chicago Press.

Skogan, W. G. (1989). Communities, crime, and neighborhood organization. *Crime and Delinquency*, 35, 437–457.

Skogan, W. G., & Maxfield, M. G. (1981). *Coping with crime: Individual and neighborhood reactions.* Beverly Hills, CA: Sage.

Smith, D. H. (1966). The importance of formal voluntary organizations for society. *Sociology and Social Research*, 50, 483–494.

Smith, D. H. (1972). *Voluntary activity in eight Massachusetts towns.* Chestnut Hill, MA: Institute of Human Sciences.

Smith, G. B., & Lab, S. P. (1991). Urban and rural attitudes toward participating in an auxiliary policing crime prevention program. *Criminal Justice and Behavior*, 18, 202–216.

Smith, D. H., Reddy, R. D., & Baldwin, B. R. (1972). Types of voluntary action: A definitional essay. In D. H. Smith, R. D. Reddy, & B. R. Baldwin (eds.), *Voluntary action research* (pp. 154–183). Lexington, MA: D. C. Heath.

Staub, E. (1974). Helping a distressed person: Social, personality, and stimulus determinants. In L. Berkowitz (ed.), *Advances in experimental social psychology* (pp. 184–205). New York: Academic.

Taub, R., Taylor, D. G., & Dunham, J. (1984). *Patterns of neighborhood change: Race and crime in urban America.* Chicago: University of Chicago Press.

Tomeh, A. K. (1973). Formal voluntary organizations: Participation, correlates, and interrelationships. *Sociological Inquiry*, 43, 89–122.

U.S. Department of Justice. (1977). *Guidelines manual: Guide to discretionary grant programs.* Washington, DC: U.S. Government Printing Office.

Wandersman, A., & Giamartino, G. A. (1980). Community and individual difference characteristics as influences on initial participation. *American Journal of Community Psychology*, 8, 217–228.

Wandersman, A., Jakubs, J. F., & Giamartino, G. A. (1981). Participation in block organizations. *Journal of Community Action*, 1, 40–47.

Whitaker, C. J. (1986). *Crime prevention measures: Bureau of Justice Statistics Special Report.* Washington, DC: U.S. Department of Justice.

White, C. R., & Eidner, S. M. (1981). Participation in neighborhood organizations. *Journal of Community Action,* 1, 17–28.

Wilson, J. Q. (1975). *Thinking about crime.* New York: Basic Books.

Wright, C., & Hyman, H. (1958). Voluntary association membership of American adults: Evidence from national sample surveys. *American Sociological Review,* 23, 284–94.

Yin, R. K. (1979). What is citizen crime prevention? In National Criminal Justice Reference Service (ed.), *How well does it work?* Washington, DC: U.S. Government Printing Office.

Yin, R. K., Vogel, J., Lavrakas, P. J., & Green, S. (1977). *National evaluation program—Phase I summary report: Citizen Patrol Projects.* Washington, DC: National Institute of Justice.

3

𝕍

Organizing and Empowering the Community

Collective Surveillance Programs

The concepts of "community mobilization" and "community empowerment" are extremely popular today and represent a broad array of efforts to stimulate citizen participation in activities to alleviate local community problems. These concepts conjure visions of community volunteers working together to create self-regulating, safer neighborhoods—places where residents feel more control over, and responsibility for, the events that occur. In the domain of community crime prevention, collective responses to crime are broadly defined as any activity by a group of volunteers to prevent crime and disorder in a geographically defined area. The reader should note that "community" has many definitions in the literature and, consequently, has been heavily debated in sociological circles. At the most basic level, the term can refer to a geographic area, such as a neighborhood, or to a set of social ties that link individuals or groups (Hunter & Riger, 1986).[1] With community crime prevention, we are often referring to both—that is, a *neighborhood* or *smaller area* where people organize themselves into *groups* or *networks* to prevent (either directly or indirectly) local crime and other problems. These collective strategies are the focus of this chapter.

---

1. We should note that the definitions of "community" and "neighborhood" are substantially more complex than this discussion suggests. There are many levels of social networks, with smaller communities nested within larger ones. For a review, see Bursik and Grasmick (1993).

In the 1960s, as levels of violence escalated to unprecedented heights, Americans responded in the only way they knew how—with increased fear and avoidance of dangerous situations. They retreated to the safety of their homes, adding locks, bars, alarms, and, sometimes, guards. Research now suggests that such restrictions of behavior and security purchases are often effective in reducing an *individual's* risk of property loss (for reviews, see Lavrakas, Normoyle, Skogan, Herz, Salem, & Lewis, 1980; Rosenbaum, 1988), but the price might have been higher than expected. Concerned about this type of restrictive crime prevention behavior, the National Advisory Commission on Criminal Justice Standards and Goals (1973, p. 46) observed that "although these prophylactic measures may be steps in self-protection, they can lead to a lessening of the bonds of mutual assistance and neighborliness." Indeed, community researchers have suggested that one primary explanation for high levels of crime, disorder, and fear of crime in specific neighborhoods is the absence of "community" (Greenberg, Rohe, & Williams, 1985; Jacobs, 1961; Kelling & Coles, 1996; Skogan, 1990). In any event, the 1970s witnessed a nationwide call for *collective* crime prevention actions. Given the public's preference for "private-minded" anticrime measures designed to protect themselves and their immediate property and family, local community leaders saw a clear need to get people out of their homes and involved in the process of protecting the *neighborhood*. In turn, this "public-minded" approach should have benefits for both the community and its individual members. The rationale for these expected benefits can be found in criminological theories about why and how crime occurs in a community context.

THEORETICAL FOUNDATIONS

Collective crime prevention practices are consistent with at least three theoretical models—social disorganization, social support, and opportunity reduction theories of crime. We will briefly describe each as it provides a framework for understanding community crime prevention interventions.

Social Disorganization Model

Social disorganization theory emerged from the "Chicago School" in the 1920s and 1930s: Theorists such as Clifford Shaw and Henry McKay began to identify the community variables that were responsible for differences in community-level crime rates (1931; 1942). Noting that high-crime communities were characterized by heterogeneity of class and ethnicity, high levels of transiency, and large numbers of youths, these theorists argued that the driving force behind the crime problem was "social disorganization," that is, a weakened capacity of local institutions and organizations to regulate social behavior. In essence, families, schools, churches, and ethnic activities that once held these communities together and defined appropriate social behavior are no longer functioning in this capacity. Although social disorganization theory has been attacked many times over the years (see Carey, 1975; Matza, 1969), today this model has received renewed interest from a new generation of scholars who have shown greater precision with their concepts, methods, and approaches to data analysis (see Bursik & Grasmick, 1993; Reiss, 1986; Sampson & Groves, 1989).

The argument for collective citizen action against crime, as derived from social disorganization theory, can be stated very simply as follows:

> If social disorganization is the problem and if traditional agents of social control no longer are performing adequately, we need to find alternative ways to strengthen informal social control and restore a "sense of community." . . . (T)he objective is to "organize" the neighborhood and thus encourage the types of behaviors that are believed to provide the basis for regulating or controlling social behavior, beginning with the encouragement of more frequent social interaction. (Rosenbaum, 1988, p. 327)

Greenberg and her colleagues define social control as "the use of rewards or punishments to insure that members of a group—such as a family, organization, neighborhood, or society—will obey the group's rules or norms" (1985, p. 4). In contrast with *formal* social control, which is derived from written rules and laws and is enforced by the police and courts, *informal* social control is derived from local customs and norms, and is enforced by ordinary citizens through behaviors such as surveillance, verbal reprimands, rejection, warnings, and other pressures to achieve conformity. More precisely, Hunter (1985) identifies three levels of social control networks—private, parochial, and public. Private social control involves intimate, primary ties among friends and family members, and control is often exercised by withdrawing affection, support, and esteem and by physical punishment. Parochial social control involves relations among neighbors (via community groups, schools, churches, local businesses) and might include efforts to influence social behavior through community group activities, surveillance of suspicious or deviant behavior, and social intervention as needed. Finally, public social control involves relations with agencies outside the neighborhood (such as police departments and other government and social service agencies) and includes efforts to bring more resources and services to the neighborhood. In this chapter, we focus primarily on the role of community groups as they attempt to exercise both parochial and public social control in their neighborhoods.

Social Support Model

In practice, social disorganization and social control models focus on the process of control and conformity, achieved primarily through various punitive responses to nonconformists. However, collective neighborhood responses to crime could, in theory, be derived from a more positive, supportive approach to preventing antisocial conduct. Cullen (1994) offers such an alternative model by developing a "social support" explanation of criminality. After a careful review of research and existing theories of crime, Cullen makes a compelling argument that social support reduces criminal involvement. Social support can be defined as "the perceived or actual instrumental and/or expressive provisions supplied by the community, social networks, and confiding partners." (Lin, 1986, p. 18). Essentially, the social support model suggests that neighborhood crime and disorder are fueled by a community (and society) that is "not organized, structurally or culturally, to be socially supportive" (Cullen, 1994, p. 531). Driven by self-interest and individualism, Americans have little time to express "communitarian" concerns for neighbors, show compassion for the less fortunate, or exhibit other types of support for persons outside their immediate family.

Interestingly enough, Cullen argues that high-crime community characteristics that are traditionally interpreted as signs of social disorganization— such as family disruption, weak friendship networks, and low rates of citizen participation in voluntary organizations—can just as easily be interpreted as signs of weak social support in these environments. In essence, the absence of informal *helping* networks can contribute to criminality in the neighborhood as much as the absence of informal *social control*.

These models can suggest different solutions to neighborhood crime and disorder problems by focusing on either the restoration of social control or the strengthening of social support mechanisms needed to prevent antisocial and dysfunctional behavior. However, as Cullen notes, the solutions can be complementary and mutually dependent because social support, trust, and respect are often prerequisites for exercising social control in a relationship.[2] Nevertheless, voluntary community groups tend to give more attention to social control strategies, and, therefore, these approaches are the focal point of the present chapter. Social support strategies, such as youth-oriented programs and early intervention projects, are given greater attention in Chapter 10.

Opportunity Reduction Model

Perhaps the most appropriate model for understanding community crime prevention practices is the opportunity reduction approach. In a nutshell, opportunity theories suggest that criminal behavior is driven by the opportunity to commit crime presented by a particular location, time, and set of circumstances. Therefore, the removal or reduction of these opportunities, according to this model, should lead to a reduction in crime in that particular setting and under those conditions.

For a crime to occur, four basic elements must be present: criminal law, an offender, a target or victim, and a place or environment. The opportunity models have emerged from research focusing on different aspects of the criminal

---

2. Stated in interpersonal terms, a youth might say to a control agent (not necessarily in these words), "You have no control or influence over me because I don't respect you, trust you, or believe that you care about me and are acting in my interest."

event. Environmental criminology, influenced by the writings of Jeffrey (1971) and Newman (1972), helped us understand how changes in the *physical environment* (urban design and architecture) would influence crime and perceptions of safety in particular neighborhoods (see Chapter 7). More recently, research focusing on the thoughts and behaviors of *offenders* has led to the development of important opportunity theories of crime, including routine activities models (Cohen & Felson, 1979) and offender decision-making or rational choice models (Brantingham & Brantingham, 1984; Cornish & Clarke, 1986; Rengert, 1989).

The routine activities model provides the clearest illustration of how opportunity is the key element in the commission or prevention of crime. This model suggests that a crime is more likely to occur in places where there is a convergence of "motivated offenders," "suitable targets," and the absence of "guardians" who can prevent the offense. The limited rational choice decision-making theories help us understand how offenders select particular neighborhoods, plan their offenses, and select their targets, but again, the key element is the offender's assessment of whether the right opportunity to maximize benefit and minimize costs exists. Indeed, research has established a link between environmental opportunity/risk and criminal behavior (for example, Clarke, 1992; Cohen & Felson, 1979; Mayhew, 1990; Rengert, 1980).

The implications of opportunity theories for community crime prevention are clear. Community groups and individuals concerned about the neighborhood must do everything possible to make crime more difficult or costly for offenders by either removing or reducing opportunities in specific locations. Clarke and his colleagues have delineated and classified the different ways this can be accomplished (Clarke, 1992). Generally speaking, opportunity reduction strategies are designed to (1) increase the level of effort required to commit a crime, (2) increase the risk of detection and apprehension, or (3) reduce the rewards associated with crime (see Chapter 8 for a more detailed discussion of "situational crime prevention" measures). Here, we are interested in collective citizen actions as they pertain to neighborhood-based crime prevention. Our emphasis is on interventions designed to directly influence the social behavior of neighborhood residents rather than on interventions that focus on changes to the physical environment. Nevertheless, we recognize the close interdependency of physical and social variables in crime prevention.

Although voluntary community organizations sometimes get involved in strategies to increase the effort needed to commit a crime (for example, educating local residents about target hardening or access control measures) or strategies to reduce the rewards for offending (for example, property marking, graffiti cleaning), historically, their primary agenda has been to encourage human surveillance of public spaces to detect and prevent criminal activity. In the language of opportunity theory, local residents, through neighborhood watches and patrols, seek to increase the number of "guardians" who will protect the neighborhood and decrease the number of "suitable targets" by supervising the behavior of youth. If offenders come to the conclusion that the risk of detection and apprehension are higher in a particular neighborhood or on a particular block as a result of human surveillance, they should be less inclined to perpetrate crimes in that geographic area.

The theoretical explanations offered by the three models just described are more complementary than they are conflictual when applied to community crime prevention practices. Indeed, neighborhood guardians, individually and collectively, employ a wide variety of strategies to prevent crime and maintain order. These include the provision of social supports, in combination with social control sanctions, to encourage local youths to act in prosocial ways. In addition to helping local youths desist from offending and avoid victimization by being "streetwise," neighborhood guardians are on the lookout for predatory and property offenders who might be deterred by surveillance and intervention or, if necessary, by police action. Even though considerable uncertainty and debate exists about the extent of nurturing and supportive behaviors in urban neighborhoods, there is little question that neighborhoods are organizing to fight back against known offenders (see, for example, Chapter 6 for antidrug initiatives). Hence, in this chapter, we will examine the nature and effectiveness of the most popular and persistent collective crime prevention programs—watches and patrols. First, however, we will examine the role of voluntary community organizations in neighborhood life.

COLLECTIVE ACTION AND COMMUNITY ORGANIZATIONS

"Organizing" the community has become a common response to neighborhood and community problems. Across the nation, literally thousands of grassroots community organizations have sought to organize and empower local residents given perceived threats such as crime, toxic chemicals, noise pollution, traffic safety, and other environmental stressors (Heller, 1990). Collective grassroots action is considered necessary when the public believes that traditional, formal responses from governmental and service agencies have been (or will be) ineffectual at best, or, at worst, harmful to the community. Grassroots community activism for the purpose of community empowerment has experienced a major rebirth in recent years, beginning in the late 1970s (Boyte, 1980; 1987). There are many different approaches to community empowerment. Dreier (1996) identified three distinct strategies for empowering the community: (1) "community organizing" efforts to mobilize people against specific problems and increase their voices in decisions affecting their lives; (2) "community-based development" to improve the physical and economic conditions through job creation, business development, housing, and so on; and (3) "community-based service provision" that will enhance people's skills and opportunities, such as job training, child care, and parenting skills.

This chapter focuses on the first empowerment strategy, namely, community organizing efforts to mobilize local residents against the problems of crime, gangs, and drug abuse. Nevertheless, we begin with the recognition that voluntary community organizations have approached the problem of crime from different angles with diverse anticrime strategies.

Collective responses to crime can take many forms and be conceptualized in different ways (see Bickman, Lavrakas, Green, North-Walker, Edwards, Vorkowski, DuBow, & Wuerth, 1976; DuBow, McCabe, & Kaplan, 1979; Greenberg, Rohe, & Williams, 1985; Rosenbaum, 1988; Yin, 1979; Yin, Vogel, Chaiken, & Both, 1976). Programs vary depending on the extent to which they focus on preventing offending or preventing victimization (Lewis & Salem, 1981), are initiated by efforts indigenous or exogenous to the neighborhood (Bursik & Grasmick, 1993; Greenberg, Rohe, & Williams, 1985), address social problems at the root of crime or opportunities for crime (Podolefsky & DuBow, 1981; Rosenbaum, 1988; Skogan, 1990), and engage in social action to advocate the cause of disadvantaged groups or to preserve the status quo by reinforcing common values and practices (Lewis, Grant, & Rosenbaum, 1988; Skogan, 1987). Many of these distinctions are overlapping. For example, groups whose primary interest is victimization prevention tend to focus their efforts on reducing opportunities for crime, defending the neighborhood from criminal behavior, and reinforcing the status quo through social control mechanisms. Some are single-issue watch groups, whereas others are multi-issue community organizations. In contrast, groups whose primary interest is the alleviation of social problems facing the neighborhood tend to attack crime by providing social services (for example, drug treatment, housing for the homeless, employment training) and by advocacy efforts that target governmental and service agencies. In the latter case, crime prevention is a by-product of efforts to improve the neighborhood and strengthen human capital rather than a primary objective of the group (see Chapter 10 for a discussion of the social problems approach). In this chapter, the focus is on direct anticrime efforts by community organizations.

Research strongly suggests that local voluntary organizations are an important vehicle for collective crime prevention activities in urban neighborhoods (Lavrakas et al., 1980; Podolefsky & DuBow, 1981). Neighborhood surveys in major cities during the late 1970s indicate that between 10 and 20 percent of neighborhood residents participated in local voluntary organizations and even fewer participated in crime prevention activities through these groups. More recent national survey data confirm these findings and provide documentation of changes in collective participation rates over time. A national sample survey in 1981 found that approximately 12 percent of the adult population belonged to a neighborhood group that was involved in crime prevention activities (O'Keefe & Mendelsohn, 1984). This figure increased dramatically in the decade that followed. Another national survey using the same question in 1992 found that the percentage of adults belonging to a neighborhood group involved in crime prevention had increased to 31 percent (O'Keefe, Rosenbaum, Lavrakas, Reid, & Botta, 1996).

NEIGHBORHOOD WATCH

The dominant form of collective citizen crime prevention in the United States during the past 25 years has been "Neighborhood Watch" or "Block Watch." Watch programs, which are widely supported by community organizations and law enforcement agencies, typically involve "citizens coming together in relatively small groups (usually block clubs) to share information about local crime problems, exchange crime prevention tips, and make plans for engaging in surveillance ('watching') of the neighborhood and crime-reporting activities." (Rosenbaum, 1987, p. 104). Two national sample surveys conducted by O'Keefe and his colleagues measured changes in levels of citizen participation in crime prevention behaviors from the early 1980s to the early 1990s, including watch-type activities (O'Keefe et al., 1996). The results indicate that watching a neighbor's house while the neighbor is away (and vice versa) increased substantially during this decade, but getting together formally with a group of neighbors to discuss crime prevention actually declined. Specifically, the percentage of households that reported "always" "keeping a helpful watch on neighbors and their property" rose from 43 percent in 1981 to 61 percent in 1992. Similarly, from 1981 to 1992, there were noticeable increases in the percentage of households that "always" ask a neighbor to watch their homes when away (55 percent vs. 74 percent) and ask a neighbor to stop deliveries or bring in the mail (46 percent vs. 69 percent). However, participation in group meetings to "discuss steps to take against crime" dropped from 47 percent in 1981 to 30 percent in 1992. Thus, ad hoc defensive actions to protect one's own property and that of one's *immediate* neighbors continues to rise in the United States, but more formal group meetings to discuss crime prevention actions appear to have declined in frequency. Nevertheless, Neighborhood Watch remains a popular program. Although comparable data are not available from 1981, the 1992 survey revealed that 42 percent of all households in America reported having a Neighborhood Watch program in their neighborhood, and more than two-thirds said that the program was "extensively" implemented.

Theory-Based Expectations

From the perspective of social control and social support theories, the expectation is that watch-type activities increase social contact and social interaction, thus helping to strengthen social control bonds, increase social support, enhance social cohesion, and reduce fear of crime by reducing isolation and distrust (DuBow & Emmons, 1981; Greenberg, Rohe, Williams, 1985; Rosenbaum, 1987; Silloway & McPherson, 1985; Yin, 1979). From the perspective of opportunity theories, watch-type programs are expected to reduce opportunities for crime by enhancing human surveillance of, and intervention in, suspicious or criminal activity as described earlier. At the foundation of many opportunity theories, including environmental design models (Jeffrey, 1971; Newman, 1972) is Jacobs's (1961) idea that "eyes on the street" are very important for deterring crime. Through social intervention (rather than physical design), watch programs are intended to stimulate intentional (rather than casual) surveillance of the neighborhood, with the intent of reducing criminal opportunities. The opportunity model suggests that fear of crime will decrease as the neighborhood becomes safer and residents perceive a decrease in their risk of victimization. Thus, watch programs, by asking residents to become "the eyes and ears" of the police, seek to increase collective surveillance of the block or neighborhood. In addition, such programs serve other crime prevention functions. According to a national survey of 550 watch programs (Garofalo & McLeod, 1986), many of these groups engaged in property marking (81 percent), home security surveys (68 percent), meetings to exchange information (61 percent), and the distribution of newsletters (54 percent). Generally, these activities can be characterized as self-protective, victimization prevention strategies within the opportunity reduction framework.

Empirical Support

Two distinct types of empirical evidence are relevant to the question of whether watch-type interventions are useful and effective strategies of crime prevention. The first is a substantial number of neighborhood studies on citizen reactions to crime (for reviews, see DuBow, McCabe, & Kaplan, 1979; Greenberg, Rohe, & Williams, 1985). The second is a body of evaluation research that focuses directly on assessing watch programs (see Rosenbaum, 1987; 1988). We will summarize the key aspects of these literatures.

Neighborhood research on reactions to crime and studies of small groups are generally consistent with the theories behind collective crime prevention programs—both types of research highlight the importance of social influence. For example, research on group dynamics indicates that more frequent social contact among group members is associated with stronger group cohesion (Shaw, 1981), which is consistent with the goal of "community building." Also, network studies have demonstrated that greater social interaction is associated with stronger informal social control (Fischer, Jackson, Stueve, Gerson, & Jones, 1977).

In theory, community organizations and watch-type programs provide neighborhood residents with opportunities to have more social contact and interaction. In turn, this interaction is expected to increase familiarity with neighbors, stimulate information exchange, and enhance social integration and cohesion (DuBow & Emmons, 1981; Greenberg, Rohe, & Williams, 1985; Rosenbaum, 1987; Skogan, 1987). Indeed, studies indicate that "participators" in local grassroots organizations exhibit higher levels of neighborhood social interactions than "nonparticipators" (Ahlbrandt & Cunningham, 1979; Axelrod, 1956; Bell & Boat, 1957; Fellin & Litwak, 1963; Greer, 1956; Hunter, 1975; Kasarda & Janowitz, 1974).

Some neighborhood studies have examined the relationship between specific social control responses (or social support, depending on one's interpretation) and the rate of local crime problems. In support of community crime prevention theories, crime rates and related problems are lower in neighborhoods where residents report more attachment to the neighborhood (Taub, Taylor, & Dunham, 1984; Warren, 1969), feel more responsibility for events in the area (Taylor, Gottfredson, & Brower, 1981), report a greater willingness to intervene in criminal activity (Maccoby, Johnson, & Church, 1958), and believe that their neighbors would intervene (Newman & Franck, 1980).[3] Contrary to predictions from these models, however, crime rates are not associated with "neighboring" activities (for example, surveillance), having friends in the neighborhood, or the ability to recognize strangers (see Greenberg, Rohe, & Williams, 1985). Recently, Sampson, Raudenbush, and Earls (1997), in a large study of 343 Chicago neighborhoods, found lower rates of violence in neighborhoods that were high in "collective efficacy," that is, high social cohesion among neighbors combined with people's willingness to intervene on behalf of the common good.

Finally, additional support for crime prevention theory comes from neighborhood studies that suggest that levels of disorder or incivility[4] are lower in neighborhoods where residents interact more frequently, engage in less avoidance and withdrawal behavior, express more community solidarity or cohesion and cooperate more in crime prevention activities (Skogan, 1990).

Bringing citizens together to fight crime is expected to reduce fear of crime either directly (by reducing crime and disorder) or indirectly (by increasing familiarity, mutual trust and support, and feelings of control). Neighborhood studies indicate that fear of crime is lower in neighborhoods where residents report more responsibility and control over events in the area (Greenberg, Rohe, & Williams, 1982; Skogan & Maxfield, 1981), levels of disorder and incivility are low (Skogan & Maxfield, 1981; Skogan, 1990; Taub, Taylor, & Dunham, 1981), and neighbors are perceived as available when needed to provide assistance (Sundeen & Mathieu, 1976).

Although cross-sectional neighborhood studies suggest that specific social processes might help regulate levels of crime, disorder, and fear, they tell us little about whether these variables are *causally connected* and whether watch-type programs can activate the social processes implicit in theories underlying the program. For example, a tremendous amount of self-selection occurs (for example, the decision to participate in anticrime programs and the decision to live in certain neighborhoods), which might explain differences in neighborhood outcomes. Participation in community groups or watches is not a

3. These findings are supported by data from controlled experiments on bystander intervention, which indicate that witnesses to a crime are more likely to intervene or call the police if they know the victim, know the witnesses, are encouraged to intervene, or are familiar with the environment (Bickman & Rosenbaum, 1977; Gills & Hagan, 1982; Latané & Darley, 1970; Moriarity, 1975; Ross, 1971). For more information, see Chapter 2.

4. Disorder refers to a range of neighborhood problems that concern local residents but traditionally have not been a priority of the police. These include acts of social incivility and physical deterioration, including graffiti, litter, boarded-up buildings, abandoned autos, youths hanging out, public drunkenness, prostitution, drug sales, and so on.

random process. As noted in Chapter 2, research indicates that participators are more likely to be middle class, married with children, homeowners, and well educated (Lavrakas et al., 1980; Skogan & Maxfield, 1981; Wandersman, Jakubs, & Giamartino, 1981). Participation in watch programs is also a middle-class activity according to national studies (Garofalo & McLeod, 1989; Whitaker, 1986) and is more likely to emerge in neighborhoods with racial and economic homogeneity (Greenberg, Rohe, & Williams, 1982). Research also informs us that middle-class neighborhoods exhibit stronger levels of informal social control and support than high-crime, lower-income areas. Specifically, residents report more control over events, greater willingness to intervene, more responsibility for crime prevention, and more similarity to their neighbors (Boggs, 1971; Greenberg, Rohe, & Williams, 1982; Hackler, Ho, & Urquhart-Ross, 1974; Taub, Taylor, & Dunham, 1982; Taylor, Gottfredson, & Brower, 1981). These findings, when viewed separately, could be misconstrued to suggest that watch programs are effective at stimulating citizen participation and social interaction, strengthening social control behaviors, and reducing crime, disorder, and fear. This type of misinterpretation would be unfortunate. The problem can be summarized as follows:

> [This research] leaves unanswered the fundamental question of whether the *introduction* of a community crime prevention program (and Neighborhood Watch in particular) can make a difference in the perceptions, attitudes, and behaviors of local residents. The important question here is whether informal social control (and other processes supposedly activated by watch-type programs) can be *implanted* in neighborhoods where they have not naturally developed. Let us refer to this as the Implant hypothesis. (Rosenbaum, 1987, p. 108)

This brings us to the second type of data—evaluations of watch programs, especially those interventions designed to implant collective surveillance and social control processes in neighborhoods where such behavior is weak or nonexistent. In support of watch-type programs, numerous studies have found that participants report less property victimization than do nonparticipants, and a smaller subset of studies shows sizable drops in property crime in target areas after implementation of the program (see Greenberg, Rohe, & Williams, 1985; Titus, 1983). However, the vast majority of these findings are based on very weak research designs. For example, we identified 111 programs claiming success with Neighborhood Watch and found that 92 percent used a simple one-group pretest-posttest design (Lurigio & Rosenbaum, 1986), which is subject to numerous threats to validity (see Cook & Campbell, 1979). Some of the better evaluations of community crime prevention programs also show reductions in property crime and fear of crime (see Rosenbaum, 1986), but often they are assessing comprehensive programs, and the independent effects of watch activities cannot be easily determined.

The best, most scientifically collected data on the effectiveness of watch-type programs comes from four large-scale evaluations in Chicago (Rosenbaum, Lewis, & Grant, 1985; 1986), London, England (Bennett, 1987),

Minneapolis (Pate, McPherson, & Silloway, 1987), and Seattle (Cirel, Evans, McGillis, & Whitcomb, 1977). The findings from these studies were very different than those reported in the typical evaluation of Neighborhood Watch. The general pattern of results in these large-scale studies can be summarized as follows: (1) residents' awareness of, and participation in, the program increased as hypothesized; (2) crime rates generally did not change or increase contrary to expectation; (3) fear of crime did not change or increased contrary to expectation; (4) social cohesion generally did not change; and (5) other intermediate social processes did not change. The last set of findings is perhaps the most critical and can be summarized this way:

> Perhaps the most important set of findings to emerge from these evaluations is that community organizing was unable to activate the intervening social behaviors that are hypothesized as necessary (according to informal social control and opportunity reduction models) to produce the desired changes in crime, fear, and social integration. Specifically, the researchers reported very few changes in social interaction, surveillance, stranger recognition, crime reporting, home protection behaviors, feelings of control, efficacy, and responsibility, satisfaction with the neighborhood, and attitudes toward the police. (Rosenbaum, 1988, p. 362)

In summary, the most rigorous evaluations provide scant support for the implant hypothesis. In retrospect, one implication of these studies is that community leaders, policy makers, and academicians expected too much from these programs in the 1970s and 1980s. Furthermore, they were forced to explain some surprising and unexpected findings, such as significant increases in fear of crime after residents participated in watch meetings. On closer scrutiny, these fear-of-crime results were not so difficult to explain. Researchers have suggested that fear will be heightened when residents meet and exchange information about local crime and victimization experiences (Greenberg, Rohe, & Williams, 1985; Rosenbaum, Lewis, & Grant, 1985; Skogan & Maxfield, 1981). Indeed, fieldwork in Chicago and a review of community organizing manuals in Chicago and Seattle revealed that organizers of block watch meetings are trained to encourage a discussion of crime and victimization experience as a method of increasing participants' motivation for action (see Rosenbaum, 1987).

From these evaluations, we also learned that mobilizing citizens and maintaining their participation in collective activities is most difficult in neighborhoods where crime prevention programs are needed the most. In low-income, high-crime, heterogeneous neighborhoods, participation levels tend to be very low even after substantial organizing efforts (McPherson & Silloway, 1987). As it turns out, in these target areas, many of the assumptions behind watch programs are questionable at best (Rosenbaum, 1987). For example, asking residents to work together, keep an eye out for "suspicious persons," and report crime to the police is asking too much in neighborhoods defined by high levels of disorder, crime, fear of crime, mutual distrust, high transience, numerous "strangers," and a history of poor police-community relations. In a nutshell, attempts to implant middle-class norms about "neighboring" or re-porting "illegal" behavior reflect an ignorance of the inner-city social ecology. In a similar vein, local residents in high-crime communities define the prob-lem not as one of "suspicious persons" but, rather as unemployment, poor schools, drug abuse, and other social problems that can contribute to gangs, violence, and contact with the criminal justice system. Consequently, local voluntary organizations in these neighborhoods are often more inclined to promote a social-problems approach to crime prevention, as described in Chapter 10, rather than to pursue watch-type programs (Bennett & Lavrakas, 1988; Podolefsky, 1983).

CITIZEN PATROLS

Neighborhood and Block Watch programs generally involve passive surveil-lance, whereby local residents are asked to "keep an eye out" for suspicious or criminal activity as part of their daily, routine activities. A more aggressive and structured type of watch program—the citizen patrol[5]—is also available to residents in many urban areas. Many types of citizen patrols have been orga-nized in the United States during the past 30 years (see Garofalo & McLeod, 1986; Pennell, Curtis, & Henderson, 1985; Podolefsky & DuBow, 1981; Yin et al., 1976). In the 1960s, African American groups initiated citizen patrols to protect their communities from urban police abuses (for example, Black Pan-thers in Oakland, California) and from racist groups in the south (Garofalo & McLeod, 1986; Marx & Archer, 1971). In the 1970s and early 1980s, the typical citizen patrol was used as the mobile "eyes and ears" of the police to prevent and detect residential crime (especially burglary) in middle-class neighborhoods. In the 1980s and 1990s, citizen patrols became popular in inner-city neighborhoods as a weapon against open-air drug markets and known drug houses (see Chapter 6; Also see Davis, Lurigio, & Rosenbaum, 1993; Rosenbaum, Bennett, Lindsay, & Wilkinson, 1994). Today, citizen pa-trols appear in diverse neighborhoods and focus on a wide range of crime and disorder problems as part of a new problem-solving partnership between local residents and local police (see Chapter 9).

Citizen patrols can be distinguished along several dimensions (Yin et al., 1976). They differ in their function (for example, protection of individual residents, deterrence of crime and disorder, identification of problem areas), surveillance area (for example, buildings, neighborhood streets, public trans-portation, college campuses), mode of transportation (for example, foot, bicy-cle, or motorized patrol), and policies about responding to incidents (for example, reporting only versus intervention or arrest). Patrol groups also differ

---

5. Today, many citizen patrols are also called watches, so these labels have become interchangeable to many local groups. However, the level of active participation continues to vary, as some groups do not patrol their neighborhoods.

in size. Most citizen patrols are local neighborhood groups, but others are city-wide or national in scope. The Guardian Angels, for example, is a national network serving dozens of U.S. cities (Pennell, Curtis, & Henderson, 1985).

The number and type of citizen patrols in the United States today is difficult to estimate. In 1975, a national study estimated the number of patrols at only 800 (Yin et al., 1976). Certainly, the number of patrols has grown considerably during the past 20 years. A 1992 national telephone survey, for example, found that 10 percent of U.S. households report having an active citizen patrol in their neighborhood, which implies that there are literally thousands of patrols nationwide. In larger U.S. cities, the number of participants in citizen patrols can be substantial. Pennell and her colleagues (1985) refer to reports that estimated 150,000 Philadelphia participants and a similar number in New York City in the first half of 1980.

Patrols are sometimes affiliated with Neighborhood Watch programs. In 1984, a national mail survey of Neighborhood Watch programs found that 12 percent of these programs had a formal surveillance component and the majority of these were motorized patrols (Garofalo & McLeod, 1986).

Research suggests that the "typical" citizen who participates in citizen patrols is very similar to the Neighborhood Watch member—middle-class, homeowner, well-educated, married with children, and so forth. Consistent with the pattern of participation in passive Watch programs, citizen patrols are likely to appear in areas experiencing gentrification (McDonald, 1986). The pattern of participation in organized citizen patrols, however, is not identical to that of Watch programs. One difference is that men are more likely to participate than women (Lavrakas et al., 1980; Pennell, Curtis, & Henderson, 1985; Troyer, 1988). Also, the mobilization of inner-city residents in the war against drugs in the late 1980s prompted more participation among low-to-middle income residents and persons of color (Davis, Lurigio, & Rosenbaum, 1993; Rosenbaum et al., 1994), and in public housing developments (Popkin et al., 1996). However, because of the added risk of retaliation by drug dealers, the preferred antidrug strategies in high-crime neighborhoods involve participation in large ad hoc rallies and vigils or covert surveillance in support of police operations rather than scheduled, visible patrols of the area (Rosenbaum et al., 1994).

Are citizen patrols effective? How are they perceived by the police and the community? Despite the popularity of citizen patrols in urban neighborhoods, there has been little research on their effectiveness (see Pennell, Curtis, & Henderson, 1985, for a review). Relying on anecdotal evidence, the only national evaluation of citizen patrols (Yin et al., 1977) concluded that *building* patrols "may be" effective in preventing crime and increasing residents' perceived safety at home, but other types of patrols have less empirical support. Consistent with this conclusion, a major evaluation of anticrime strategies in Chicago public housing—which included tenant patrols as a key program component—showed significant beneficial effects on perceived levels of violence, fear of crime, and other quality of life measures (Popkin et al., 1996). Unfortunately, because tenant patrols were only one component of a comprehensive antidrug initiative, the evaluators were unable to disentangle the effects of different interventions.

Neighborhood patrols as a single intervention have been studied in several cities, but the results are mixed. A well-organized walking patrol in Columbus, Ohio, was associated with reductions in several types of reported crime, especially burglary and auto theft (Latessa and Allen, 1980). In San Diego, the presence of a Guardian Angels patrol had no impact on violent crime rates, but was associated with short-term declines in property crime during peak visibility periods (Pennell, Curtis, & Henderson, 1985). These evaluation findings, however, should be viewed with caution because of the limitations of the research designs.

Perhaps the more important question at this point is how the police and the public view citizen patrols. Generally speaking, the public has been very supportive of citizen patrols, including aggressive patrols where citizens intervene in criminal situations. For example, surveys of community residents in San Diego and eastern transit riders indicate that they view the Guardian Angels (who are not afraid to stop violent crimes in progress) as effective in reducing crime and that they feel more safe when the Angels are patrolling (Pennell, Curtis, & Henderson, 1985). The police, however, have been slow to recognize and accept citizen patrols, especially patrols that desire to do more than be the "eyes and ears" of law enforcement.

Police administrators have been fearful that endorsing citizen patrols could lead to "vigilantism" and "hate violence."[6] Clearly, the media and the criminal justice system have recently given increased attention to extreme groups (for example, neo-Nazis, "skinheads," KKK affiliates) who have demonstrated hatred toward persons of color, homosexuals, Jews, and others (Bureau of Justice Assistance, 1997). Furthermore, our nation has a long history of vigilantism, both before and after the transfer of responsibility for law enforcement functions from the citizenry to paid officials (see Brown, 1970; DuBow, McCabe, & Kaplan, 1979). Before the mid nineteenth century, when paid law enforcement was nonexistent or inadequate, vigilantism was considered helpful to government. However, after this period, vigilantism became a vehicle for the expression of hatred and control over racial and ethnic groups, which provides the basis for modern police concerns about lawless citizen patrols. Despite these concerns, there is little reason to believe that the typical citizen patrol is prone to vigilantism or hate crime (Yin et al., 1977).

This is not to suggest that prejudice and racism play no part in modern citizen patrols and watches. Actually, a more subtle process of racism can occur with watch-type anticrime programs. Watches and patrols often start in middle-class neighborhoods at a time when local residents perceive a sharp rise in crime or have experienced a dramatic crime incident (Garofalo &

---

6. Hate crimes, or bias-motivated crimes, are defined as "offenses motivated by hatred against a victim based on his or her race, religion, sexual orientation, handicap, ethnicity, or national origin." (Bureau of Justice Assistance, 1997, p. ix.)

McLeod, 1986). Talk about crime is likely to increase fears about victimization and concern about neighborhood decline (see Rosenbaum, 1987), and patrols are more likely to form in neighborhoods with some racial transition. Given widespread prejudice in our society, it is all too easy for watch/patrol participants to blame certain groups for what is perceived as a growing crime problem. The concern is that "the issues of crime, race, ethnicity, religion, and neighborhood transition can become confused and intertwined in the minds of fearful residents. Fear of strangers, newcomers (even those of the individual's same race or religion), and other ethnic or racial groups can easily be misconstrued as fear of crime" (Rosenbaum, Hernandez, & Daughtry, 1991, p. 107). Hence, part of the responsibility of community organizers (and watch/patrol leaders) is to keep the focus on crime-related problems and not on persons of color moving into (or through) the neighborhood. Unfortunately, the tendency to associate minorities with crime has led some watch groups to direct their surveillance activities disproportionately at minorities. Being African American or Hispanic should not be grounds for suspicion, but this is a real possibility with watch and patrol groups, as it has been with some police officers.

Although subtle racism should concern police and community leaders, the primary concern of police administrators seems to be the possibility of the blatant vigilantism and law suits that can result from overzealous citizens on patrol (Rosenbaum, Hernandez, & Daughtry, 1991). The Guardian Angels illustrate this problem. Many big-city police chiefs do not recognize or support this national patrol group, despite the positive review it has received in a national evaluation (Pennell, Curtis, & Henderson, 1985). The Guardian Angels encourage their members to intervene in criminal or emergency situations, which has scared away many law enforcement agencies.

Most police leaders today remain opposed to citizen intervention in crime situations, but their support for the typical "eyes and ears" patrol has grown substantially. This change in attitude, which might reflect the influence of the community policing movement (see Chapter 9), has translated into closer working relationships with citizen patrols. There are many excellent examples. The Mobile Neighborhood Watch in Salt Lake City, Utah, a nonprofit patrol organization, is housed at the police department headquarters, where federal grant support is provided for equipment, staff, and training (Rosenbaum & Kaminska, 1997). After 16 hours of training, pairs of citizens in personal cars (marked "Mobile Watch") patrol for either two- or three-hour shifts. They have mobile phones with direct access to the police dispatcher or field commander and are expected to file a report at the conclusion of each shift that will be read by the beat officer. Membership has climbed from about 450 in 1995 to approximately 800 volunteers in 1997. Citizen patrols are also blossoming in Fort Worth, Texas. Here, the police department also provides space and works very closely with local citizen volunteers on training issues and field operations (Skogan & Rosenbaum, 1997). Unlike Salt Lake City, Fort Worth is a decentralized operation in which independent citizen patrols have developed their own relationship with neighborhood police stations in different regions of the city.

SUMMARY AND CONCLUSION

In this chapter we have reviewed efforts to prevent neighborhood crime through collective citizen action. There are many strategies for empowering citizens to attack neighborhood problems, but in the field of crime prevention, community organizing through voluntary community groups has been the predominant approach. The rationale for collective, as opposed to individual, anticrime efforts is consistent with three major theories of crime—social disorganization, social support, and opportunity theories.

Historically, most collective crime prevention activities are defined by two types of programs—Neighborhood Watch and citizen patrols. Despite growing citizen participation in these programs, evaluations have been unable to find consistent benefits in crime reduction or quality of life measures. Certainly, these programs provide additional "eyes and ears" for the police, and these partnerships with the police can improve police-community relations or lead to an increase in the number of arrests for certain types of offenses, although evaluators have yet to document such results. Considerable evidence indicates that vigilant citizens have been successful in using community antidrug initiatives to close drug houses and remove open-air drug markets (see Chapter 6). But no empirical evidence indicates that Watches and patrols can successfully "implant" social order, social control, and social support in neighborhoods where such processes are naturally lacking. Also, there is limited evidence that such programs can reduce crime and disorder, except for drug activity.

The failure to find scientific evidence of effective watch-type programs is likely due to various factors. First, we must emphasize there have been very few scientifically rigorous evaluations of community crime prevention programs involving voluntary collective citizen actions. Most evaluations are seriously flawed (Lurigio & Rosenbaum, 1986). A series of well-controlled experiments or quasi-experiments might yield more promising results. However, given that several major studies have produced null results, we must ask why. There are many possible explanations, including false assumptions about the social ecology of high-crime neighborhoods and the failure to think creatively about strategies to prevent crime. During the past 25 years, our nation's "cookie cutter" approach to neighborhood crime prevention policy has led to the widespread promotion of watch-type programs, even in neighborhoods where they are inappropriate (see Rosenbaum, 1987). For example, in heterogeneous neighborhoods with a high rate of renter turnover and high levels of crime, the idea of having a social gathering with trusted neighbors to develop a system for surveillance and mutual support against "strangers" and "suspicious persons" makes little sense. Virtually everyone is a stranger in this setting. However, meetings can be tailored to the social requirements of the neighborhood and help residents creatively solve local problems. Today, we see this happening with much greater frequency.

Even in neighborhoods where watch-type programs are appropriate, these activities will not survive unless organizers are attentive to the factors that contribute to longevity. Most watch programs are discontinued within a short time—usually when the initial crisis has subsided and members lose interest. The successful maintenance of collective citizen crime prevention requires strong leadership, continuous group structure, links to outside resources, a full agenda, decentralized planning, good communication channels, and regular efforts to reward citizens for their efforts (Bennett & Lavrakas, 1988; Chavis, Florin, Rich, Wandersman, & Perkins, 1987; Garofalo & McLeod, 1986). For these reasons, researchers and community leaders have encouraged local residents to create multi-issue community organizations that address a wide range of neighborhood problems and are not limited to the issue of crime.

To effectively attack crime, drugs, gangs, and disorder in inner-city neighborhoods, communities will also need more resources to mount serious programs. We have little reason to expect that the typical community-based intervention will significantly affect neighborhood conditions, primarily because the "dosage" of the "treatment" (to borrow some medical terms) is far too weak. As evaluators, we are always surprised at how little money (if any) is given to community organizations to develop and implement crime prevention programs. This state of affairs can be attributed to a general distrust of grassroots organizations by government funding agencies, combined with the popular misconception that crime prevention programs run by "voluntary" community organizations should be "free" to the taxpayers. Although crime prevention activities often reflect donated hours of time by volunteers (thus lowering program costs), nevertheless, credible interventions still require funding for personnel, equipment, and materials.

Finally, community leaders will need to think more creatively about crime prevention. This should include efforts to reach beyond the mobilization of local residents to form partnerships with other agencies and organizations both inside and outside the neighborhood. The ability to leverage resources outside the neighborhood (police, social services, city services) is especially important in high-crime areas where local institutions are weak and financial disinvestment is widespread. Watches and patrols—although they play an important defensive role in the neighborhood—only scrape the surface of what is possible through voluntary community action. For example, local community organizing efforts produced the successful national "community reinvestment" movement to stop the problem of bank redlining in low-income and minority neighborhoods (see Dreier, 1996). Clearly, community groups can play an important role in bringing government attention to issues of housing, health, education, city services, the environment, and economic development. By carefully defining the problems that contribute to crime and neighborhood decline, community organizations can play an important role in shaping the agenda for long-term solutions.

REFERENCES

Ahlbrandt, R. S., Jr., & Cunningham, J. V. (1979). *A new public policy for neighborhood preservation.* New York: Praeger.

Axelrod, M. (1956). Urban structure and social participation. *American Sociological Review* 21, 13–18.

Bell, W., & Boat, M. D. (1957). Urban neighborhoods and informal social relations. *American Journal of Sociology* 62, 391–398.

Bennett, S., & Lavrakas, P. J. (1988). *How neighborhood groups decide what to do about crime.* Paper presented at the annual meeting of the American Society of Criminology, San Diego.

Bennett, T. (1987). *An evaluation of two neighborhood watch schemes in London.* Executive summary of final report to the Home Office Research and Planning Unit. Cambridge: Cambridge University, Institute of Criminology.

Bickman, L., Lavrakas, P. J., Green, S. K., North-Walker, N., Edwards, J., Vorkowski, S., DuBow, S. S., & Wuerth, J. (1976). *Citizen crime reporting projects.* National Evaluation Program, Phase I summary report. Washington, DC: Department of Justice.

Bickman, L., & Rosenbaum, D. P. (1977). Crime reporting as a function of bystander encouragement, surveillance, and credibility. *Journal of Personality and Social Psychology* 35, 577–586.

Boggs, S. (1971). Formal and informal crime control: An exploratory study of urban, suburban and rural orientation. *Sociological Quarterly* 12, 319–327.

Boyte, H. (1980). *The backyard revolution: Understanding the new citizen movement.* Philadelphia: Temple University Press.

Boyte, H. (1987). *Commonwealth: A return to citizen politics.* New York: Free Press.

Brantingham, P. J., and Brantingham, P. L. (1984). *Patterns in crime.* New York: Macmillan.

Brown, R. M. (1970). The American vigilante tradition. In H. D. Graham and T. R. Gurr (eds.), *The history of violence in America* (pp. 154–217). New York: Bantam.

Bureau of Justice Assistance (1997). *A policymaker's guide to hate crime.* Washington, DC: U.S. Department of Justice, Bureau of Justice Assistance.

Bursik, R. J., Jr., & Grasmick, H. G. (1993). *Neighborhoods and crime: The dimensions of effective community control.* New York: Lexington.

Carey, J. T. (1975). *Sociology and public affairs: The Chicago School.* Beverly Hills: Sage.

Chavis, D. M., Florin, P., Rich, R. C., Wandersman, A., Perkins, D. D. (1987). *The role of block associations in crime control and community development: The Block Buster Project.* Final report to the Ford Foundation. New York: Citizens Committee for New York City, Inc.

Cirel, P., Evans, P., McGillis, D., & Whitcomb, D. (1977). *Community crime prevention program in Seattle: An exemplary project.* Washington DC: Department of Justice, National Institute of Justice.

Clarke, R. V. (ed.) (1992). *Situational crime prevention: Successful case studies.* Albany, NY: Harrow and Heston.

Cohen, L. E., & Felson, M. (1979). Social change and crime rate trends: A routine activities approach. *American Sociological Review* 44, 588–608.

Cook, T. D. & Campbell, D. T. (1979). *Quasi-experimentation: Design and analysis issues for field settings.* Chicago: Rand McNally.

Cornish, D. B., and Clarke, R. V. (1986). *The reasoning criminal: Rational choice perspectives on offending.* New York: Springer-Verlag.

Cullen, F. T. (1994). Social support as an organizing concept for criminology: Presidential address to the Academy of Criminal Justice Sciences. *Justice Quarterly* 11, 527–559.

Davis, R. C., Lurigio, A. J., & Rosenbaum, D. P. (1993). *Drugs and the
community.* Springfield, IL: Charles C.
Thomas.

Dreier, P. (1996). Community empowerment strategies: The limits and potential of community organizing in urban
neighborhoods. *Cityscape: A Journal of
Policy Development and Research 2,*
121–159.

DuBow, F., & Emmons, D. (1981). The
community hypothesis. In D. Lewis
(ed.) *Reactions to crime.* Beverly Hills,
CA: Sage.

DuBow, F., McCabe, E., & Kaplan, G.
(1979). *Reactions to crime: A critical
review of the literature.* Washington,
DC: U.S. Department of Justice,
National Institute of Justice.

Fellin, P., & Litwak, F. (1963). Neighborhood cohesion under conditions of
mobility." *American Sociological Review*
28, 364–376.

Fischer, C. S., Jackson, R. M., Stueve,
C. A., Gerson, K., & Jones, L. M.
with Baldassare, M. (1977). *Network
and places: Social relations in the urban
setting.* New York: Free Press.

Garofalo, J. & McLeod, M. (1986). *Improving the effectiveness and utilization of
Neighborhood Watch Programs.* Draft
final report to the National Institute
of Justice. Albany: State University of
New York at Albany, Hindelang
Criminal Justice Research Center.

Garofalo, J. & McLeod, M. (1989). Struc-
ture and operations of Neighborhood
Watch programs in the United States.
Crime and Delinquency 35(3), 326–344.

Gills, A. R., & Hagan, J. (1982). *Bystander
apathy and the territorial imperative.*
Toronto: University of Toronto,
Centre for Urban and Community
Studies.

Greenberg, S. W., Rohe, W. M., &
Williams, J. R. (1982). *Safe and secure
neighborhoods: Physical characteristics and
informal territorial control in high and low
crime neighborhoods.* Washington, DC:
U.S. Department of Justice, National
Institute of Justice.

Greenberg, S. W., Rohe, W. M., &
Williams, J. R. (1985). *Informal citizen
action and crime prevention at the neighborhood level.* Washington, DC: U.S.
Department of Justice, National Institute of Justice.

Greer, S. (1956). Urbanism reconsidered:
A comparative study of local areas in a
metropolis. *American Sociological Review*
21, 19–25.

Hackler, J. C., Ho, K. Y., & Urquhart-
Ross, C. (1974). The willingness to
intervene: Differing community
characteristics. *Social Problems* 21,
328–344.

Heller, K. (1990). Social and community
intervention. *Annual Review of Psychology* 41, 141–168.

Hunter, A. (1975). The loss of community: An empirical test through replication. *American Sociological Review* 40,
537–552.

Hunter, A. (1985). Private, parochial, and
public school orders: The problem of
crime and incivility in urban communities. In G. D. Suttles, and M. N.
Zald (eds.), *The challenge of social control: Citizenship and institution building
in modern society.* Norwood, NJ:
Ablex.

Hunter, A., & Riger, S. (1986). The
meaning of community in community
mental health. *Journal of Community
Psychology* 14, 55–71.

Jacobs, J. (1961). *The death and life of great
American cities.* New York: Vintage.

Jeffrey, C. R. (1971). *Crime prevention
through environmental design.* Beverly
Hills, CA: Sage.

Kasarda, J. D. & M. Janowitz. (1974).
Community attachment in mass
society. *American Sociological Review* 39,
328–339.

Kelling, G. L, & Coles, C. M. (1996).
*Fixing broken windows: Restoring order
and reducing crime in our communities.*
New York: Free Press.

Latané, B., & Darley, J. (1970). *The unre-
sponsive bystander: Why doesn't he help?*
New York: Appleton-Century-
Crofts.

Latessa, E. J., & Allen, H. F. (1980). Using citizens to prevent crime: An example of deterrence and community involvement. *Journal of Police Science and Administration* 8(1), 69–74.

Lavrakas, P. J., Normoyle, J., Skogan, W. G., Herz, E. J., Salem, G., & Lewis, D. A. (1980). *Factors related to citizen involvement in personal, household, and neighborhood anticrime measures.* Final report. National Institute of Justice. Evanston, IL: Northwestern University, Center for Urban Affairs and Policy Research.

Lewis, D. A., Grant, J. A., & Rosenbaum, D. P. (1988). *The social construction of reform: Community organizations and crime prevention.* New Brunswick, NJ: Transaction.

Lewis, D. A., & Salem, G. (1981). Community crime prevention: An analysis of a developing perspective. *Crime & Delinquency* (July), 405–421.

Lin, N. (1986). Conceptualizing social support. In N. Lin, A. Dean, & W. Edsel (eds.), *Social support, life events, and depression* (pp. 17–30). Orlando, FL: Academic.

Lurigio, A. J. & Rosenbaum, D. P. (1986). Evaluation research in community crime prevention: A critical look a the field. In D. P. Rosenbaum (ed.), *Community crime prevention: Does It work?* (pp. 19–44). Beverly Hills: Sage.

Maccoby, E. E., J. P. Johnson, & R. M. Church. (1958). Community integration and the social control of juvenile delinquency. *Journal of Social Issues* 14, 38–51.

Marx, G. T., & Archer, D. (1971). Citizen involvement in the law enforcement process: The case of community police patrols. *American Behavioral Scientist* 15, 52–72.

Matza, D. (1969). *Becoming deviant.* Englewood Cliffs, NJ: Prentice-Hall.

Mayhew, P. (1990). Opportunity and vehicle crime. In D. M. Gottfredson & R. V. Clarke (eds.), *Policy and theory in criminal justice.* Aldershot, UK: Avebury.

McDonald, S. C. (1986). Does gentrification affect crime rates? In A. L. Reiss, Jr., & M Tonry (eds.). *Communities and crime* (Vol. 8, pp. 231–311). Chicago: University of Chicago Press.

McPherson, M., & Silloway, G. (1987). The implementation process: Effort and response. In A. Pate, M. McPherson, & G. Silloway (eds.), *The Minneapolis community crime prevention experiment.* Draft evaluation report (pp. 4–1 to 4–38). Washington, DC: Police Foundation.

Moriarity, T. (1975). Crime, commitment, and the responsive bystander: Two field experiments. *Journal of Personality and Social Psychology* 31, 370–376.

National Advisory Commission on Criminal Justice Standards and Goals (1973). *A National strategy to reduce crime.* Washington, DC: Government Printing Office.

Newman, O. (1972). *Defensible space: Crime prevention through urban design.* New York: Macmillan.

Newman, O., & Franck, K. A. (1980). *Factors influencing crime and instability in urban housing developments.* Washington, DC: U.S. Government Printing Office.

O'Keefe, G. J., & Mendelsohn, H. (1984). *Taking a bite out of crime: The impact of a mass media crime prevention campaign.* Washington, DC: U.S. Department of Justice, National Institute of Justice.

O'Keefe, G. J., Rosenbaum, D. P., Lavrakas, P. J., Reid, K, & Botta, R. A. (1996). *Take a bite out of crime: The impact of a national prevention campaign.* Newbury Park, CA: Sage.

Pate, A. M., McPherson, M., & Silloway, G. (eds) (1987). *The Minneapolis community crime prevention experiment.* Draft evaluation report. Washington, DC: Police Foundation.

Pennell, S., Curtis, C., & Henderson, J. (1985). *Guardian Angels: An assessment of citizen responses to crime* (Vol. 2). Technical report to the National Institute of Justice. San Diego: San Diego Association of Governments.

Podolefsky, A. M. (1983). *Case studies in community crime prevention.* Springfield, IL: Charles C. Thomas.

Podolefsky, A., & DuBow, F. (1981). *Strategies for community crime prevention: Collective responses to crime in urban America.* Springfield, IL: Charles C. Thomas.

Popkin, S. J., Gwiasda, V. E., Amendolia, J. M., Anderson, A. A., Hanson, G., Johnson, W. A., Martel, E., Olson, L. M., & Rosenbaum, D. P. (1996). *The hidden war: The battle to control crime in Chicago's public housing.* Final report. Washington, DC: U.S. Department of Justice, National Institute of Justice.

Reiss, A. J. Jr. (1986). Why are communities important in understanding crime? In A. J. Reiss Jr. and Michael Tonry (eds.), *Communities and crime* (Vol. 8., pp. 1–33). Chicago: University of Chicago Press.

Rengert, G. F. (1980). Spatial aspects of criminal behavior. In D. E. Georges-Abeyle & K. D. Harries (eds.), *Crime: A spatial perspective.* New York: Columbia University Press.

Rengert, G. F. (1989). Behavioral geography and criminal behavior. In D. J. Evans & D. T. Herbert (eds.), *The Geography of Crime.* London: Routledge.

Rohe, W., & Greenberg, S. (1982). *Participation in community crime prevention programs.* Chapel Hill: University of North Carolina, Department of City and Regional Planning.

Rosenbaum, D. P. (ed.) (1986). *Community crime prevention: Does It work?* Beverly Hills, CA: Sage.

Rosenbaum, D. P. (1987). The theory and research behind Neighborhood Watch: Is it a sound fear and crime reduction strategy? *Crime and Delinquency* 33, 103- 34.

Rosenbaum, D. P. (1988). Community crime prevention: A review and synthesis of the literature. *Justice Quarterly* 5, 323–395.

Rosenbaum, D. P., Bennett, S. F., Lindsay, B., & Wilkinson, D. L. (1994). *Community responses to drug abuse: A program evaluation.* Washington, DC: National Institute of Justice.

Rosenbaum, D. P., Hernandez, E., & Daughtry, S., Jr. (1991). Crime prevention, fear reduction and the community. In W. A. Geller (ed.), *Local government police management* (Golden anniversary edition, pp. 96–130). Washington, DC: International City Management Association.

Rosenbaum, D. P., & Kaminska, S. J. (1997) *Salt Lake City's Comprehensive Communities Program: A case study.* Cambridge, MA: BOTEC Analysis Corporation.

Rosenbaum, D. P., Lewis, D. A., & Grant, J. A. (1985). *The impact of community crime prevention programs in Chicago: Can neighborhood organizations make a difference?* Evanston, IL: Northwestern University, Center for Urban Affairs and Policy Research.

Rosenbaum, D. P., Lewis, D. A., & Grant, J. A. (1986). Neighborhood-based crime prevention: Assessing the efficacy of community organizing in Chicago. In D. P. Rosenbaum (ed.), *Community crime prevention: Does it work?* Beverly Hills, CA: Sage.

Ross, A. S. (1971). Effect of increased responsibility on bystander intervention: The presence of children. *Journal of Personality and Social Psychology* 19, 306- 310.

Sampson, R. J. & Groves, W. B. (1989). Community structure and crime: Testing social-disorganization theory. *American Journal of Sociology* 94, 774–802.

Sampson, R. J., Raudenbush, S. W., & Earls, F. (1997). Neighborhoods and violent crime: A multilevel study of collective efficacy. *Science* 277, 918–924.

Shaw, M. E. (1981). *Group dynamics.* 3rd edition. New York: McGraw-Hill.

Shaw, C. R., & McKay, H. D. (1931). *Social factors in juvenile delinquency.* Vol. 2, No. 13. Washington, DC: U.S. Government Printing Office.

Shaw, C. R., & McKay, H. D. (1942). *Juvenile delinquency and urban areas.* Chicago: University of Chicago Press.

Silloway, G., & McPherson, M. (1985). *The limits to citizen participation in a government-sponsored community crime prevention program.* Presented at annual meeting of the American Society of Criminology, San Diego.

Skogan, W. G. (1987). Community organizations and crime. In M. Tonry and N. Morris (eds.), *Crime and Justice: A Review of Research* (Vol. 10., pp. 39–78). Chicago: University of Chicago Press.

Skogan, W. G. (1990). Disorder *and* decline: *Crime and the spiral of decay in American neighborhoods.* New York: Free Press.

Skogan, W. G., & Maxfield, M. G. (1981). *Coping with crime.* Beverly Hills, CA: Sage.

Skogan, W. G., & Rosenbaum, D. P. (1997). *Fort Worth's Comprehensive Communities Program: A case study.* Cambridge, MA: BOTEC Analysis Corporation.

Sundeen, R. A., & Mathieu, J. T. (1976). Fear of crime and its consequences among elderly in three urban areas. *Gerontologist* 16, 211–219.

Taub, R. P., Surgeon, G. P., Lindholm, S., Otti, P. B., & Bridges, A. (1977). Urban voluntary associations: Locality based and externally induced. *American Journal of Sociology* 83, 425–442.

Taub, R. P., Taylor, D. G., & Dunham, J. D. (1981). *Crime, fear of crime, and the deterioration of urban neighborhoods.* Chicago: National Opinion Research Center.

Taub, R. P., Taylor, D. G., & Dunham, J. D. (1982). *Safe and secure neighborhoods: Territoriality, solidarity, and the reduction of crime.* Final report, National Institute of Justice. Chicago: National Opinion Research Center.

Taub, R. P., Taylor, D. G., & Dunham, J. D. (1984). *Patterns of neighborhood change: Race and crime in urban America.* Chicago: University of Chicago Press.

Taylor, R. B., Gottfredson, S., & Brower, S. (1981). Informal control in the urban residential environment. Final Report to the National Institute of Justice. Baltimore: Johns Hopkins University.

Titus, R. M. (1983). *Residential burglary and the community response.* Paper presented at the Home Office workshop on residential burglary, Cambridge, England, July.

Troyer, R. J. (1988). The urban anticrime patrol phenomenon: A case study of a student effort. *Justice Quarterly* 5, 397–419.

Wandersman, A., Jakubs, J. F., & Giamartino, G. A. (1981). Participation in block organizations. *Journal of Community Action* 1, 40–47.

Warren, D. I. (1969). Neighborhood structure and riot behavior in Detroit: Some exploratory findings. *Social Problems* 16, 464–484.

Whitaker, C. J. (1986). Crime prevention measures. *Bureau of Justice Statistics Special Report.* Washington, DC: U.S. Department of Justice.

Yin, R. K. (1979). What is citizen crime prevention? In National Criminal Justice Reference Service (ed.), *How Well Does It Work?* Washington, DC: Government Printing Office.

Yin, R. K., Vogel, M. E., Chaiken, J. M., & Both, D. R. (1976). *Patrolling the neighborhood beat: Residents and residential security.* Santa Monica: Rand.

Yin, R. K., Vogel, M. E., Chaiken, J. M., & Both, D. R. (1977). *Citizen patrol projects (Phase I summary report).* National evaluation program. Washington, DC: U.S. Department of Justice, National Institute of Justice.

p.58 = blank

4

✿

Crime Prevention
Through the
Mass Media

The amount of violent crime in the United States is far beyond that of other industrialized nations. When seeking to explain this phenomenon, many researchers have cited the mass media as a coconspirator with firearms. Pervasive sex and gun violence on prime-time television are considered more than a mere reflection of American society—they are considered a major *cause* of these conditions in real life. If, indeed, the media is a powerful change agent, perhaps it can be employed for prosocial purposes as well. In this chapter, we discuss the use of the mass media to help solve and prevent crime.

Other chapters draw attention to the limits of neighborhood-based crime prevention strategies, including the possible displacement of criminal activity outside the program's target area. As Lab (1988) notes, "One logical solution to the problem of displacement is the initiation of more extensive crime prevention activities across larger geographic areas" (p. 67). Anticrime programs that use the mass media have the distinct advantage of reaching large numbers of individuals and, thus, the promise large-scale impact at the city, state, or national level. In this chapter, we examine several types of media programs: (1) national crime prevention campaigns, with particular attention to the McGruff program; (2) crime-solving media programs, with particular attention to Crime Stoppers; and (3) community newsletters.

MEDIA RESEARCH

The development of anticrime media programs is best understood when placed in the context of research on the mass media. During the past three decades, numerous studies of the mass media (especially television) have focused on a variety of topics, including media content, audience characteristics, and media effects (for reviews, see Comstock, Chaffee, Katzman, McCombs, & Roberts, 1978; Cook, Kendzierski, & Thomas, 1983; Leibert & Schwartzberg, 1977; National Institute of Mental Health, 1982; Oskamp, 1984; Roberts & Bachen, 1981). Much of this work has focused on the presentation of crime and aggression in media news and entertainment. Research has taught us, for example, that the media provide a distorted picture of crime by overrepresenting violent offenses, inflating the frequency of crime, and showing only partial or inaccurate information about victims, offenders, and crime incidents.

This type of unrealistic television violence has affected its audience in several undesirable ways. The National Institute of Mental Health (1982), after reviewing more than a decade of intensive research, concluded that there is "overwhelming" evidence that television violence causes aggressive behavior in children. Although this has been a hotly debated subject for many years, most researchers now agree that the bulk of the evidence from laboratory studies, survey research, and field experiments supports this conclusion.

Gerbner and his colleagues have gone further to suggest that media violence contributes to a "cultivation effect," whereby viewers are conditioned to think that violence is a common and acceptable part of everyday life (Gerbner, Gross, Elay, Jackson-Beeck, Jeffries-Fox, & Signorielli, 1978; Gerbner, Gross, Morgan, & Signorielli, 1980). They have also suggested that heavy television viewing, because of the exposure to the "scary world" of television crime, is associated with higher levels of fear of crime (Gerbner, Gross, Jackson-Beeck, Jeffries-Fox, & Signorielli, 1977; Gerbner et al., 1978). But these correlational findings have been challenged by other researchers, who have found no fear effect after controlling for background differences associated with heavy television viewing (Doob & Macdonald, 1979; Hughes, 1980; O'Keefe, 1984; Skogan & Maxfield, 1981). The most compelling evidence on this issue, however, comes from the analysis of national panel survey data by O'Keefe and Reid-Nash (1987).[1] The authors conclude that "individuals who pay greater attention to televised news about crime are more fearful of crime and are more concerned about protecting themselves from being victimized" (p. 158). Because the sample was reinterviewed, this study also adds additional confidence to the conclusion that television viewing leads to increased fear of crime rather than the other way around.

In summary, research suggests that media violence can distort one's view of the world, enhance one's tendency to aggress against others, and perhaps

---

1 In this panel sample, 426 respondents were reinterviewed after two years.

increase fear and concern about crime. Researchers have since turned their attention to questions of "how?" and "why?," seeking, for example, to identify social and psychological variables that can explain the media-aggression relationship (see Huesmann & Malamuth, 1986). The available research has its limitations and the need for additional longitudinal work is apparent. Taken as a whole, however, the research suggests that the mass media can be an important agent for modifying public perceptions, attitudes, and behaviors toward crime. The question here is whether the power of the media can be rechanneled to produce *prosocial changes* in the general public—changes that will contribute to the control or prevention of crime rather than to its escalation and perpetuation.

Growing evidence indicates that exposure to prosocial media can have positive effects on children (see Oskamp, 1984; Rushton, 1979). By watching programs such as *Sesame Street* and *Mr. Rogers' Neighborhood,* preschoolers can learn cooperation, helping, self-control, and other prosocial behaviors. Even episodes of the classic television shows such as *The Waltons* (Baran, Chase, & Courtright, 1979) and *Lassie* (Sprafkin, Leibert, & Poulos, 1975) can enhance prosocial cooperation and helping behavior. Because virtually all the studies on the media's prosocial effects have been conducted in laboratory settings, the question remains whether similar effects would be found in natural settings or would persist over time. Nevertheless, this research suggests that the media has the potential for encouraging prosocial behavior.

This potential for positive effects, along with the escalation of crime and other social problems in the 1970s, served as the impetus for the creation of media-based anticrime programs. National and local media outlets were asked, as a public service, to promote citizen participation in crime prevention activities and to work with law enforcement to solve known crimes. We will review the most popular programs in the following sections.

PUBLIC INFORMATION CAMPAIGNS:
"McGRUFF"

In October 1979, the "Take a Bite Out of Crime" campaign was initiated as a joint venture involving the Crime Prevention Coalition, the Advertising Council, and the federal Office of Justice Assistance, Research, and Statistics (now the Office of Justice Programs, U.S. Department of Justice). Featuring "McGruff," the crime dog, this national information campaign encouraged citizen involvement in crime prevention efforts, especially precautionary measures against burglary and street crime. The campaign, guided by the National Crime Prevention Council (NCPC), has expanded over the years to include other issues, such as neighborhood watch, child abduction, drug abuse, and violence. Essentially, two aspects of crime prevention have been promoted by the campaign (now called the National Citizens' Crime Prevention Campaign). The media spots teach people (1) to "watch out," that is, protect themselves and their property, and (2) to "help out," that is, provide mutual assistance and become involved in collective neighborhood activities.

The major media vehicle for communicating McGruff's message to "take a bite out of crime" is the public service announcement (PSA). The trench-coated dog has appeared in thousands of PSAs designed for television, radio, newspapers, magazines, billboards, and posters.

Although the national media spots provide the central element in the McGruff campaign, these are supplemented and reinforced by a wide range of state and local activities involving government, businesses, schools, law en-forcement, and community groups. Thus, the campaign is national in scope, but its success depends on local efforts by each community, such as the distri-bution of booklets containing crime prevention tips, the participation of local law enforcement agencies, and the donation of media time or space.

The "Take a Bite Out of Crime" media campaign was the subject of a for-mal impact evaluation by O'Keefe and his colleagues (see O'Keefe, 1985; 1986; O'Keefe & Reid, 1989). Essentially, this evaluation included a national probability sample survey of 1,200 adults that was conducted in 1979 at the start of the campaign, and a pretest-posttest panel survey of 426 adults in three cities, with the posttest interviews conducted in 1981.

The evaluation results indicate that, unlike most campaigns directed at the abuse of alcohol, drugs, or cigarettes, the McGruff campaign was effective in achieving its objectives. During the first two years, the McGruff ads had a sig-nificant impact on the American public. Survey results indicated that more than half the respondents recalled seeing or hearing one or more McGruff PSAs (usually on television), and the ads were very positively evaluated by the viewers. The campaign was able to reach a broad cross-section of the nation, although elderly residents were underexposed.

Although campaign exposure was quite diverse, attentiveness to the mes-sage was more selective. As O'Keefe (1986) notes, "a greater amount of atten-tion was paid by persons who saw themselves as more knowledgeable about prevention and those more confident about being able to protect themselves from crime." (p. 258). Unfortunately, as often happens with other prevention programs, persons who were the least likely to need crime prevention infor-mation were the most likely to be attentive to the media spots.

The McGruff campaign appears to have had a positive effect on citizens' knowledge, attitudes, and behaviors relating to crime prevention. Nearly 1-in-4 persons exposed to the campaign reported having learned something new about prevention, and about 1-in-2 said the PSAs reminded them of things they had forgotten. Persons who recalled the PSAs were more likely to report confidence in their ability to protect themselves and express more con-fidence in the efficacy of crime prevention measures.

The behavioral changes were less dramatic, but still significant. In the national sample, nearly 1-in-4 persons exposed to the PSAs reported having taken some preventative action as a result of McGruff. The campaign's two main themes—improving household security and cooperating with neighbors—were mentioned most often as areas where respondents had changed their behavior. The strongest evidence of behavioral change comes from the panel study:

> Prior to the campaign, the panel interviewees were asked about the extent to which they carried out 25 specific prevention actions. Of these activities, 7 were subsequently given particular emphasis in the McGruff PSAs, including locking doors, leaving on lights, and various neighborhood cooperative efforts. Panel members were then asked again about the same 25 activities when reinterviewed two years after the initiation of the campaign. Panelists exposed to the ads registered statistically significant gains over those who were not exposed in 6 of the 7 activities recommended in the PSAs. There were no such increases in the 18 nonrecommended actions. (O'Keefe, 1986, p. 260)

These discriminant outcomes strengthen the conclusion that McGruff was responsible for the observed changes. The presence of behavioral change on outcome measures targeted by the intervention, and the absence of similar change on measures not so targeted, suggests that the program was affecting the American public.

The Follow-Up Evaluation

The McGruff campaign continued to flourish throughout the 1980s, as it switched from crime to drugs to violence. After 10 years of support, the Justice Department decided to take a second look at the program, funding a national follow-up evaluation (see O'Keefe, Rosenbaum, Lavrakas, Reid, & Botta, 1996). In 1992, O'Keefe and his colleagues conducted national sample surveys of crime prevention practitioners, media gatekeepers, and citizens, using many survey questions from the original 1981 study. The evaluators concluded that "we find no indications of decreases over the years in public attention or involvement with the campaign messages; on the contrary, the campaign appears to have continued to gain in popularity and impact over the past decade" (p. 122). Roughly 80 percent of the nation could recall the McGruff campaign in 1992, and more than three-fourths saw the ads as effectively promoting crime prevention to adults and children. The campaign was most effective at increasing awareness of crime prevention techniques among females, African-Americans, persons of lower income, and the less educated. Citizens who were more attentive to the McGruff public service announcements reported more crime prevention activities, but they also saw their neighborhood as less safe and were more fearful than citizens with less exposure to the ads. Some moderate level of fear-arousal might be optimal for stimulating changes in crime prevention behaviors. Consistent with this argument, Americans who reported taking preventive actions saw themselves as more at risk of victimization and more fearful than citizens who did not take any action.

Findings from the follow-up evaluation of the national crime prevention campaign suggest that McGruff ads might be having a positive influence on citizens' attention, information gain, and crime prevention behaviors.

However, caution should be exercised because the data from this evaluation, although subjected to controlled regression analyses, provide only a cross-sectional look at attitudes, perceptions, and behaviors.

PUBLIC INFORMATION CAMPAIGNS
IN GENERAL

The McGruff results, although encouraging, should be placed in the larger context of research on public information campaigns. Generally speaking, campaigns have been useful for increasing knowledge regarding the problem, and often (but to a lesser extent) have been effective in changing beliefs, perceptions, and attitudes. However, changes in crime prevention behaviors as a result of mass media exposure are uncommon in the literature. On the one hand, crime prevention campaigns in Jerusalem (Geva & Israel, 1982) and the Netherlands (van Dijk & Steinmetz, 1981) apparently produced some enhancements in individual crime prevention behaviors similar to the McGruff program. On the other hand, programs in Canada (Sacco & Silverman, 1981), Sweden (Schafer, 1982), and a series of campaigns in Britain (see Riley & Mayhew, 1980) have shown few, if any, effects on behavioral precautions.

In essence, mass media crime prevention programs have produced mixed results, and there are many possible explanations for these inconsistent findings. Sacco and Trotman (1990), after reviewing the evaluation literature, identified the following as factors that contribute to the likelihood of campaign impact: (1) audience members receive widespread exposure to campaign materials, (2) audience members perceive campaign themes as salient, (3) campaign themes are not contradicted by other powerful information sources, (4) campaign goals are modestly and realistically defined by program planners, (5) campaign materials are focused on specific types of attitudinal or behavioral change, (6) intended campaign effects are supported by informal interpersonal communications, (7) barriers to attitudinal or behavioral change are effectively met by campaign materials, and (8) audience members are properly targeted for lifestyle, beliefs, and media preferences and habits.

The early success of the McGruff program has been attributed to some of these factors. As O'Keefe (1986) observes, crime was a very salient issue on the U.S. agenda in 1981 when the campaign was in full swing, thus perhaps contributing to the appeal of the message. (The same was true during the reevaluation period). Furthermore, the campaign was supported by a substantial grassroots movement to establish neighborhood watch and other crime prevention initiatives at the community level. Researchers have noted the importance of interpersonal communication and local community organizations as a vehicle for crime prevention activity (Lavrakas, 1985; Podolefsky & DuBow, 1981; Rosenbaum, 1988; Skogan, 1990) and, in some cases, have documented how media effects are enhanced by local action (Maccoby & Solomon, 1981).

Because fear of crime is an important issue in the prevention field, the role of fear arousal in media campaigns should be briefly mentioned. Experts have not always agreed about the appropriate level of fear arousal that is desirable in public education campaigns. For many years, campaign planners (and marketing experts) have known that some level of fear arousal about the risks of not taking preventive action was necessary to stimulate such behavior. Many local and national groups, frustrated by low levels of citizen participation, operate under the assumption that higher levels of fear will motivate more citizen involvement (see Rosenbaum & Heath, 1990). The psychological research literature suggests, however, that fear is a complex response—communications that do not have a fear component are unlikely to capture the attention of the audience, whereas high-fear communications can cause people to avoid or reject the message (for reviews, see Higbee, 1969; Sutton, 1983). If this curvilinear relationship between fear and preventive action can be applied to media-based crime prevention, the suggestion is that *moderate* levels of fear arousal would be optimal (Surette, 1992). Weinstein (1987) argues that, in the field of prevention campaigns, little evidence suggests that target audience behavior will be restricted or immobilized because the communication aroused too much fear. He argues for stronger appeals on the grounds that campaigns are "usually weak and short-lived, incapable of sustaining preventive self-protective behavior" (p. 327).

From marketing research we have learned something about the effects of different types of fear-arousing threats. Research suggests that campaigns will be more effective if the threat of physical harm is directed toward a surrogate target, such as a spouse or child, rather than toward the target audience (see Surette, 1992). In recent years, mass media appeals in the areas of crime and drugs have carried fairly strong fear-arousal messages. The impact of these effects remains unknown.

ANTICRIME MEDIA SHOWS:
CRIME STOPPERS

The unwillingness of ordinary citizens to get involved in crime fighting activities is not just a problem for those promoting victimization prevention programs—it has been a long-standing problem for law enforcement agencies that rely on information supplied by citizens to make arrests. Reliable information from witnesses and informants is the lifeblood of the criminal justice system. Research indicates that without a witness who can identify the suspect, the probability of solving most offenses is dramatically reduced (Skogan & Antunes, 1979). More than three-fourths of all arrests are the result of reports initiated by citizens, and very few are produced by police surveillance alone (Black, 1970; Smith & Visher, 1981). Thus, the unstoppable sleuths of fictional literature, who piece together a complex puzzle of crime, have little to do with the real world of criminal investigations. Furthermore, given that only slightly more than one-third (36 percent) of all personal and household crimes are ever reported to the police (Maguire & Pastore, 1996, p. 250), law enforcement has virtually no opportunity to solve the two-thirds of the crimes that occur and never come to their attention.

Frustrated by the lack of citizen participation and cooperation with law enforcement, Greg MacAleese, a police officer in Albuquerque, New Mexico, started a program called "Crime Stoppers" in 1976. MacAleese reasoned that citizens are unwilling to provide information to the police either because of apathy or fear of retaliation.[2] To address these problems, the new Crime Stoppers program offered cash rewards and anonymity to persons who provided information that led to the arrest or indictment or both of suspected criminals. Although the Albuquerque program was preceded by other programs in the early 1970s that used cash rewards and anonymity as incentives, such as the WE-TIP (We Turn in Pushers) program in southern California (Bickman & Lavrakas, 1976), MacAleese was the first to feature the media in a central role. He convinced local newspapers and television stations to publicize selected unsolved crimes and to educate citizens about the rewards for participation. The mass media provide a modern version of the old West's "Wanted" posters, with the obvious advantage of reaching large populations instantaneously. The idea that thousands (even hundreds of thousands) of citizens can participate in criminal investigations without leaving their homes was considered innovative and worthy of further examination. In addition, these programs have the potential benefit of reminding citizens, on a weekly basis, that law enforcement cannot always solve crimes by itself and that the public's role is essential.

The Crime Stoppers program has become extremely popular since its inception. As a result of this growth, the National Institute of Justice funded a national evaluation of the program (see Rosenbaum, Lurigio, & Lavrakas, 1986a). Let us look closely at the operations and effects of this bold initiative. The major advantages and disadvantages for the communities involved are explored in the following sections.

Program Operations

In different parts of the United States, Crime Stoppers is known by various names, including "Crime Solvers," "Secret Witness," and "Crime Line." These self-sustaining programs involve the mass media, the community, and law enforcement in a unique partnership created to stimulate citizen cooperation with the police. Each program has a board of directors staffed by community volunteers that is responsible for setting policy, coordinating fund raising directed at both public and private contributors, and allocating rewards to citizen who participate. The media play a major role by publicizing facts about

---

2 The reasons for nonreporting or noncooperation by citizens are actually more complex and diverse, and researchers have debated whether apathy is a legitimate motivating force. Nevertheless, the program was based on these premises.

the program's objectives, general operations, and previous successes. The media's most salient role is to publicize the details of unsolved crimes by presenting a reenactment or narrative description of a selected "Crime of the Week."

The law enforcement role in Crime Stoppers involves receiving and processing crime tips from anonymous callers and then forwarding these leads to detectives for further investigation. The police coordinator also functions in a variety of other roles, such as selecting the Crime of the Week, drafting press releases and radio feeds, consulting on the production of the televised reenactments, keeping records on the program, and serving as a liaison with the board of directors and the media.

Program Success

Our national and local surveys found that Crime Stoppers programs are very popular with law enforcement agencies, the media, and the general public (Lurigio & Rosenbaum, 1991; Rosenbaum & Lurigio, 1989; Lavrakas, Rosenbaum, & Lurigio, 1990). In several media markets, television viewers have rated Crime Stoppers as one of the top programs. Indeed, these programs have been modeled at the national level by popular anticrime shows such as "America's Most Wanted" and "Unsolved Mysteries." Although media representatives often depict Crime Stoppers programs as the equivalent of public service announcements (at prime time), there is little doubt that such programs would be dropped if their ratings began to slide.

Clearly, Crime Stoppers is a popular and rapidly growing program. In 1981, there were only 48 programs in the United States. By 1984, the number had grown to nearly 500, and by 1997, there were an estimated 900 programs.

Looking beyond its popularity, the question becomes this: Does Crime Stoppers effectively solve crime and increase citizen participation in this process? At the national level, the statistics are sizable. As shown in Table 4-1, as of April 1997, Crime Stoppers programs have solved more than 634,000 felony cases, recovered more than 3.3 billion dollars worth of narcotics and stolen property, and convicted 99 percent of the felony suspects prosecuted through the program. To achieve this level of productivity, community members have raised and paid out more than 41 million dollars in cash rewards to anonymous callers, averaging $718 per case cleared.

Even though these statistics seem impressive, it would be misleading to conclude that Crime Stoppers is a panacea for our nation's crime problem. Our national evaluation found that, on average, only 6.5 percent of all crimes cleared by the cooperating law enforcement agencies were the result of the Crime Stoppers program. Furthermore, *all* clearances constitute only about one-fifth of the felony crimes reported to the police, which in turn, constitute only one-third of all felony crimes committed. Thus, there is little reason to expect that the crime rate will be substantially reduced by the introduction or promotion or such programs, although a 6 percent enforcement boost is helpful.

Table 4-1 Crime Stoppers Statistics

Felony Crimes Solved	634,106
Conviction Rate	99%
Stolen Property and Narcotics Recovered	
Property	$1,047,303,472
Narcotics	$2,299,751,524
Total	$3,447,054,996
Average Amount Recovered	$5,721
Rewards Paid	$41,765,174
Average Reward Size	$718

SOURCE: Crime Stoppers International. Based on statistics reported by more than 900 programs through April 1997.

Without question, Crime Stoppers programs deserve credit for solving some "dead-end" felony cases that were unlikely to be cleared through regular criminal investigations or by devoting a "reasonable" amount of law enforcement resources to these cases. With the help of widespread media coverage, the promise of anonymity, and the opportunity of a sizable reward, Crime Stoppers programs have been able to "crack" some difficult cases.

The effectiveness of these programs seems to vary by type of crime. Crime Stoppers seems to be especially effective in solving cases that involve fugitives, bank robberies, and narcotics. The widespread media coverage of the suspect's photograph or composite seems to be the key ingredient in catching fugitives and bank robbers, whereas the promise of anonymity and a cash reward are believed to play an important role in solving narcotics cases. (Local programs reported that about one-third of the anonymous calls they received involve drugs).

An important question is whether Crime Stoppers is effective at encouraging citizen participation and cooperation with the police. Clearly, the arrest, clearance, and reward statistics cited suggest that citizens are involved in a big way. They become involved as callers, financial contributors, board members, and members of the media. The base of community support, however, comes primarily from two segments of the community. The business community provides financial support for the program and is well represented on the board of directors. Criminals and their friends are widely suspected of being overrepresented as callers and reward recipients (Rosenbaum, Lurigio, & Lavrakas, 1986b). Because offenders and "fringe players" (that is, persons who affiliate with offenders) are the most knowledgeable about criminal activity in the community, they are in the best position to use the Crime Stoppers program for financial gain, retaliation, or other personal reasons. According to program coordinators, fringe players provide the best information to the program on a consistent basis. Conversely, little evidence indicates that Crime Stoppers has been successful at gaining the participation of a broad cross-section of the community.

To better estimate the mass media effects of Crime Stopper on the general public, we conducted a quasi-experimental evaluation in Indianapolis, Indiana, where a new program was scheduled for implementation (Lurigio & Rosenbaum, 1991). Random samples of city residents and business owners were surveyed by telephone three months *before* media exposure to the Crime Stoppers program, and again six months *after* the program was unveiled via television, radio, and newspaper. Media coverage produced a substantial increase in program awareness, reaching 96 percent in the business community and 93 percent in the general public at the posttest. However, the Crime Stoppers program had few effects on the attitudes and behaviors of the target audience. At best, the media improved the public's attitude regarding the effectiveness of Crime Stoppers in generating arrests and increased the public's willingness to accept the notion of paying informants to cooperate with the police. The absence of other effects was encouraging in one respect—fear of victimization was *not* heightened, as one might expect, from a strong dosage of violent reenactments.

The Indianapolis study, although the first of its kind, was limited to a six-month follow-up. The impact of Crime Stoppers over a longer period, for better or worse, remains unknown.

The "Down Side" of Crime Stoppers

Given the overwhelming popularity of the Crime Stoppers program, how could there be any drawbacks? The very nature of the program—with its reliance on cash rewards, anonymous tips, and dramatic reenactments—makes it vulnerable to attack from several fronts. As the program grows, so do the complaints from defense attorneys, civil rights advocates, journalists, and academicians (see Rosenbaum & Lurigio, 1985). Many question the theoretical underpinning of the program and its long-term impact on society. Whether these criticisms reflect serious program liabilities for society or overblown worries, it is too early to determine. Nevertheless, these misgivings are summarized here so you can reach your own conclusions.

Complaint #1: Citizens have a moral and legal responsibility to report crime-related information to the police and, therefore, should not be paid to perform their civic duty. Beyond this ethical and legal issue, psychological research suggests that paying citizens money to cooperate with the police can undermine their intrinsic motivation to do so in the absence of payment (see Rosenbaum & Lurigio, 1985, for a review). Advocates of Crime Stoppers programs argue that the rewards are targeting those individuals who feel no civic duty or obligation to cooperate with the police. However, everyone exposed to the program receives the message. This position also raises another issue that is bothersome to the public, namely, the idea of paying large sums of money to criminals to assist the police (in larger cities, some informants have been known to make as much as $15,000 to $20,000 in reward money per year).

Complaint #2: Large rewards and a promise of anonymity will encourage false accusations, violations of civil liberties, and mutual distrust. Crime Stoppers can result in innocent citizens being watched, accused, and arrested, which can create permanent, sometimes unofficial, police files. Furthermore, there is concern that this program will encourage betrayal rather than mutual trust among neighbors, who will be more inclined to monitor their neighbor's activities rather than respect their privacy. Our society has mixed feelings about "snitching," seeing it as moral but despicable (Himmelfarb, 1980; Pfuhl, 1992). As a result, some Crime Stoppers programs are going into the classroom to encourage students to challenge the social norm against snitching.

The intensity of the current "war on drugs" and the widespread use of illegal substances adds to the critic's apprehension about Crime Stoppers. Encouraging citizens to spy on their neighbors is reminiscent of Nazi Germany and George Orwell's *1984*. As we seek to expand the pool of criminal justice informants and encourage average citizens to report every criminal act, we should be fully aware of the many factors that compel individuals to become informants (Horgan, 1974; Moore, 1977; O'Hara, 1976; Rosenbaum, Lurigio, & Lavrakas, 1986b). These include (1) fear—concern for personal safety or the safety of loved ones; (2) vanity—attempts to feel important or useful to the police; (3) ingratiation—seeking the favor of the police to earn special treatment or regard; (4) revenge—a vindictive attempt to "get even" with another; (5) repentance—removing guilt or making amends for previous wrongdoing; (6) jealousy—actions to humiliate others who have earned greater accomplishments or possessions; (7) remuneration—informing for financial or other material gain; (8) avoidance of punishment—volunteering information for the promise of leniency; (9) civic mindedness—efforts to protect the community from crime; (10) gratitude—informing to express appreciation; and (11) competition—informing to undermine those who are pursuing the same criminal interest. In summary, the motives of police informants are not always pure and in the best interest of society. Hence, efforts to enhance informing behavior should be approached with caution. The anonymity component of Crime Stoppers might eliminate certain of these motives (for example, ingratiation), but it can exacerbate others. Psychologists have observed that anonymity can facilitate a process of "deindividuation" (Zimbardo, 1970), whereby individuals are more inclined to act in an aggressive, antisocial, or irresponsible manner because their personal identities are hidden or blurred. The Klu Klux Klan is a good example.

Complaint #3: Offers of cash and anonymity, as well as pretrial publicity, create special problems for the criminal justice system and threaten to derail the promise of a fair trial. There are several key issues: Should anonymous tips be allowed as credible evidence in court, or does the defendant have the right to know his or her accuser? Should programs be allowed to dramatically increase the size of the reward to encourage informants to testify in court, or does this incentive also increase the likelihood of false testimony? Finally, does pretrial publicity in the form of media reenactments or narrative reports bias the testimony (recall) of witnesses? There have been several court cases regarding Crime Stoppers, and the primary focus has been the credibility of anonymous callers. Generally, the courts have ruled in favor of the program, allowing such tips as evidence and protecting the "privilege" of anonymity, so long as the information provided by the anonymous source is corroborated by other information (see Surette, 1992, for specific cases).

Taking a defensive posture on other matters, Crime Stoppers programs have been forced to seek legal protection in a variety of law suits, including claims of false arrest and imprisonment, defamation of character, invasion of privacy and other violations of civil rights, breach of contract, illegal fundraising activities, and the misappropriation and unauthorized use of protected properties.

The issue of pretrial publicity has not been resolved. Whether media reenactments will bias the accuracy and completeness of witness testimony is uncertain, but a large body of research on factors that contribute to biased recall is not encouraging for program advocates (see Loftus, 1979).

Complaint #4: The direct involvement of the press in this type of program undermines its role as the watchdog of government agencies, especially the police. Media organizations might be less willing to conduct a thorough investigation of a law enforcement agency with which it jointly produces a program on a weekly basis. Our national survey of media organizations found that some (especially newspapers) were reluctant to participate because it might interfere with their efforts to provide objective coverage of the police or crime news, or because they disagreed with the basic philosophy that underlies Crime Stoppers. However, the majority of media outlets praised the program, and of those whose community did *not* have such a program, two-thirds said their organization would be "very likely" to participate if a Crime Stoppers program were available (Lavrakas, Rosenbaum, & Lurigio, 1990).

Complaint #5: Publicizing a dramatic, often violent "Crime of the Week" gives the general public a distorted view of the crime problem in their community and perpetuates old stereotypes. Surette's (1986) analysis of the media content at one program over a two-year period is consistent with our conclusions from the national study: "On the whole, the program portrayed criminality as an attribute of a young, violent, dangerous class of criminals composed mostly of minorities. Crime was portrayed as largely stranger-to-stranger injurious or fatal encounters in which handguns play a dominant role." (Surette, 1992, p. 172). Of course, the electronic media prefer this type of reenactment because of its entertainment value, but the long-term impact on public perceptions and fear of crime remain unknown. Certainly, one could argue that the public's strong support for incapacitation and punishment of young offenders (in contrast with their support for prevention and treatment services) can be partially attributed to the demonization of these kids as super predators by the news media.

Complaint #6: Media coverage of arrests generated by calls to Crime Stoppers gives the public the impression that the program is a highly effective method of dealing with the community's overall crime problem. Essentially, citizens are led to believe that an anonymous call to the police is all that is necessary, whereas collective community involvement and comprehensive partnerships are more likely to have a lasting impact on public safety through the development of a broad range of prevention programs.

ANTICRIME NEWSLETTERS

In recent years, the distribution of anticrime newsletters by police and community organizations has become a popular crime prevention strategy. Traditional media campaigns to increase citizen crime prevention behaviors have generally met with limited success for a number of reasons. The newsletter is not hindered by all of the same problems.

Tyler (1984) has argued that traditional media reports are uninformative, either because they focus on infrequent or unusual crimes that are not relevant to the average citizen or the media coverage is too broad to refer to local crimes. In contrast, a local newsletter can (1) give local residents a more accurate picture of the nature and extent of crime at the neighborhood level, and (2) provide specific crime prevention advice that is tailored to the problems at hand, unlike the typical media campaign, and (3) report local "success stories" as a motivational tool for continued action.

One important question raised by police administrators, mayors, and city managers (especially those who are reluctant to release crime statistics to the public) is whether such information will increase, decrease, or have no impact on residents' fear of crime. At best, program planners were hoping that the publication of crime statistics and crime prevention tips would educate the public and raise concern about local crime and the need for community action. One critical question is whether a newsletter can raise public *concern* about the crime problem (and therefore, heighten motivation to engage in crime prevention behaviors) without simultaneously heightening *fear* of victimization? Research indicates that concern about crime is associated with participation in neighborhood-based anticrime activities, whereas fear is associated with avoidance behaviors (Lavrakas, Normoyle, Skogan, Herz, Salem, & Lewis, 1981; Rosenbaum & Heath, 1990).

In 1981, a series of studies were conducted in Evanston, Illinois, to assist in the development and evaluation of a comprehensive community crime prevention program (Rosenbaum & Kaminski, 1982). One policy recommendation to emerge from this work was the development and distribution of an experimental newsletter that would be the joint product of the Evanston Police Department and a new consortium of local community organizations. Although this was not the nation's first newsletter, this was the first time, to our knowledge, that a newsletter was distributed in a controlled manner to evaluate its impact on local residents (for a full presentation of the results, see Lavrakas, Rosenbaum, & Kaminski, 1983).

The evaluation involved a quasi-experimental design, with Evanston residents assigned to one of three newsletter conditions: (1) neighborhoods that received a newsletter *without crime statistics*; (2) neighborhoods that received a newsletter *with crime statistics*; and (3) a citywide random sample that *did not receive a newsletter*. Households in all conditions were interviewed by telephone. The results indicate that persons exposed to either version of the newsletter saw the local crime problem as greater and more severe than persons who did not receive a newsletter, but the groups did not differ in their fear of crime. Most important, residents who received the newsletter (especially the version with crime statistics) were more likely than nonrecipients to report engaging in a variety of crime prevention measures and more likely to express positive attitudes about police-community partnerships. Furthermore, the version *with* crime statistics was rated more favorably than the version *without* crime statistics.

These findings were encouraging and suggested to us that a newsletter might be a useful vehicle for stimulating citizen concern about crime and boosting protective behavior without raising fear of crime. However, the evaluation design was relatively weak and the generalizability of the results to other cities remained uncertain.

The promising nature of these results caused the Police Foundation to attempt a replication of the newsletter model as a component of the Houston-Newark Fear Reduction project. (For a full description of these evaluations, see Brown & Wycoff, 1987; Lavrakas, 1986; Williams & Pate, 1987.) In a nutshell, the follow-up demonstrations were less successful. The only consistent finding across all three sites is that residents enjoyed receiving the newsletters. In Houston and Newark, the newsletter had few effects on fear of crime, perceptions regarding the magnitude of the crime problem (concern), perceptions of crime prevention activities, or self-reported crime prevention behaviors. On the positive side, recipients of the newsletters in both cities reported that the newsletter made them feel more confident in their ability to avoid victimization.

A few unexpected negative findings emerged that were more central to the evaluation and more carefully assessed. In Houston, exposure to the newsletter *with crime statistics* was associated with a significant *increase* in fear of property crime victimization. In Newark, exposure to either version of the newsletter was associated with significantly *fewer* household protection behaviors.

The Houston and Newark results conflict with the Evanston results and should not be lightly dismissed. Lavrakas (1986) offers several explanations for the differences in results across these evaluations: (1) differences in the strength of the treatment—a substantial number of households in the Houston and Newark target areas reported no exposure to the newsletter; (2) differences in mode of dissemination—in Houston and Newark, the newsletters were mailed, but in Evanston, they were hand delivered by local community organizations; (3) differences in educational levels—Evanston recipients reported a significantly higher level of education than the Houston or Newark samples.

In addition, the importance of local rates of crime and disorder should be factored into the equation. When levels of crime and disorder are high, the dissemination of crime statistics might increase fear of crime and immobilize residents, or at best, have no effect. Beyond residents' favorable evaluation of the newsletter itself, the capacity of this tool to have a significant impact in low-income, high-crime neighborhoods has yet to be established. At this point, it would be safe to say only that community-based dissemination (and ownership) of newsletters might be more effective than mailing from the police agency and that effects are greater with more educated audiences that enjoy reading. Clearly, there is considerable room for additional research on this topic.

CONCLUSIONS

The power of the media to reach large audiences, create awareness of social problems, and enhance prosocial behavior in children has led to the development of various anticrime programs that seek to enhance citizen participation in crime prevention and law enforcement activities. Public education campaigns have sought to change awareness, attitudes, and behaviors regarding crime prevention, but the level of success in achieving these objectives has been mixed. Media campaigns have been effective in creating public awareness, but attitudinal and behavioral effects have been inconsistent. The "McGruff" national crime prevention campaign has been the most successful, and several factors might have contributed to its success (see O'Keefe et al., 1996, p. 124), including the use of commercial advertising research and planning strategies; segmenting the public into target audiences with messages tailored to each; the use of coordinated efforts across media (television, radio, newspapers, magazines, billboards); the use of entertaining characters to convey information; sponsorship by reputable organizations; linking of the campaign to local community issues; and enlisting support from local groups.

Reaching agreement on the optimal level of fear arousal for media spots has not been easy for researchers or policy makers. Although most experts agree that too much fear can backfire, it is debatable whether the typical media campaign has generated enough fear to motivate the target audience to take action and is sufficiently relevant to their personal lives. The McGruff campaign appears to have been effective at stimulating public concern, and even fear, about crime and drug abuse, but it also focuses on the types of preventive behaviors that citizens can take to eliminate the threat and the benefits to be realized from such actions.

To promote greater citizen involvement and cooperation with law enforcement, hundreds of media anticrime programs have emerged in recent years. The Crime Stoppers model is the most popular and has led to the arrest and conviction of many felony suspects. Unfortunately, the use of cash rewards, anonymous callers, and dramatic reenactments has made these programs vulnerable to criticism from defense attorneys, civil rights groups, and others who question whether the benefits of these "Wanted" messages are outweighed by the long-term costs to society.

Finally, anticrime newsletters have become a popular strategy to create public awareness about the extent and nature of local crime and to promote crime prevention behaviors. Research indicates that local residents enjoy reading these newsletters and want them continued. However, the effectiveness of newsletters in changing fear, perceptions of local crime, and crime prevention behaviors remains uncertain. A successful demonstration in one city suggests that hand delivery (versus mail) and coauthorship between the police and community organizations can improve the impact on crime prevention behaviors. Personal and social factors might be important as well, such as the readers' education level and the amount of crime in the target neighborhood.

REFERENCES

Baran, S. J., Chase, L. J., & Courtright, J. A. (1979). Television drama as a facilitator of prosocial behavior: "The Waltons." *Journal of Broadcasting* 23, 277–285.

Bickman, L., B., & Lavrakas, P. J. (1976) *Citizen crime reporting projects: National evaluation summary report.* Washington, DC: U. S. Government Printing Office.

Black, D. J. (1970). Production of crime rates. *American Sociological Review* 35, 733–748.

Brown, L. P. & Wycoff, M. A. (1987). Policing in Houston: Reducing fear and improving service." *Crime and Delinquency* 33, 71–89.

Comstock, G., Chaffee, S., Katzman, N., McCombs, M., & Roberts, D. (1978). *Television and human behavior.* New York: Columbia University Press.

Cook, T. D., Kendzierski, D. A., & Thomas, S. V. (1983). The implicit assumption of television research. *Public Opinion Quarterly* 47, 161- 201.

Doob, A. N. & Macdonald, G. E. (1979). Television viewing and fear of victimization: Is the relationship causal ? *Journal of Personality and Social Psychology* 37, 170–79.

Gerbner, G., Gross, L., Elay, M., Jackson-Beeck, M., Jeffries-Fox, S., & Signorielli, N. (1978). Cultural indicators: Violence profile no. 9. *Journal of Communication* 28, 176–207.

Gerbner, G., Gross, L., Jackson-Beeck, M., Jeffries-Fox, S., & Signorielli, N. (1977). TV violence profile no. 8. *Journal of Communication* 27, 171–180.

Gerbner, G., Gross, L., Morgan, M., & Signorielli, N. (1980). The "main-streaming" of America: Violence profile no. 11. *Journal of Communication* 30, 10–29.

Geva, R. & Israel, I. (1982). Anti-burglary campaign in Jerusalem: Pilot project update. *Police Chief* 49, 44–46.

Higbee, K. (1969). Fifteen years of fear arousal: Research on threat appeals, 1953–1968. *Psychological Bulletin* 72, 426–444.

Himmelfarb, S. (1980). Reporting and nonreporting of observed crimes: Moral judgments of the act and actor. *Journal of Applied Social Psychology* 10, 56–70.

Horgan, J. J. (1974). *Criminal investigation.* New York: McGraw-Hill.

Huesmann, L. R. & Malamuth, N. M. (1986). Media violence and anti-social behavior: An overview. *Journal of Social Issues* 42, 1–6.

Hughes, M. (1980). The fruits of cultivation analysis: A reexamination of some effects of television watching. *Public Opinion Quarterly* 44, 287–302.

Lab, S. (1988). *Crime prevention: Approaches, practices and evaluations.* Cincinnati: Anderson.

Lavrakas, P. J. (1985). Citizen self-help and neighborhood crime prevention policy. In L. A. Curtis (ed.) *American violence and public policy.* New Haven, CT: Yale University Press.

Lavrakas, P. J. (1986). Evaluating police-community anti-crime newsletters: The Evanston, Houston, and Newark field studies. In D. P. Rosenbaum (ed.) *Community crime prevention: Does it work?* Beverly Hills: Sage.

Lavrakas, P. J., Normoyle, J., Skogan, W. G., Herz, E. J., Salem, G. & Lewis, D. A. (1981). *Factors related to citizen involvement in personal, household, and neighborhood anti-crime measures: An executive summary.* Washington, DC: U.S. Government Printing Office.

Lavrakas, P. J., Rosenbaum, D. P., & Kaminski, F. (1983). Transmitting information about crime and crime prevention to citizens: The Evanston newsletter quasi-experiment. *Journal of Police Science and Administration* 2, 463–473.

Lavrakas, P. J., Rosenbaum, D. P., Lurigio, A. J. (1990). Media cooperation with the police: The case of Crime Stoppers. In R. Surette (ed.) *The Media and Criminal Justice Policy* (pp. 225–241). Springfield, IL: Charles C. Thomas.

Leibert, R. M., & Schwartzberg, N. S. (1977). Effects of mass media. *Annual Review of Psychology* 28, 141–173.

Loftus, E. F. (1979). *Eyewitness testimony.* Cambridge, MA: Harvard University Press.

Lurigio, A. J., & Rosenbaum, D. P. (1991). The effects of mass media on crime prevention awareness, attitudes, and behavior: The case of Crime

Stoppers. *American Journal of Criminal Justice* 15, 82–105.

Maccoby, N., & Solomon, D. (1981). The Stanford community studies in health promotion. In R. Rice & W. Paisley (eds.), *Public communications campaigns.* Beverly Hills, CA: Sage.

Maguire, K., & Pastore, A. L. (1996, eds.) *Sourcebook of criminal justice statistics 1995.* U.S. Department of Justice, Bureau of Justice Statistics, Washington, DC: U.S. Government Printing Office.

Moore, M. H. (1977). *Buy and bust.* Lexington, MA: Lexington.

National Institute of Mental Health (1982). *Television and behavior: Ten years of scientific progress and implications for the eighties.* Washington, DC: U. S. Government Printing Office.

O'Hara, C. E. (1976). *Fundamentals of criminal investigation.* Springfield, IL: Charles C. Thomas.

O'Keefe, G. J. (1984). Public views on crime: Television exposure and media exposure. In R. N. Bostrom (ed.), *Communication yearbook 8* (pp. 513–536). Newbury Park, CA: Sage.

O'Keefe, G. J. (1985). Taking a bite out of crime: The impact of a public information campaign. *Communication Research* 12, 147–178.

O'Keefe, G. J. (1986). The McGruff national media campaign: Its public impact and future implications. In D. P. Rosenbaum (ed.), *Community crime prevention: Does it work?* (pp. 252–268). Beverly Hills, CA: Sage.

O'Keefe, G. J., & Reid-Nash, K. (1987). Crime news and real-world blues: The effects of the media on social reality. *Communication Research* 14, 147–163.

O'Keefe, G. J., & Reid, K. (1989). The McGruff crime prevention campaign. In R. E. Rice & C. K. Atkin (eds.), *Public communication campaigns.* (2nd ed., pp. 210- 211). Newbury Park, CA: Sage.

O'Keefe, G. J., Rosenbaum, D. P., Lavrakas, P. J., Reid, K., & Botta, R. A. (1996). *Taking a bite out of crime: The impact of the National Citizens' Crime Prevention Media Campaign.* Thousand Oaks, CA: Sage.

Oskamp, S. (1984). *Applied social psychology.* Englewood Cliffs, NJ: Prentice-Hall.

Pfuhl, E. H., Jr. (1992). Crimestoppers: The legitimation of snitching. *Justice Quarterly* 9, 505–528.

Podolefsky, A. & DuBow, F. (1981). *Strategies for community crime prevention.* Springfield, IL: Charles C. Thomas.

Riley, D., & Mayhew, P. (1980). *Crime prevention publicity: An assessment.* London, England: Her Majesty's Stationery Office. Home Office research study no. 63.

Roberts, D. F., & Bachen, C. M. (1981). Mass communication effects. *Annual Review of Psychology* 32, 307–356.

Rosenbaum, D. P. (1988). Community crime prevention: A review and synthesis of the Literature. *Justice Quarterly* 5, 323–395.

Rosenbaum, D. P., & Heath, L. (1990). The "psycho-logic" of fear reduction and crime prevention programs. In J. Edwards, E. Posavac, S. Tindel, F. Bryant, & L. Heath (eds.) *Applied Social Psychology Annual* (Vol. 9, pp. 221–247). New York: Plenum.

Rosenbaum, D. P., & Kaminski, S. (1982, eds.). *Crime and preventative strategies in Evanston: Research findings and policy implications.* Evanston, IL: City of Evanston.

Rosenbaum, D. P., & Lurigio, A. J. (1985). Crime Stoppers: Paying the price. *Psychology Today* June, 56–61.

Rosenbaum, D. P., & Lurigio, A. J. (1989). Enhancing citizen participation and solving serious crime: A national evaluation of Crime Stoppers programs. *Crime and Delinquency* 35, 401–420.

Rosenbaum, D. P., Lurigio, A. J., & Lavrakas, P. J. (1986a). Crime Stoppers: A national evaluation. *Research in*

Brief Series. Washington, DC: National Institute of Justice, U.S. Department of Justice.

Rosenbaum, D. P., Lurigio, A. J., & Lavrakas, P. J. (1986b). *Crime Stoppers: A national evaluation of program operations and effects.* Final report. Washington, DC: U.S. Department of Justice, National Institute of Justice.

Rushton, J. P. (1979). Effects of prosocial television and film material on the behavior of viewers. In L. Berkowitz (ed.), *Advances in experimental social psychology* (Vol. 12). New York: Academic.

Sacco, V. F., & Silverman, R. A. (1981). Selling crime prevention: The evaluation of a mass media campaign. *Canadian Journal of Criminology* 23, 191–202.

Sacco, V. F., & Trotman, M. (1990). Public information programming and family violence: Lessons from the mass media crime prevention experience. *Canadian Journal of Criminology* 32, 91–105.

Schafer, H. (1982). Frauj bei nacht— Women by night: Analysis of a warning-leaflet campaign. In E. Kuhlhorn & B. Svensson (eds.), *Crime prevention.* Stockholm: The National Swedish Council for Crime Prevention.

Skogan, W. (1990). *Disorder and decline: Crime and the spiral of decay in American neighborhoods.* New York: Free Press.

Skogan, W. G. & Antunes, G. (1979). Information, apprehension, and deterrence: Exploring the limits of police productivity. *Journal of Criminal Justice* 47, 217–241.

Skogan, W. G., & Maxfield, M. E. (1981). *Coping with crime.* Newbury Park, CA: Sage.

Smith, D., & Visher, C. A. (1981). Street level justice: Situational determinants of police arrest and decisions. *Social Problems* 29, 169–177.

Sprafkin, J. N., Liebert, R. M., & Poulos, R. W. (1975). Effects of a prosocial televised example on children's helping. *Journal of Experimental Child Psychology* 20, 119–126.

Surette, R. (1986). The mass media and criminal investigations: Crime Stoppers in Dade County, Florida. *Journal of Justice Issues* 1, 21–38.

Surette, R. (1992). *Media, crime, and criminal justice: Images and realities.* Pacific Grove, CA: Brooks/Cole.

Sutton, S. R. (1983). Fear-arousing communications: A critical examination of theory and research. In J. Eiser (ed.), *Social psychology and behavioral medicine.* London: Wiley.

Tyler, T. R. (1984). Assessing the risk of crime victimization: The integration of personal victimization experience and socially transmitted information. *Journal of Social Issues* 40, 27–38.

van Dijk, J. J. M., & Steinmetz, C. H. D. (1981). *Crime prevention: An evaluation of the National Publicity Campaigns.* The Hague, Netherlands: Ministry of Justice.

Weinstein, N. D. (1987). Cross-hazard consistencies: Conclusions about self-protective behavior. In N. D. Weinstein (ed.), *Taking care: Understanding and encouraging self-protective behavior* (pp. 325–335). Thousand Oaks, CA: Sage.

Williams, H., & Pate, A. M. (1987). Returning to first principles: Reducing fear of crime in Newark. *Crime and Delinquency* 33, 53–70.

Zimbardo, P. G. (1970). The human choice: Individuation, reason, and order versus deindividuation, impulse, and chaos. In W. J. Arnold & D. Levine (eds.), *Nebraska symposium on motivation, 1969.* Lincoln: University of Nebraska Press.

PART III

Fighting Back: Protecting Oneself and One's Neighborhood

p.80 = blank

5

◉

Personal Defense

Protecting Oneself From Victimization

Individuals engage in a wide variety of behaviors for the purpose of protecting themselves against confrontational crimes, such as rape, robbery, and assault. Such behaviors might include, for example, avoiding "dangerous" areas or situations, taking self-defense classes, buying a large dog, carrying a weapon, or dressing differently in public. Also, during victim-offender encounters, victims might decide to resist offenders in a variety of ways. In this chapter, we will explore the nature, extent, and effectiveness of these self-protective responses.

Individual self-protective measures can be conceptualized as two distinct groups (compare Suttles, 1972): (1) those behaviors intended to *reduce* the risk of victimization, and (2) those behaviors intended to *manage* the risk of victimization when crime is unavoidable. The latter responses attempt to make the criminal act more difficult to complete or to minimize the victim's losses (that is, property loss or injury). The former responses attempt to reduce risk primarily through avoidance of high-risk situations. In this chapter, we will examine both types of self-protection. We focus on self-protective behaviors directed at confrontational crimes that might occur outside one's home. (Various crime prevention measures to secure or protect one's dwelling unit are covered in Chapters 3, 7, and 8). However, one household protective action— owning a gun for protection—will be covered in this chapter because of its importance to crime prevention both inside and outside the home.

RISK-AVOIDANCE BEHAVIORS

One of the most common responses to crime by individual citizens is to engage in "risk-avoidance" activities (Lavrakas, Normoyle, Skogan, Herz, Salem, & Lewis 1980). Many residents believe they can avoid becoming a victim of crime by staying at home, by avoiding certain areas of the city or neighborhood when they do go out, or by avoiding certain types of people on the streets. Urban neighborhood surveys generally find that 25 to 45 percent of the residents have recently refrained from going out at night because of crime (Biderman, Johnson, McIntyre, & Weir, 1967; Harris, 1969; Reiss, 1967; Skogan & Maxfield, 1981). The tendency to stay home varies from one location to the next, but this response is most frequent in high-crime, inner-city neighborhoods and least frequent in small towns (Lavrakas, Hartnett, Merkle, & Rosenbaum, 1992).

Other common risk-avoidance behaviors include avoiding specific areas within the city or neighborhood. In the mid-1970s, victimization surveys in eight large U.S. cities revealed that more than one-third of the respondents avoided certain areas of the city at night, and one-fifth avoided these areas during the day (Garofalo, 1977a). A nationwide survey in 1992 found that 49 percent of adults avoid certain places at night (O'Keefe, Rosenbaum, Lavrakas, Reid, & Botta, 1996). Other surveys have shown that the tendency to avoid areas at night can be as high as 70 percent in large cities such as Chicago (Lavrakas et al., 1980). The downtown area and public parks are often mentioned as specific areas to be avoided. In addition, individuals tend to avoid encounters with strangers and youth gangs by crossing the street if necessary to avoid trouble (Lavrakas et al., 1980; Yaden, Folkstand, & Glazer, 1973).

Risk-avoidance is a much broader and subtler set of behaviors than research suggests. People are so used to restricting their behavior on a routine, daily basis that they might be unaware that crime was the original impetus for many of their decisions. Driving instead of walking, parking in a certain location, using remote control car keys, and many other daily actions are likely the result of a perceived crime threat.

Many risk avoidance behaviors are heavily influenced by fear of crime. The most fearful groups within the general population—women and older citizens—are the most likely to engage in extreme avoidance behaviors (Biderman et al., 1967; Garofalo, 1977b; Lavrakas et al., 1980; Skogan & Maxfield, 1981). Other groups inclined toward avoidance behaviors include African-Americans, low-income residents, and persons living in high-crime neighborhoods (Boggs, 1971; see DuBow, McCabe, & Kaplan, 1979).

A fundamental question is whether risk-avoidance behaviors are effective at reducing the risk of victimization, and the empirical evidence suggests that restricting one's behavior is a good way to avoid crime. Studies have shown that individuals who engage in risk-avoidance behaviors (for example, not going out at night, avoiding certain areas or persons) are less likely to be victims of crime than persons who do not restrict their behavior on a regular basis (Biderman et al., 1967; Garofalo, 1977b; Kleinman & David, 1973;

Lavrakas, 1982; Rifai-Young, 1976; Skogan & Maxfield, 1981). However, a cause-and-effect-relationship has not been established firmly. Studies in this area often do not control for age, gender, race, neighborhood, and other pertinent variables when assessing the relationship between avoidance activity and risk of victimization.

Nevertheless, the apparent effectiveness of avoidance behaviors makes good sense from a theoretical and logical standpoint. As Rosenbaum (1988, p. 333) notes, "Unless one lives with a violent family member, staying at home behind locked doors and not venturing outside should lower a person's risk of personal victimization because most violent crime occurs outdoors." Indeed, patterns of victimization appear to be strongly connected to one's daily activities and, therefore, to one's exposure to risk. This observation can be predicted from Cohen and Felson's (1979) routine activities theory, which has become an important theoretical framework in criminology.[1]

According to the routine activities model, a crime is likely to occur when the following conditions converge at the same time and location: (1) a likely offender, (2) a suitable target (that is, something or someone that is visible, valued by, accessible to the offender), and (3) the absence of capable guardians who can prevent or stop the crime. This theory highlights the importance of criminal opportunities, and, as Cohen and Felson note, such opportunities have increased dramatically in recent years as people move outside their homes with greater frequency: "College enrollment, female labor force participation, urbanization, suburbanization, vacations, and new electronic durables provide various opportunities to escape the confines of the household while they increase the risk of predatory victimization" (p. 605). Although this theory does not focus directly on the behavior of potential victims, it does provide a framework for arguing that an individual's actions can play an important role in determining his or her risk of victimization.

Large differences in the rates of victimization for different subgroups of the population, as shown by the National Crime Victimization Survey, suggest that individual lifestyle factors and routine activities can play a significant role in victimization (see Bureau of Justice Statistics, 1988). African-American males have a 1-in-30 lifetime risk of being a homicide victim, nearly six times higher than the risk for white males (1-in-179). African-American females have a 1-in-132 risk of being murdered, nearly 4 times higher than the risk for white females (1-in-495). More generally, the National Crime Victimization Survey shows that victims of violent crime are more often young, male, African-American, single (or divorced or separated), unemployed, low income, and living in an urban area. In contrast, older citizens, whites, and females—persons who engage in the greatest number of avoidance behaviors—are the least likely to experience crimes of violence or theft.

---

1. Also, Hindelang, Gottfredson, and Garofalo (1978) offer the centrality of lifestyle theory, which emphasizes that different lifestyles are associated with different probabilities of criminal victimization.

These data should not be used to blame the victim. Undoubtedly, an extreme lifestyle that includes gang activity, drug trafficking, or crime will dramatically increase the chances of victimization; however, the majority of residents living in high-crime, low-income neighborhoods are law-abiding citizens whose risk of victimization is higher than normal because of where they live. Not only is violent crime concentrated in specific neighborhoods, but recent research has identified "hot spots" where criminal activity clusters (Sherman, Gartin, & Buerger, 1989; Maltz, Gordon, & Friedman, 1991). Certain taverns, school yards, gas stations, street corners, or residential addresses will experience a disproportionate amount of criminal activity and disorder.

Clearly, victims and neighborhoods across the United States are *not* chosen at random by criminals. The simple point here is that persons who live, work, recreate, hang out in, or simply pass through high-crime environments (regardless of their own criminality) run a higher risk of victimization than persons who do not use these environments. This is not to suggest that such persons could easily reduce their risk of victimization by engaging in risk-avoidance behaviors. There is little evidence that citizens who use these high-risk environments have control over their most important routine activities or can be influenced by educational initiatives. Most people, for example, perceive little freedom to change where they live and work as a crime prevention measure. Furthermore, their lifestyles (for example, recreational and social activities) are influenced by years of socialization, current socioeconomic status, and other relevant factors that are not easily modified.

Although avoidance behaviors can be effective at lowering one's risk of victimization, this response is not a panacea for the community's crime or drug problems, nor does it necessarily yield a net benefit to the individuals who engage in these precautions. The additional safety that is achieved by avoidance measures has a stiff price tag that includes a loss of behavioral freedom and possibly increased fear of crime. Researchers are still uncertain about whether high levels of fear increase behavioral restrictions or whether the restrictions increase fear of crime, or both (for example, Rosenbaum & Heath, 1990). Liska, Sanchirico, and Reed (1988) find support for a reciprocal model, wherein fear leads to avoidance, which in turn, leads to increased fear.

What is indisputable is that women and older citizens experience a major loss of mobility because of crime. The added psychological burden that all women carry because of their physical vulnerability to predatory and sexual crime is only compounded by constant restrictions on their behavioral freedom—restrictions that are considered necessary and rational in an urban environment (for example, women are considered "crazy" if they go out alone at night in many neighborhoods). Clearly, the adverse impact of crime on individuals reaches far beyond the actual incidence of victimization to affect one's quality of life.

In recent years, the cost of avoidance behavior has been felt strongly in inner-city neighborhoods where gangs and drug trafficking have increased. For example, in testimony before the Chicago City Council, residents of a gang-infested neighborhood complained that drive-by-shootings have eliminated the family tradition of sitting on the front porch on hot summer days (Davis, 1992). Instead, residents in these neighborhoods have been confined to their homes without the benefit of air conditioning on muggy summer evenings.

Risk avoidance not only carries a price tag for the individual but can also have adverse effects on the community when such behavioral restrictions become widespread and reach a certain threshold. If, for example, a substantial number of residents stop using the streets and sidewalks in the evening, this reaction could undermine the community's capacity to exercise informal social control. Under these conditions, criminally inclined persons are likely to recognize that public surveillance is at a minimum, that detection and apprehension are improbable, and therefore, that crimes can be committed in this area without punishment. Community self-regulation is considered essential for preventing crime and disorder, and individual avoidance runs counter to the collective presence in public spaces that is needed to constrain deviant behavior.

Finally, one extreme form of risk-avoidance is to move to another neighborhood or leave the city (Skogan & Maxfield, 1981). Although this can be an effective crime prevention technique for the individual or family, the widespread flight of high-income whites to the suburbs has contributed to the problems of unemployment, housing, and crime in the neighborhoods left behind (Kasarda, 1976; Skogan, 1986). Indeed, the continued abandonment of inner-city neighborhoods by businesses and others has only exacerbated the concentration of poverty and crime in these areas (Wilson, 1987).

RISK-MANAGEMENT BEHAVIORS

When high-risk environments cannot be avoided entirely, individuals will often engage in a variety of behaviors designed to make it more difficult to commit the crime or make crime less costly to themselves. Survey data suggest that approximately 7-in-10 urban residents will avoid carrying large sums of money when going outdoors (Lavrakas et al., 1980), nearly half will take a car rather than walk to avoid crime (Skogan & Maxfield, 1981), and one-fourth to one-half will take an escort when going out at night (Biderman et al., 1967; Kleinman & David, 1973; Reiss, 1967; Skogan & Maxfield, 1981). Furthermore, to make themselves less attractive as targets of crime, individuals have been known to dress or act in certain ways to give the impression of self-assuredness, aggressiveness, or having limited possessions (DuBow, McCabe, & Kaplan, 1979).

Many of these risk management behaviors are similar to the avoidance activities described earlier in that they are relatively common, passive attempts to avoid crime or reduce its impact. They are also employed more frequently by women, older persons, and other high-fear groups. In contrast, some risk-management behaviors involve more aggressive attempts to protect oneself from predatory, confrontational crime by increasing one's ability to resist or possibly deter nearby offenders. Surveys indicate that nearly 15 percent of the citizenry will take something with them when going out that could be used for self-defense, such as a dog, a whistle, a knife, or a gun (Kelling, Pate, Dieckman, & Brown 1974; Kleinman & David, 1973; Mangione & Noble, 1975; McIntyre, 1967). Generally, researchers have shown that these behaviors—often referred to as "self-protection" or "personal security"—are empirically distinguishable from the avoidance behaviors described earlier (Greenberg, Rohe, & Williams, 1984; Lab, 1990; Lavrakas & Lewis, 1980; Skogan & Maxfield, 1981). There is less agreement, however, about who engages in these self-protective actions. Using national survey data, Lab (1990) concluded that personal security responses (defined as firearms for protection at home, dogs owned for protection, and carrying protection when away from home) are most likely among older, more educated, lower-income, female residents. Generally, however, other researchers have found that bringing along a weapon or a dog when going out or taking self-defense training are responses more likely among males and young people than among females or older citizens (DuBow, McCabe, & Kaplan, 1979).[2]

Today, some convergence of responses from these different demographic groups might be occurring. The profile of the person inclined toward self-defense on the street is no longer limited to the traditional youth male. Females' willingness to challenge the barriers to their mobility, as well as their growing fear of sexual assault, have led to their increased participation in these more aggressive forms of self-protection in recent years. Large numbers of women have enrolled in self-defense or martial arts classes to provide additional protection against confrontational crimes, especially rape.

The basic question is whether risk-management behaviors are effective for the individual and society. When high-risk areas cannot be avoided, changing one's means of travel seems like a sensible risk-management strategy. Traveling by car (or even bicycle) rather than on foot would appear to be a safer means of mobility in high-crime areas. However, offenders have changed their modus operandi in recent years to catch these individuals. "Smash and grab" tactics— in which the offender smashes the window of a stopped car and grabs a purse or other property within reach—have grown increasingly common in urban areas. Also, minor car accidents are used as a ploy to stop and assault lone drivers. In many urban areas, "carjackings"—where the victim is not only robbed (often at a traffic signal or after a contrived accident), but asked to turn over his or her car at gunpoint—have become a popular crime (Levin, 1991). Undoubtedly, car travel still remains less risky than walking or biking, but, again, losing the freedom to move about freely is a price that cannot be ignored.

---

2. To some extent, the discrepancy in findings might reflect the different orientation of the questions—2 of the 3 National Crime Victimization Survey questions used by Lab could be interpreted as indicative of self-protection at home (behaviors that are more characteristic of older residents and females), whereas the typical citywide survey question used by other researchers focuses on protection outdoors (more characteristic of young males, where the risk of violent confrontation is greater).

Carrying less, or less valuable, property when outdoors will obviously reduce your losses in the event of victimization. This has motivated a national advertising campaign to discourage teenagers from wearing designer clothes that could cost them their lives. In Milwaukee, Wisconsin, the "Dress Smart—Stay Alive" campaign is a good example, showing the outline on the street where someone has been murdered for refusing to relinquish his or her designer clothes to attackers. Yet these initiatives clearly highlight the cost of crime prevention behaviors—the message is that students must dress down to avoid being attacked by street gangs.

Self-Defense Against Rape

Rape is a serious confrontational crime that requires women to engage in risk-management behaviors for self-protection. Being confronted by a rapist is a fear that haunts most women in the United States and has forced them to consider their response options (see Gordon & Riger, 1988). Rape is a prevalent problem in the United States and one that, for years, has been grossly underestimated by federal police statistics and even the National Crime Victimization Survey (NCVS). Independent data sources indicate that rape incidences might be 6 to 10 times higher than original NCVS estimates (Koss, 1992). Results from the redesigned NCVS indicate that there were an estimated 167,530 completed rapes and 148,610 attempted rapes in the United States in 1994, bringing the total to 316,140 (Bureau of Justice Statistics, 1995).[3]

How do women respond when attacked by a rapist, and are the chosen resistance strategies the most sensible and efficacious? Data from the 1994 NCVS indicate that 82 percent of all rape or sexual assault victims took self-protective measures. Women generally tried multiple strategies, including seeking help, threatening or arguing, resisting without force, or forceful resistance, including using weapons in 1 to 2 percent of the cases. The most important question is whether these resistance strategies are effective, and at what price. Does the available research on this subject provide women with any practical information that they can use when facing an assailant?

In rape situations, a woman is forced to make an immediate decision about whether or not to resist, and if so, in what way. From a research and public policy standpoint, Ullman and Knight (1992, p. 32) describe the problem in these terms:

> In weighing the viability of various resistance strategies, a clear assessment of the severity and probability of the consequences of each strategy is essential. The amount of psychological trauma resulting from a completed rape, the impact of the survivor's actions during the assault on her subsequent self-esteem, the probable success of various strategies in

---

3. The 316,140 estimated rapes and attempted rapes is a figure that does not include an estimated 116,570 nonrape sexual assaults.

avoiding the completion of the rape, and the relative risks of physical injury have to be considered in assessing the efficacy of potential resistance strategies.

A growing body of research has focused on the efficacy of rape resistance strategies (see Ullman, 1997, for a review). Essentially, four basic strategies of resistance have been identified by researchers: forceful physical resistance, forceful verbal resistance, nonforceful physical resistance, and nonforceful verbal resistance. Examples of each type of strategy are provided in Figure 5-1, along with the results that can be expected with each type of resistance, according to the research literature. The findings from resistance studies can be summarized as follows: *Forceful physical resistance* (for example, hitting, kicking) generally helps to reduce the probability of severe sexual abuse or rape completion (Bart & O'Brien, 1985; Block & Skogan, 1986; Kleck & Sayles, 1990; Ullman & Knight, 1993), but this approach appears to increase the risk that the victim will be attacked and physically injured (Bart & O'Brien, 1985; Block & Skogan, 1986; Ruback & Ivie, 1988; Siegel, Sorenson, Golding, Burman, & Stein, 1989; Ullman & Knight, 1993). *Forceful verbal resistance* (for example, screaming, threatening the offender) generally reduces the chances of rape completion (Kleck & Sayles, 1990; Ruback & Ivie, 1988; Siegel et al., 1989; Ullman & Knight, 1993), but shows no consistent relationship to injury (Ruback & Ivie, 1988). *Nonforceful physical resistance* (for example, fleeing or pushing the offender away) also appears to reduce the chances of rape completion (Bart & O'Brien, 1985; Block & Skogan, 1986) and has no effect on the likelihood of injury (Block & Skogan, 1986; Skogan & Block, 1983). Finally, *nonforceful verbal resistance* (for example, pleading, crying, reasoning) generally contributes to a greater probability of rape completion but is unrelated to physical injury (Bart & O'Brien, 1985; Ullman & Knight, 1993).[4]

In summary, the traditional advice dispensed by police departments nationwide might not lead to the best outcome for the victim. For years, women have been told to remain passive and not fight back in sexual assault situations. However, research indicates that resistance is generally an effective means of rape avoidance, with the exception of nonforceful verbal strategies. (Crying, pleading, and attempting to reason with the rapist is counterproductive to rape avoidance and can play into the offender's well-known desire to control and dominate a weaker person; see also Groth, Burgess, & Holmstrom, 1977.) If the victim's goal is to avoid additional physical injury, the literature suggests that most resistance strategies have no effect on injury, with the exception of forceful physical resistance, which could make matters worse. However, the link between fighting back and injury that appears in so many studies might be spurious and explainable by the offender's violence *before* the rape, which is

---

4. Research on the use of resistance in cases of robbery are fewer in number. Generally, all types of resistance seem to reduce the likelihood of the robber's success, but forceful physical resistance often leads to increased injury to the victim (Block & Skogan, 1986; Hindelang, 1976; Kleck, 1988; Kleck & DeLone, 1993).

Type of Resistance

	Physical	Verbal
Forceful	*Behavior:* Hitting, kicking, biting, using weapon *Results:* • Reduces probability of rape completion • Increases risk of attack and injury	*Behavior:* Screaming, calling for help, threatening the offender *Results:* • Reduces probability of rape completion • Effects on injury unclear
Nonforceful	*Behavior:* Fleeing scene, pushing offender away, shielding onself *Results:* • Reduces probability of rape completion • No effect on injury	*Behavior:* Pleading, crying, reasoning with offender *Results:* • Increases porbability of rape completion • No effect on injury

Level of Force

FIGURE 5-1 Rape Victim Resistance Strategies: Summary of Research Findings

likely to cause the victim to physically fight back (Quinsey & Upfold, 1985; Ullman & Knight, 1992). In a rare study that analyzes the *sequencing* of behaviors in the offender-victim interaction, Ullman and Knight (1992) found that women who fought back in response to an offender's physical attack were more likely to avoid rape and did not increase their level of physical injury. However, the physical resistance must be equal to that of the offender's attack to avoid rape (Siegel et al., 1989; Ullman & Knight, 1992). There is some evidence that forceful resistance with a weapon also has no adverse effect on injury but, rather, helps achieve rape avoidance (Kleck & Sayles, 1990; Lizotte, 1986). Thus, forceful physical resistance might not be a dysfunctional strategy after all and is generally more effective than nonforceful verbal strategies at stopping a rapist. But clearly, risks are involved with these more aggressive attempts to fight back, and, therefore, every victim should use her own judgment and common sense to assess the unique set of circumstances she is facing.

Self-Defense Training

Self-defense is not simply an issue of estimating the probability of victimization or injury and responding accordingly. All too often, women live with a fear of harm by male aggressors and do not feel efficacious in their ability to fight back. Controlling fear is an important objective when one wants to maintain a high quality of life and maximum mobility. As it turns out, a relationship exists between perceived self-defense skills and fear of crime. Women who view themselves as strong and fast report less fear of crime than women who describe themselves as weak and slow (Gordon & Riger, 1988). To improve feelings of efficacy and control in threatening situations, women have been attracted to self-defense training programs. Although these programs have not been thoroughly evaluated, there is some evidence that they can have beneficial effects for women. A study by Cohen, Kidder, and Harvey (1978) found that women who enrolled in a self-defense course felt more control over their bodies and less fear of crime after the class than before and felt more control relative to women who were not enrolled in the course. Thus, training programs can improve women's self-confidence when they are dealing with confrontational offenders. If the acquisition of self-defense skills can reduce fear of crime, then it might reduce unnecessary avoidance behaviors and allow women to move about freely in low-to-moderate risk environments. (For a closer look at the research on self-defense training, see Cummings, 1992; Follansbee, 1983; Smith, 1984.)

Firearms

One of the most prevalent, and clearly the most controversial, means of self-protection by private citizens is the purchase of firearms. The number of firearms in the United States is substantial and growing. Results from a national survey conducted annually by the National Opinion Research Center indicate that, between 1973 and 1994, the percentage of U.S. households that report having a gun of some type fluctuated between 40 percent and 51 percent (Maguire & Pastore, 1996). During the past 30 years, the number of privately owned weapons has increased at an alarming rate, from an estimated 80 million in 1968 to 120 million in 1978 (Wright, Rossi, & Daly, 1983), to as many as 200 million in 1992 (see Eckholm, 1992; Wright, 1995). An estimated four million new firearms are added to the total supply each year.

The real issue in this country is not guns, per se, but handguns, which are involved in a disproportionate number of violent crimes. During the period from 1979 to 1987, handguns were used by offenders in 44 percent of all homicides, 18 percent of all robberies, 22 percent of all aggravated assaults, and 7 percent of all rapes (Rand, 1990). Since 1985, the rate of homicide committed by juveniles with guns has more than doubled (Blumstein, 1995), causing many criminologists to take a closer look at the contribution of guns to urban violence. Furthermore, new handguns are being added to the current U.S. supply at a rate of two million per year.

Perceiving an increase in criminal violence, as communicated by the media, many urban Americans have responded by purchasing handguns for protection. Of the households that possess one or more firearms, approximately one-in-four owns a handgun (Maguire & Pastore, 1996). Although most Americans own a firearm for recreational purposes (Wright, Rossi, & Daly, 1983), almost half of surveyed *handgun* owners indicate their ownership is motivated by fear of crime or a need for protection. Wright and his colleagues refer to this latter motivation as the "fear and loathing" hypothesis, but argue that fear is *not* a major driving force behind gun ownership.

Although policy analysts have debated whether the literature supports this hypothesis, a growing body of research suggests that fear and perceived crime risk *are* important motivational forces behind the purchase of weapons (Kleck, 1984; Lizotte, Bordua, & White, 1981; Smith & Uchida, 1988; Whitehead & Langworthy, 1989). Consistent with this conclusion, a national survey by the YWCA (1996), which asked U.S. adults to list the "main reason" for keeping a gun in their home, found that 37 percent listed "protection from criminals"—second only to "hunting or recreation" at 46 percent.

Major events seem to provide more compelling evidence for the fear-and-loathing hypothesis than does controlled research. The 1992 race riots in Los Angeles illustrate the extent to which firearm purchases are driven by fear and the desire for self-protection. More than 20,000 guns were bought in California during the first 11 days following the riots, reflecting a 50 percent increase over the previous year (Egan, 1992).

Female gun ownership is another indicator of the fear response in recent years. Paralleling a 21 percent increase in the rate of reported sexual assault during the 1980s (Federal Bureau of Investigation, 1989), female gun ownership appears to have increased during this period (see Quigley, 1989). In a 1995 Gallup poll, 22 percent of American women responded affirmatively to the question, "Do you personally own a gun?" (Maguire & Pastore, 1996). Gun retailers report that female purchases have increased dramatically in recent years, and some national survey data support this observation (See Quigley, 1989). As Zimring (1985) observes, because females are physically vulnerable to sexual violence, they are likely to play an important role in future public policy debates about the ownership of handguns for self-defense purposes.

In the inner city, there is little question that residents purchase handguns for protection as well as for self-respect. Gang violence and drug markets have forced law-abiding citizens and gang members alike to carry handguns for self-protection (Blumstein, 1995; Wilkinson, 1998). In one national survey, 66 percent of the urban handgun owners mentioned "protection from criminals" as the "main reason" for keeping a firearm (YWCA, 1996).

Given that a number of Americans are inclined to purchase handguns for safety reasons, the fundamental question is whether this is an effective anti-crime strategy for the individual and a good policy for our society as a whole. Do handguns protect individuals from criminals or do they increase the chances of suffering a more serious victimization? Do handguns provide their carriers with a feeling of safety and security or do they create additional anxieties? Finally, do handguns reduce or aggravate the overall level of crime in American cities?

Impact on Crime

The relationship between guns and crime has been the subject of much debate as a result of controversial gun control initiatives. Walker (1989) does a nice job of summarizing the arguments posited by both advocates and opponents of gun control. The advocates point to unusually high levels of both gun ownership and violent crime in the United States relative to other countries. Opponents of gun control point to the failure of the criminal justice system to punish weapon offenders, the failure of existing gun legislation, and the rights of private citizens to own firearms.

Unfortunately, the question of whether firearms cause criminal violence is difficult to answer. Wright and his colleagues (1983) argue there is little empirical evidence linking handgun ownership directly with changes in criminality at the individual level. Most research has relied on comparisons of crime and weapon ownership rates across large geographic areas (nations, states, counties), which differ in too many ways to make strong causal statements. If we rely on these statistics, however, the international comparisons provide the most dramatic statement about guns and crime. The United States is nearly "off the chart" for the amount of violent crime and the volume of firearms relative to other developed countries. (Deane, 1990; Gartner, 1990; Killias, 1990; Kleck, 1991; Kopel, 1995). These comparisons, however, are not good science because of the vast number of cultural differences between nations other than the propensity to buy firearms and to commit violent crime.

Within the United States, the estimated 20,000 gun control laws at the federal, state, and local level should, in theory, provide a test of the hypothesis that reducing firearms will reduce the violent crime rate. Existing research provides little evidence that such laws will reduce the amount of violent crime in the target jurisdiction (see Wright, Rossi, & Daly 1983). Kleck and Patterson (1989) conducted an extensive multivariate analysis of data gathered from 170 U.S. cities. They concluded that "gun ownership levels have no net effect on total violence rates." The problem, however, is apparent in their second conclusion—"gun control restrictions have no net effect on gun ownership levels." Weak gun control laws have not been successful at reducing the number of firearms in the jurisdiction, which, in effect, precludes any compelling test of the firearm–crime hypothesis. Without some type of ban at the national level, citizens have numerous opportunities to purchase or steal weapons, and therefore, a reasonable test of the general gun control hypothesis is not possible.[5]

The study by Kleck and Patterson (1989), however, does point to some benefits linked to specific gun control legislation. Two types of gun control seem to affect total violence rates—mandatory penalties for unlawful carrying are associated with reductions in robbery rates, and state or local licensing of gun dealers is associated with reductions in assaults. These data do not directly test the link between the availability of guns and crime but do suggest that specific restrictions might help in specific ways.

---

5. Certainly, the Brady federal gun control law, which imposes a waiting period and a background check for handgun purchases, would have little impact on the opportunities to use a handgun. With an estimated 200 million firearms in circulation today (50 million handguns), a total ban on handguns would have a limited effect for many years.

At another level, recent efforts by law enforcement to remove guns from the streets in selected "hot spot" neighborhoods provides a limited test of the notion that the volume of guns can influence local crime rates. In Kansas City, after the police were trained to detect and seize concealed weapons, gun seizures in the target neighborhood increased by 60 percent and gun crimes declined by 49 percent (Sherman, Shaw, & Rogan, 1995). In another demonstration initiative, Boston gang members and probationers were strongly discouraged by the police from carrying guns. Qualitative evidence indicates that the target groups are complying with the police request and that the number of juvenile gun homicides has dropped precipitously (Kennedy, Piehl, & Braga, 1996).

The relationship between guns and crime can also be examined from a community perspective. Rather than *disarming* the offenders, what would be the effect of *arming* the community on a large scale for self-protection? Would this deter offenders who might be afraid of facing armed targets? The Orlando rape self-defense program is often cited by gun enthusiasts as evidence of the deterrent effect of gun ownership. Following a dramatic increase in the rate of sexual assault in 1966, the Orlando Police Department provided a training course in handgun self-defense, which was taken by approximately 6,000 women over a six-month period. The media gave considerable attention to the program (suggesting that women were now armed and dangerous). The rate of sexual assault dropped by nearly 90 percent in the year following the program, while surrounding communities showed either no change or increases. (Benson, 1984; Robin, 1991). Although "regression to the mean" might help to explain this drop in the number of rapes (after a tripling of rates in the previous year), nevertheless, the possibility of a deterrent effect exists because of the media coverage (see also Green, 1987).

Impact on Personal Safety

Most relevant to this chapter (and perhaps most relevant to the gun control issue down the road) is the question of how much personal protection is provided by the ownership and deployment of a handgun. Are people safer owning a gun or does ownership only provide a false sense of security, while increasing the risk of injury to self or loved ones? Gun control advocates point to the problem of accidental deaths and injuries caused by firearms, the increasing number of suicides involving guns, and the increasing amount of weapon violence among youth. Gun control opponents, aside from their interest in preserving the right to bear arms, point to the benefits of armed self-protection. Our primary objective here is to interject a few facts into this debate.

Paralleling the domestic arms build up, the rate of suicide has climbed dramatically since the 1960s, and the percentage of suicides involving firearms has also increased (Wright, Rossi, & Daly, 1983; Centers for Disease Control and Prevention, 1992). The gun-crime statistics are also indisputable: Between 1979 and 1987, handguns were used to commit an average of 639,000 violent crimes per year in the United States (Rand, 1990). This includes killing an average of 9,200 people per year.

Children remain a major source of concern in the gun debate. An estimated 1500 to 3400 youths commit suicide with a firearm each year, and another 400 are unintentional firearm fatalities (Treanor & Bijlefeld, 1989). In addition, the problem of children bringing firearms to school has become a national concern in the context of school violence (Bailey, Flewelling, & Rosenbaum, 1997). The Centers for Disease Control and Prevention (1995) found that in 1993 approximately 1–in–5 (21 percent) high school students brought a weapon to school within the past 30 days, and other studies indicate that approximately 5 percent of high school students have carried a gun to school at some time (PRIDE, 1995).

Perhaps the most striking statistics are those documenting the rise of inner-city violence by young people and the role posited by firearms. Blumstein (1995) attributes the recent nationwide doubling in juvenile homicides and juvenile gun homicides to the emergence of the crack markets around 1985, which required the recruitment and arming of youth as employees in this violent business. Guns were needed primarily for self-protection and became increasingly indispensable as the number of guns in the neighborhood exploded. Consequently, between 1985 and 1993, the number of juvenile arrests for weapons offenses increased more than 100 percent (Greenfield & Zawitz, 1995).

Although these statistics are troubling, gun control opponents look to another set of facts to support the use of firearms by private citizens. The *American Rifleman*, a monthly publication of the National Rifle Association, contains numerous stories each month of how armed, law–abiding citizens have successfully defended themselves against criminal attacks at home or away from home. However, the actual use of firearms by victims in the United States is very rare, especially given that nearly half of all households have a gun. Analyzing the National Crime Victimization Survey data, Marshall and Webb (1994) found that in only 2 percent of the cases of physical forceful resistance did the victim fire a gun. McDowall and Wiersema (1994) also examined the NCVS data and found that victims used a firearm in only 0.83 percent of all violent offenses.

A look at gun death statistics illustrates the infrequency of defensive firing as a self-protective measure. *Time* magazine (Magnuson, 1989) offered a snapshot view of 464 gun deaths in the United States that occurred during the week of May 1 through May 7, 1989: Only 14 of these gun deaths were the result of defensive firing, 216 were suicides, 22 were accidents, and many of the rest were homicides by acquaintances or relatives. (Magnuson, 1989). Similarly, the often–cited Seattle study of 398 gunshot deaths over a six-year period in homes with firearms showed only 2 self-defensive shootings of intruders (Kellerman & Reay, 1986). There were 12 accidental deaths, 41 homicides of family members or acquaintances, and 333 suicides. The infrequent use of guns for self-defense in the home can be attributed to the fact that residential burglars seek to avoid confrontation, but when confrontation does occur, the offender is likely to catch the victim off-guard and unprepared to deploy a firearm.

Thus, although guns might save lives (and the size of the numbers is uncertain here), more reliable evidence at this point indicates that they facilitate the taking of lives and that the opportunities to confront the offender in home invasions and burglaries are limited. The counter argument offered by gun advocates is that residential burglary rates are lower in the United States than in many other developed countries primarily because of the deterrent effect of gun ownership, that is, burglars are afraid to enter homes that are protected by firearms (see Kopel, 1995).

Residents should be more concerned about violence from relatives and "friends" rather than from intruding strangers. National homicide data indicate that in 44 percent of all firearm homicides the victim knew the killer, in 24 percent of the cases the victim and offender were friends or acquaintances, and in 13 percent of the cases the killer was a relative or intimate of the victim (Zawitz, 1996). More generally, 3-in-10 female homicide victims are killed by their husbands or boyfriends, and arguments accounted for 34 percent of all homicides (FBI, 1991). In this context, the use of handguns at home for self-defense is not a simple matter and can backfire in a domestic dispute. The mere opportunity to use a handgun in the heat of a domestic fight will increase the likelihood of a fatal outcome.

Two large public health studies help answer the question of whether having guns in the home provides increased protection or increased risk of injury (see Kellerman, 1996). Interviews were conducted with surviving next-of-kin in cases of suicides and homicides, as well as with adults in neighboring "control" households that were matched on a wide range of demographics. After statistically controlling for numerous variables that were independently predictive of suicide and homicide, the researchers found that households *with guns* were nearly five times more likely to experience a suicide and nearly three times more likely to experience a homicide than comparable households *without guns*. Hence, these data suggest that keeping a gun at home can dramatically increase the risk of suffering a violent death in that setting.

Protection on the Street

The remaining question is whether a firearm can serve as an effective means of self-protection outside the home. Two major questions have been addressed by researchers: (1) What is the effect of *armed* victim resistance on the likelihood that the offender will complete the crime? (2) How does armed resistance affect the likelihood that the victim will be injured? Unfortunately, very few studies have directly examined these questions. Researchers often elect not to separate armed from unarmed resistance and sometimes rely on police records (rather than victimization surveys) for their data, which introduces significant sample biases.[6] The most extensive work has focused on the crime

---

6. Police records underestimate the extent and successfulness of victim resistance (see Kleck, 1992).

of robbery. The available research suggests that armed resistance is associated with a lower probability of robbery completion (that is, property loss) than unarmed resistance (Kleck, 1988; Ziegenhagen & Brosnan, 1985). Furthermore, Kleck's (1988) analysis of National Crime Victim Survey data showed that victims who resist by using a gun reported the lowest completion rates among eight types of self-protection.

The relationship between *armed* victim resistance and victim *injury* is less clear in the case of robbery. Forceful resistance in general is associated with higher rates of victim injury, but few researchers have separated armed and unarmed resistance. Two studies, using victim survey data, showed that armed resistance was associated with *lower* rates of injury (Kleck, 1988; Ziegenhagen & Brosnan, 1985), whereas another study, using police data, showed that armed resistance was associated with *higher* rates of injury (McDonald, 1975).[7] Finally, a more controlled study by Kleck and DeLone (1993) found a nonsignificant (but negative) relationship between resistance with a gun and injury. One main finding from Kleck's work is that most forms of resistance to personal robbery are unrelated to injury (that is, do not increase or decrease the chances of injury), yet resistance tends to decrease the chances of a successful crime.

Armed resistance by potential rape victims has been the subject of two empirical studies. In both cases, the researchers found that women who resisted their attacker with a weapon were more likely to avoid rape, yet the presence of the weapon did not increase their risk of physical injury (Kleck & Sayles, 1990; Lizotte, 1986).

In summary, the available evidence suggests that citizens who protect themselves with a gun when confronted by a robber or a rapist are less likely to have their property taken or be raped, respectively, and are no more likely (and might be less likely) to be injured than citizens who do not take such actions.

A third question that has received little attention is how gun ownership affects fear of crime or feelings of safety. One would suspect that purchasing a gun for self-protection would help reduce fear of crime. The problem is that, to our knowledge, researchers have not adequately tested this hypothesis. Surveys generally show that gun owners are less fearful than nongun owners (Maxfield, 1977), but as Stinchcombe and his colleagues demonstrate, this relationship is likely to be spurious: Gun owners are typically males living in rural areas. Males are less fearful of crime than females in the first place, and rural areas are characterized by low fear and low crime rates (Stinchcombe, Heimer, Iliff, Scheppele, Smith, & Taylor, 1978). With a growing number of female gun owners, a better test of the ownership-fear hypothesis will be possible in the future. Also, differences between urban, suburban, and rural environments are likely to influence the ownership-fear relationship.

---

7. Given the sample biases in the police data, the victim survey data are more compelling.

CONCLUSIONS

Individual citizens use a wide variety of self-protective behaviors to reduce their risk of victimization or to reduce the cost of victimization when crime cannot be prevented. One of the most common forms of self-protection is avoidance, which involves restricting one's behavior to reduce the risk of victimization. Research supports the public's judgment that not going out at night, avoiding dangerous areas, and so on, will help to lower one's risk of victimization, with the exception of women who live in abusive domestic environments. The cost of these risk-avoidance behaviors are substantial, however, for women, older citizens, minorities, and other vulnerable groups who live with a constant fear of violent attack. Above all, the gain in safety must be weighted against the loss of behavioral freedom. In a free society, every citizen should have the right to move about without restriction and fear of attack. Furthermore, the irony of avoidance behaviors is that the individual may be safer but feels less safe. Not only do these crime prevention behaviors fail to lower fear levels among the high-fear population where they are practiced most frequently, but evidence indicates that some of these behaviors can exacerbate fear. Finally, and perhaps most importantly, a retreat behind locked doors is likely to *increase* (rather than decrease) the level of crime in the community by returning the streets and public places to the criminally minded. One must only observe the high frequency of avoidance behaviors in high-crime neighborhoods to realize that such actions help individuals, but they do little to help communities.

To criticize risk-avoidance behaviors is not to suggest that these measures carry no benefit for individuals. On the contrary, such actions may be the smartest (most effective) way to minimize individual risk and should be employed in moderation with the guidance of good common sense. If the individual has a choice, high-risk environments and high-risk persons should be avoided because they spell trouble. However, the criticisms stated earlier were meant to suggest that avoidance behaviors have been *overused* by some low-risk groups (for example, older females), thus contributing to feelings of powerlessness, restrictions of freedom, and in the end, reduction in their quality of life. Conversely, avoidance behaviors have been *underused* by some high-risk groups (for example, younger males), who feel invulnerable. This is one of the paradoxes of crime prevention—men are at greatest risk of victimization on the street, yet fail to take the necessary precautions in these settings. Women, in contrast, engage in a variety of avoidance behaviors to prevent victimization in public areas, but face the greatest risk of violence at home and in presumably "safe" environments with acquaintances and coworkers.

When risky environments cannot be avoided, individuals can do much to protect themselves and their property. The literature of victim resistance brings some surprises. When victims of rape, robbery, or assault engage in self-protective measures, often they can significantly lower the probability that the criminal act will be completed. Under some conditions, victims might be increasing their chances of injury by the offender, but usually this is not the case. More research is needed on this important topic to determine (with greater confidence) the degree of risk associated with various forms of self-defense.

Both women and men should be educated about the known consequences of resistance, both positive and negative. In addition, they should be aware that research cannot predict what will happen in any given situation and that common sense should prevail. Clearly, the characteristics of the offender, the victim, and the setting (for example, the presence of a weapon, the perceived level of dangerousness) will influence the outcome, and all should be assessed as part of a quick decision-making process.

For these reasons, self-defense training has never been more important. Not only does it show promise for enhancing feelings of efficacy and control among women, but it also should assist participants in distinguishing between types of self-protection that are generally functional and those that are not.

Interestingly enough, some research suggests that armed resistance is the most effective crime prevention response and does not increase the risk of injury. This is the most provocative finding and one worthy of additional study; however, such research must be weighed against the known homicides attributed to a massive gun market. Handgun ownership in urban areas is another example in which the potential gains in individual safety might accrue at the cost of public safety in the long run. As the number of guns in circulation continues to rise, the opportunities for these weapons to reach the "wrong hands" of juveniles, criminals, children, and suicidal persons also increase. In addition, increases in the prevalence of carrying a firearm are likely to increase the minimum threshold of acceptable self-protection in public places (that is, carrying a gun might become a necessity, as it is now perceived in the toughest of neighborhoods).[8]

The gun control issue is a very complex social and political problem that reaches far beyond social science research. In the final analysis, if the current media coverage of violent crime and violent "predators" continues, the perceived positive crime prevention value of guns for individuals might outweigh (in the political arena) the perceived negative crime prevention value for society.[9] In any event, we should recognize, as a society, that this gun battle is as much about our values and how to define American culture as it is a debate about the best way to reduce violence.

Returning to the issue of individual crime prevention behaviors, our current understanding of self-protection should encourage potential victims, especially high-fear groups, to pay more attention to aggressive self-defense measures. Enhanced skills and self-confidence can lead to reductions in unnecessary behavioral restrictions and a higher quality of life for many citizens.

---

8. At least 31 states have passed legislation that allows residents 18 and older to carry concealed firearms after the completion of training and background checks.

9. Public support for guns as a crime prevention tool is fairly strong. In a 1995 national survey, one-third of the respondents agreed with the statement, "Armed citizens are the best defense against criminals" (Maguire & Pastore, 1996).

Although many questions remain to be answered, it is clear that traditional police advice to potential victims is outdated. Regardless of their fears, women need to be mobile for work, recreation, and social activities, and hence, are more likely to encounter other types of (nongender) criminal victimization. Research indicates that most victims of violent crime not only resist their offender (despite law enforcement advice to the contrary), but in many situations, find their actions highly effective. Hence, the primary question is no longer whether to resist or not, but rather what type of resistance will be the most effective for the individual? In addition, public policy analysts and law makers are obligated to ask themselves the larger question—what type of resistance is the most effective for society? Unfortunately, the answers to individual and societal questions might conflict.

REFERENCES

Bailey, S. L., Flewelling, R. L., & Rosenbaum, D. P. (1997). Characteristics of students who bring weapons to school. *Journal of Adolescent Health* 20, 261–270

.Bart, P. B., & O'Brien, P. B. (1985). *Stopping rape: Successful survival strategies.* Elmsford, NY: Pergamon.

Benson, B. L. (1984). Guns for protection and other private sector responses to the fear of rising crime. In D. B. Kates (ed.) *Firearms and Violence* (pp. 329–356). San Francisco: Pacific Institute for Public Policy Research.

Biderman, A. D., Johnson, L. A., McIntyre, J., & Weir, A. W. (1967). *Report on a pilot study in the District of Columbia on victimization and attitudes towards law enforcement.* Washington, DC: U.S. Government Printing Office.

Block, R., & Skogan, W. G. (1986). Resistance and nonfatal outcomes in stranger-to-stranger predatory crime. *Violence and Victims* 1, 241–253.

Blumstein, A. (1995). Violence by young people: Why the deadly nexus? *National Institute of Justice Journal* August (229), 2–9.

Boggs, S. (1971). Formal and informal crime control: An exploratory study of urban, suburban and rural orientations. *Sociological Quarterly* 12, 319–327.

Bureau of Justice Statistics. (1988). *Criminal victimization in the United States, 1986* (NCJ-111456). Washington, DC: U.S. Department of Justice.

Bureau of Justice Statistics (1995). *Criminal victimization in the United States, 1994* (NCJ-162126). Washington, DC: U.S. Department of Justice.

Centers for Disease Control and Prevention (1992). Programs for the prevention of suicide among adolescents and young adults. *Morbidity and Mortality Weekly Report.* Washington, DC: U.S. Department of Health and Human Services, U.S. Government Printing Office. April 22.

Centers for Disease Control and Prevention (1995). Youth risk behavior surveillance—United States, 1993. *Morbidity and Mortality Weekly Report* 44 (SS-1), 1–34.

Cohen, E. S., Kidder, L. H., & Harvey, J. (1978). Crime prevention vs. victimization prevention: The psychology of two different reactions. *Victimology* 3, 285–296.

Cohen, L. E. & Felson, M. (1979). Social change and crime rate trends: A routine activities approach. *American Sociological Review* 44, 588–608.

Cummings, N. (1992). Self defense training for college students. *American Journal of College Health* 40, 183–188.

Davis, R. (1992). Loitering law clears hurdle despite fears. *Chicago Tribune,* May 19, sec. 2, p. 1.

Deane, G. (1990). Cross-national comparison of homicide: Age/sex–adjusted rates using the 1980 U.S. homicide experience as a standard. *Journal of Quantitative Criminology* 3, 215–227.

Dubow, F., McCabe, E., & Kaplan, G. (1979). *Reactions to crime: A critical review of the literature.* Washington, DC: U.S. Department of Justice, National Institute of Justice.

Eckholm, E. (1992). A basic issue: Whose hands should guns be kept out of? *New York Times* (April 3), A1–A11.

Egan, T. (1992). Los Angeles riots spurring big rise in sales of guns. *New York Times* (May 14), A1–A11.

Erskine, H. (1972). The polls: Gun control. *Public Opinion Quarterly* 36, 455–469.

Federal Bureau of Investigation (1989). *Uniform crime reports.* Washington, DC: U.S. Department of Justice.

Federal Bureau of Investigation (1991). *Uniform crime reports.* Washington, DC: U.S. Department of Justice.

Federal Bureau of Investigation (1995). *Uniform crime reports.* Washington, DC: U.S. Department of Justice.

Follansbee, P. A. (1983). Effects of a self-defense program on women's psychological health and well-being. *Dissertation Abstracts International* 43 (January, 7-B), 2388.

Garofalo, J. (1977a). *Public opinion about crime: The attitudes of victims and nonvictims in selected cities.* Washington, DC: U.S. Government Printing Office.

Garofalo, J. (1977b). *Victimization and the fear of crime in major American cities.* Paper presented at the annual meeting of the American Association for Public Opinion Research, Buck Hills Falls, PA.

Gartner, R. (1990). The victims of homicide: A temporal and cross-national comparison. *American Sociological Review* 55, 92–106.

Gordon, M. T. & Riger, S. (1988). *The female fear.* New York: Free Press.

Green, G. S. (1987). Citizen gun ownership and criminal deterrence: Theory, research and policy. *Criminology* 25, 63–81.

Greenberg, S. W., Rohe, W. M., & Williams, J. R. (1984). *Informal citizen action and crime prevention at the neighborhood level: Volume 2. Secondary analysis of the relationship between responses to crime and informal social control.* Report submitted to the National Institute of Justice. Research Triangle Park, NC: Research Triangle Institute.

Greenfield, L. A., & Zawitz, M. W. (1995). Weapons offenses and offenders. *Selected findings: Firearms, crime, and criminal justice series* (November, NCJ-155284). Washington, DC: U.S. Department of Justice, Bureau of Justice Statistics.

Groth, A. N., Burgess, A. W., & Holmstrom, L. L. (1977). Rape: Power, anger, and sexuality. *American Journal of Psychiatry* 134, 1239–1243.

Harris, R. (1969). *Fear of crime.* New York: Praeger.

Hindelang, M. J. (1976). *Criminal victimization in eight American cities.* Cambridge, MA: Ballinger.

Hindelang, M. J., Gottfredson, M. R., & Garofalo, J. (1978). *Victims of personal crimes: An empirical foundation for a theory of personal victimization.* Cambridge, MA: Ballinger.

Kasarda, J. D. (1976). The changing occupational structure of the American metropolis. In B. Schwartz (ed.), *The changing face of the suburbs.* Chicago: University of Chicago Press.

Kellerman, A. L. (1996). Understanding and preventing violence: A public health perspective. *Research Preview.* Washington, DC: U.S. Department of Justice, National Institute of Justice. June.

Kellerman, A. L. & Reay, D. T. (1986). Protection or peril: An analysis of firearms-related deaths in the home.

New England Journal of Medicine 314, 1557–1560.

Kelling, G., Pate, T., Dieckman, D., and Brown, C. (1974). *The Kansas City preventive patrol experiment*. Washington, DC: Police Foundation.

Kennedy, D. M., Piehl, A. M., & Braga, A. A. (1996). Youth gun violence in Boston: Gun markets, serious youth offenders, and a use-reduction strategy. *Law and Contemporary Problems* (Duke University School of Law), 59, 147–196.

Killias, M. (1990). Gun ownership and violent crime: The Swiss experience in international perspective. *Security Journal* 1, 169–174.

Kleck, G. (1988). Crime control through the private use of armed force. *Social Problems* 35, 1–21.

Kleck, G. (1984). The relationship between gun ownership levels and rates of violence in the United States. In Don B. Kates, Jr. (ed.), *Firearms and Violence: Issues of Public Policy* (pp. 99–132). San Francisco: Pacific Institute for Public Policy Research.

Kleck, G. (1988). Crime control through private use of armed force. *Social Problems* 35, 1–21.

Kleck, G. (1991). *Point blank: Guns and violence in America*. New York: Aldine de Gruyter.

Kleck, G., & DeLone, M. A. (1993). Victim resistance and offender weapon effects in robbery. *Journal of Quantitative Criminology* 9, 55–81.

Kleck, G. & Patterson, E. B. (1989) *The impact of gun control and gun ownership levels on violence rates*. Unpublished paper. School of Criminology, Florida State University.

Kleck, G., & Sayles, S. (1990). Rape and resistance. *Social Problems* 37, 149–162.

Kleinman, P. & David, D. (1973). Victimization and perception of crime in a ghetto community. *Criminology* 11, 307–343.

Kopel, D. B. (1995). Guns, germs, and science: Public health approaches to gun control. *The Journal of the Medical Association of Georgia* 84, 269–273.

Koss, M. P. (1992). The underdetection of rape: Methodological choices influence incidence estimates. *Journal of Social Issues* 48, 61–75.

Lab, S. P. (1990). Citizen crime prevention: Domains and participation. *Justice Quarterly* 7, 467–491.

Lavrakas, P. J. (1982). Fear of crime and behavioral restrictions in urban and suburban neighborhoods. *Population and Environment* 5, 242–264

Lavrakas, P. J., Hartnett, S. M., Merkle, D., & Rosenbaum, D. P. (1992). *Community assessment survey results in six neighborhoods: The Community Responses to Drug Abuse national demonstration program final process evaluation report* (Volume 3) Chicago, IL: Center for Research in Law and Justice, University of Illinois at Chicago.

Lavrakas, P. J., & Lewis, D. A. (1980). Conceptualizing and measuring citizen crime prevention behaviors. *Journal of Research in Crime and Delinquency* 17, 254–272.

Lavrakas, P. J., Normoyle, J., Skogan, W. G., Herz, E. J., Salem, G., & Lewis, D. A. (1980). *Factors related to citizen involvement in personal, household, and neighborhood anti-crime measures: Executive summary*. Washington, DC: U.S. Department of Justice.

Levin, D. P. (1991). 'Carjackers' in Detroit stalk drivers, stealing at gunpoint and taking off. *New York Times* (August 31), Y-8.

Liska, A. E., Sanchirico, A., & Reed, M. D. (1988). Fear of crime and constrained behavior: Specifying and estimating a reciprocal effects model. *Social Forces* 66, 827–837.

Lizotte, A. J. (1986). Determinants of completing rape and assault. *Journal of Quantitative Criminology* 2, 203–217.

Lizotte, A. J., Bordua, D. J., & White, C. S. (1981). Firearms ownership for sport and protections: Two not so divergent models. *American Sociological Review* 46, 499–503.

Magnuson. (1989). 7 deadly days. *Time Magazine* (July 17), 31–60.

Maguire, K., & Pastore, A. L. (1996, eds.) *Sourcebook of criminal justice statistics 1995*. U.S. Department of Justice, Bureau of Justice Statistics. Washington, DC: U.S. Government Printing Office.

Maltz, M. D., Gordon, A. C., & Friedman, W. (1991). *Mapping crime in its community setting: Event geography analysis*. New York: Springer-Verlag.

Mangione, T. W., & Noble, C. (1975). *Baseline survey measures including update survey information for the evaluation of a crime control model*. Survey Research Program, University of Massachusetts.

Marshall, C. E., & Webb, V. J. (1994). A portrait of crime victims who fight back. *Journal of Interpersonal Violence* 9, 45–74.

Maxfield, M. G. (1977). *Reactions to fear*. A working paper based on an examination of survey data from Portland, Kansas City and Cincinnati. Evanston, IL: Northwestern University, Center for Urban Affairs.

McDonald, J. (1975). *Armed robbery: Offenders and their victims*. Springfield, IL: Charles C. Thomas.

McDowall, D., & Wiersema, B. (1994). The incidence of defensive firearm use by U.S. crime victims, 1987 through 1990. *American Journal of Public Health* 84, 1982–1985.

McIntyre, J. (1967). Public attitudes toward crime and law enforcement. *Annals of the American Academy of Political and Social Science* 374, 34–36.

O'Keefe, G. J., Rosenbaum, D. P., Lavrakas, P. J., Reid, K., & Botta, R. A. (1996). *Taking a bite out of crime: The impact of the National Citizens' Crime Prevention Media Campaign*. Thousand Oaks, CA: Sage.

PRIDE, Inc. (1995). *1994–1995 national summary, United States grades 6–12*. Atlanta, Georgia.

Quigley, P. (1989). *Armed and female*. New York: E. P. Dutton.

Quinsey, V. L., & Upfold, D. (1985). Rape completion and victim injury as a function of female resistance strategy. *Canadian Journal of Behavioral Science* 17, 40–50.

Rand, M. R. (1990). Handgun crime victims. *Bureau of Justice Statistics special report*. Washington, DC: U.S. Department of Justice.

Reiss, A. J., Jr. (1967). *Studies in crime and law enforcement in major metropolitan areas*. Field Survey III, Vol. 1 of the President's Commission on Law Enforcement and the Administration of Justice. Washington, DC: U.S. Government Printing Office.

Rifai-Young, M. A. (1976). *Older Americans' crime research project*. Portland, OR: Multnomah County Division Public Safety.

Robin, G. D. (1991). *Violent crime and gun control*. Cincinnati: Anderson.

Rosenbaum, D. P. (1988). Community crime prevention: A review and synthesis of the literature. *Justice Quarterly* 5, 323–395.

Rosenbaum, D. P., & Heath. L. (1990). The "psycho-logic" of fear reduction and crime prevention programs. In J. Edwards, E. Posavac, S. Tindel, F. Bryant, & L. Heath (eds.) *Applied Social Psychology Annual* (Vol. 9, pp. 221–247). New York: Plenum.

Ruback, R. B., & Ivie, D. L. (1988). Prior relationship, resistance, and injury in rapes: An analysis of crisis center records. *Violence and Victims* 3, 99–111.

Sherman, L. W., Gartin, P. R., & Buerger, M. E. (1989). Hot spots of predatory crime: Routine activities and the criminology of place. *Criminology* 27, 27–55.

Sherman, L. W., Shaw, J. W., & Rogan, D. P. (1995). The Kansas City gun experiment. *Research in Brief.* Washington, DC: U. S. Department of Justice, National Institute of Justice.

Siegel, J. M., Sorenson, S. B., Golding, J. M., Burnam, M. A., & Stein, J. A. (1989). Resistance to sexual assault: Who resists and what happens? *American Journal of Public Health* 79, 27–31.

Skogan, W. G. (1986). Fear of crime and neighborhood change. In A. J. Reiss, Jr., & M. Tonry (eds.), *Communities and crime* (Vol. 8 in M. Tonry & N. Morris [eds.] *Crime and justice: An annual review of research*). Chicago: University of Chicago Press.

Skogan, W. G., & Block, R. (1983). Resistance and injury in nonfatal assaultive violence. *Victimology* 8, 215–226.

Skogan, W. G. & Maxfield, M. G. (1981) *Coping with crime: Individual and neighborhood reactions.* Beverly Hills: Sage.

Smith, D. R. (1984). A program evaluation: The effects of women's self-defense training upon efficacy expectancies, behaviors, and personality variables. *Dissertation Abstracts International* 44 (June, 12-B), 3945–3946.

Smith, D. A. & Uchida, C. D. (1988). The social organization of self-help: A study of defensive weapon ownership. *American Sociological Review* 53, 94–102.

Stinchcombe, A., Heimer, C., Iliff, R. A., Scheppele, K., Smith, T. W., & Taylor, D. G. (1978). *Crime and punishment in public opinion: 1948–1974.* Chicago: National Opinion Research Center.

Suttles, G. D. (1972). *The social construction of communities.* Chicago: University of Chicago Press.

Treanor, W. W. & Bijlefeld, M. (1989). *Kids and guns: A child safety scandal.* Washington, DC: American Youth Work Center & Educational Fund to End Handgun Violence.

Ullman, S. E. (1997). Review and critique of empirical studies of rape avoidance. *Criminal Justice and Behavior* 24, 177–204.

Ullman, S. E., & Knight, R. A. (1992). Fighting back: Women's resistance to rape. *Journal of Interpersonal Violence* 7, 31–43.

Ullman, S. E., & Knight, R. A. (1993). The efficacy of women's resistance strategies in rape situations. *Psychology of Women Quarterly* 17, 23–38.

Walker, S. (1989). *Sense and nonsense about crime: A policy guide* (2nd ed.). Pacific Grove, CA: Brooks/Cole.

Whitehead, J. T. & Langworthy, R. H. (1989). Gun ownership and willingness to shoot: A clarification of current controversies. *Justice Quarterly* 6, 263–282.

Wilkinson, D. L. (1998). *The social and symbolic construction of violent events among inner city adolescent males.* Unpublished doctoral dissertation. Rutgers University.

Wilson, W. J. (1987). *The truly disadvantaged.* Chicago: University of Chicago Press.

Wright, J. D. (1995). Ten essential observations on guns in America. *Society* March/April, 63–68.

Wright, J. D., Rossi P. H., & Daly, K. (1983). *Under the gun: Weapons, crime and violence in America.* New York: Aldine.

Yaden, D., Folkstand, S., & Glazer, P. (1973). *The impact of crime in selected neighborhoods: A study of political attitudes in four Portland census tracts.* Portland, OR: Campaign Information Counselors.

YWCA (1996). *Families taking action: A YWCA survey about making homes and communities safer.* New York: Louis Harris and Associates.

Zawitz, M. W. (1996). Firearm injury from crime. *Selected findings: Firearms, crime, and criminal justice series*, April, NCJ-160093, Washington, DC: U.S.

Department of Justice, Bureau of Justice Statistics.

Ziegenhagen, E. A. & Brosnan, D. (1985). Victim responses to robbery and crime control policy. *Criminology* 23, 675–695.

Zimring, F. E. (1985). Violence and firearms policy. In L. A. Curtis (ed.), *American violence and public policy: An update of the national commission on the causes and prevention of violence*. New Haven, CT: Yale University Press.

Zoucha-Jensen, J. M, & Coyne, A. (1993). The effects of resistance strategies on rape. *American Journal of Public Health* 83, 1633–1634.

6

❦

Neighborhood Defense

Community Antidrug
Initiatives

During the late 1980s, the community anticrime movement was given a shot in the arm by the proliferation of crack cocaine, especially in poor, inner-city neighborhoods. Centers of distribution and sale of cocaine tended to be associated with rises in burglary and larceny (Rengert, 1990). Extreme violence was often associated with drug sales as well. The rate of violent crimes climbed precipitously during the 1980s as drug sales and use increased. In the cocaine trade, violence became the preferred means for resolving territorial disputes and punishing employees or customers who reneged on payments (Boyum & Kleiman, 1995; Fagan & Chin, 1990). The extreme violence and rise in disorder brought about by drugs increased the flight of inner-city residents able to do so, made residents in some neighborhoods reluctant to use outdoor spaces, and resulted in significant deterioration of the social fabric of neighborhoods (Rengert, 1990). Most inner-city residents believed that drugs had become the number one problem (Davis, Smith, and Hillenbrand, 1991; Rosenbaum, 1991).

Drugs and the social problems they brought energized inner-city residents to mobilize against crime in an unprecedented way. Previously, experts in community anticrime programs had become pessimistic about the prospects of successfully organizing low-income neighborhoods against crime. Naturally occurring, indigenous efforts to fight crime were least likely to form and implanted programs were least likely to take hold in low-income, high crime neighborhoods—exactly those areas where programs were most needed (for example, Garofalo & McLeod, 1988; Greenberg, Rohe, & Williams, 1982).

Several large-scale efforts to implant anticrime programs in low-income neighborhoods concluded that participation rates were substantially worse than in more affluent neighborhoods (McPherson & Silloway, 1987; Rosenbaum, Lewis, & Grant, 1986; Schneider, 1986).

But by the late 1980s, the news media were awash with stories about groups of fed-up citizens banding together to take back the streets from drug dealers. Remarkably, many of these grassroots efforts were occurring in poor, high-crime neighborhoods—exactly those areas where it had been thought impossible to organize people against crime. In fact, a study by Davis, Smith, Lurigio, and Skogan (1991) found that grassroots antidrug efforts were actually *more* likely to begin in poor, high crime neighborhoods than in other urban neighborhoods. These efforts varied broadly, from neighborhood patrols by a handful of concerned residents to large, well-financed programs directly connected to law enforcement or local government agencies.

Weingart, Hartmann, and Osborne (1992) described the wide spectrum of grassroots antidrug activities as "initiatives" rather than "programs" to emphasize that many of these efforts are loosely organized and temporary. Weingart and colleagues define community antidrug initiatives as collections of individuals who join together to participate in an activity oriented against drugs. In this chapter, we will discuss what Weingart (1993) has termed "law enforcement enhancement" approaches—how citizens' actions complement enforcement actions of law enforcement agencies. In many communities, law enforcement enhancement efforts form part of a larger antidrug strategy including education and prevention, treatment for habitual drug users, leisure time activities for youth, and neighborhood clean-up and beautification.

METHODS USED BY COMMUNITY ANTIDRUG INITIATIVES

Weingart (1993) and Rosenbaum (1991) both describe the array of approaches that have been used by community antidrug efforts, which include the following:

- *Antidrug rallies.* These can be communitywide rallies or nighttime vigils at scenes of heavy drug sales or past violence. Rallies help capture the attention of neighborhood residents and demonstrate to drug dealers that the neighborhood is concerned and has the resolve to reclaim the streets. Often, rallies and vigils are the precursor to other sustained antidrug efforts.

- *Anonymous reporting and surveillance programs.* Many people fail to report drug activity out of fear of retaliation or distrust of law enforcement agencies (Davis, Smith, & Hillenbrand, 1991). Accordingly, many communities established ways for people who witness drug sales to report anonymously by telephone to civilian representatives in their neighborhoods. These reports are relayed periodically to the police, and witnesses can call back to get feedback on what was done with their information. In other communities, law enforcement agencies themselves established special "tip lines" for reporting drug activity. Callers to tip lines remain anonymous, and the information they provide is typically fed directly to central narcotics enforcement units.

- *Citizen patrols.* Citizen patrols are potentially the most confrontational form of grassroots antidrug initiative. Small groups of citizens patrol problem areas in cars or on foot (see Chapter 3). They record drug activity and report it to the police. Reporting can be either direct or (more often) indirect, through a base command post. The simple presence of citizens on patrol is believed to deter drug dealers and their customers. In some cases, patrols have become quite aggressive and attempted to intimidate drug dealers themselves, rather than summon the police.

- *Code enforcement.* Many drug sales are conducted from inside or in front of residences. Community groups have targeted such locations using enforcement of violations of local building codes to pressure property owners to clean up the location. Other groups have pressured owners' insurance companies to deny hazard insurance until such time as drug dealing is stopped. Similar actions have been applied to owners of bars or other commercial locations from which drugs are sold. In addition, some community groups have lodged complaints with local liquor control and licensing agencies threatening revocation of licenses if drug activity is not stopped.

- *Alteration of the physical environment.* In some neighborhoods, efforts have been made to alter the physical environment to deny drug dealers a safe haven for conducting business. For example, shrubbery in a park may be cut back to make activities in parks more visible to police and citizen patrols. One neighborhood in Philadelphia reduced its problem with drug selling by installing locked gates to close off alleys (Davis, Smith, Lurigio, & Skogan, 1991).

- *Drug house abatement.* The most effective tool for denying drug dealers safe havens is drug house abatement. In these actions, property owners are threatened with civil suits (which can result in fines, closure, or confiscation of the property) unless drug sales are cleaned up. Suits are brought under civil nuisance abatement statutes, which require a lower standard of proof than criminal prosecutions. Once an owner has been notified that a nuisance exists, it is his or her responsibility to abate the problem. Usually, the owner corrects the problem by evicting the problem tenant(s). The method is cheap because normally all that is required to abate a problem is a single letter to a property owner. However, questions have been raised about drug house abatement actions because (a) they often result in the eviction of persons already prosecuted and sentenced on criminal charges, (b) innocent family members or other tenants might be evicted with the drug sellers, and (c) drug dealers might simply be dispersed without curbing their selling activity.

VARIETIES OF COMMUNITY
ANTIDRUG INITIATIVES

Recently, Roehl, Wong, Huitt, and Capowich (1995) reported the results of a nationwide study that described community antidrug activities. Although they did not randomly sample local initiatives (they used a "snowball" approach to sampling, eliciting nominations from local leaders of federally funded antidrug efforts), their study represents a major systematic attempt to identify and describe community antidrug efforts.

The researchers identified several program types: loosely organized groups of citizens, block or neighborhood watch groups, grassroots groups, umbrella organizations, civic and service groups, church and religious groups, and "other" organizations. Grassroots groups were the most common program type, accounting for more than one in three initiatives in the sample. Umbrella organizations had the largest membership and budgets, whereas loosely organized citizens' groups and Neighborhood Watch groups had the least funding. In general, community antidrug initiatives had few paid staff and little external funding and one in three had no paid staff or external funding. The most common source of support came from local fund-raising efforts and individual contributions.

Roehl and colleagues also found that citizen involvement in the community antidrug initiatives generally was not high. In half of the initiatives surveyed, fewer than 1-in-10 community residents took part in the activities. Moreover, although many citizens participated in occasional marches or rallies, the programs reported that the vast majority did not become seriously involved in program activities because of apathy, denial, tolerance of drug use, practical problems, or fear. Typically, most of the work was performed by small cadres of dedicated volunteers.

Community antidrug programs vary in the extent to which they are integrated with antidrug efforts of local governments. At one extreme are programs begun solely through the efforts of local citizens without any assistance from law enforcement or other governmental agencies. Such initiatives can be openly hostile to or suspicious of municipal government: Indeed, perceived inaction by elected officials is frequently what motivates grassroots antidrug efforts by private citizens. These independent efforts are probably likeliest to form (certainly they are likeliest to be described in the media and academic literature) in poor, minority neighborhoods where distrust of police and other authorities runs high.

At the other end of the continuum are initiatives created largely through the organizing efforts of local government. Davis, Smith, Lurigio, and Skogan (1991) discuss initiatives in several neighborhoods that were the result of deliberate plans of police or other municipal agencies to organize specific neighborhoods with serious crime and drug problems. Meetings and rallies were planned by municipal officials to mobilize residents at the same time that police antidrug activities were beefed up, and building code enforcement were made a priority. Eventually, potential citizen leaders were identified and groomed to organize grassroots antidrug efforts. However, Weingart, Hartmann, and Osborne (1992) point out that such "top-top-down" approaches might not take hold in communities as well as truly indigenous grassroots efforts do.

Community antidrug efforts receive many benefits by aligning themselves with local power structures. Most important, they might receive assistance in their crusade against local pushers. The police might agree to step up patrols, set up buy-and-bust operations, or conduct drug sweeps to coincide with efforts of local citizen groups. The police can provide suggestions about how to organize local residents, training to neighborhood watch groups, or two-way radios to citizens on patrol. Local officials might agree to act as advocates with key city agencies in support of the efforts of citizen groups to close drug houses or discourage drug sales based in bars or restaurants.

Citizen antidrug organizations often have modest needs for equipment, from cameras or radios for neighborhood patrols to answering machines for block watch groups. Municipal agencies and local officials might provide funding directly to citizen antidrug groups for purchase of needed equipment or staff positions. They can also provide technical assistance and expertise to citizen groups in filing applications for funding from state or federal agencies.

Finally, collaboration with municipal agencies can give citizen groups infusions of fresh ideas. For example, governmental agencies might form coalitions of several grassroots neighborhood groups that meet regularly so that leaders can exchange tactics and bolster each other with stories of successes. This cross-pollination of ideas was an essential strategy of police-organized citizen antidrug groups in Philadelphia (Davis, Smith, Lurigio, & Skogan, 1991).

FROM INDIGENOUS INITIATIVES TO
"SEEDED" PROGRAMS

At the other extreme of the collaboration continuum are citizen antidrug efforts created by criminal justice policy makers and federal, state, or private funders. Some of these "seeded" programs have been done on a large-scale national basis. The Community Responses to Drug Abuse program funded by the Bureau of Justice Assistance incorporated 10 antidrug efforts in

10 low-income neighborhoods with serious drug and gang problems. The Robert Wood Johnson Foundation's Fighting Back program funded antidrug efforts in 15 cities. The Bureau of Justice Assistance's Weed and Seed program funded 19 sites. On an even larger scale, the Community Partnership Demonstration Program of the Center for Substance Abuse Prevention included 252 separate sites.

Most of these large-scale programs to "seed" local citizen antidrug efforts have tended to go well beyond a simple law enforcement enhancement approach: They have included substantial efforts in the areas of antidrug education, prevention, and treatment. These national approaches have also tended to be very "top-down" and bureaucratic, rather than grassroots in nature. For example, the Community Partnership Demonstration Program emphasized coalitions between health, social service, public assistance, and criminal justice agencies; schools; churches; and grassroots community organizations. The approach was based on a public health model: The partnerships emphasized public education, media campaigns, and programs for youth (Cook and Roehl, 1993).

The Justice Department's Weed and Seed program set up local bureaucratic structures with multiple interagency committees and staff liaisons to the committees. Most Weed and Seed funds were spent on law enforcement agencies for police overtime and new equipment for cracking down on drug dealers (Roehl, 1995). (Lesser "seed" monies were spent on community revitalization efforts.)

The closest thing to producing grassroots community antidrug efforts among the large-scale "seed" programs probably is Community Responses to Drug Abuse (CRDA). Funding for these sites was targeted to community-based organizations that had already demonstrated success in building communities (Rosenbaum, Bennett, Lindsay, and Wilkinson, 1994). Because significant antidrug organizing had already occurred before federal funds were received, there was a greater chance of success than if money had been given to communities to create new organizations. Sites were overseen by multi-agency task forces, which were required to develop detailed work plans with the aid of a national technical assistance team. During the first funding year, sites stuck to law enforcement enhancement approaches to community drug problems: Various sites developed neighborhood watches and citizen patrols, closed drug houses, and participated in court watch programs. The second year saw a greater appreciation of the complexity of drug problems as recreational opportunities for young people were expanded, parents were educated about drugs, and drug treatment was made available (Rosenbaum, et. al., 1994).

Realizing that citizen involvement is crucial to any successful antidrug strategy, the federal government has recently funded police agencies in several cities to implement comprehensive approaches to drug enforcement that include an important role for residents. The guiding principle behind these approaches is derived from problem-oriented and community-oriented policing (Eck & Spelman, 1987; Goldstein, 1990; Kelling & Coles, 1996; Rosenbaum, 1994; Skogan & Hartnett, 1997). In this new style of policing, police officers work cooperatively with area residents to define problems of concern to the community and to develop blueprints for solutions. Solutions can run the gamut from implementing traditional police approaches (crackdowns, undercover buys, or reverse stings) to soliciting cooperation of municipal agencies to enforce building codes, initiate drug house abatement actions, or revoke licenses of problem commercial establishments, to altering the physical environment to create defensible space (Newman, 1973). Key to these strategies is participation and cooperation of local residents.

Jersey City, New Jersey, was one of several sites of a federal effort termed the Drug Market Analysis Project (DMAP). All DMAP sites had in common the use of sophisticated computer mapping techniques for mapping drug "hot spots" (Sherman, Gartin, & Buerger, 1989). In Jersey City, a randomized experiment assigned matched pairs of hot spots to receive standard law enforcement or enhanced enforcement (Weisburd & Green, 1995). In the enhanced condition, police coupled traditional antidrug tools such as crackdowns with newer approaches. The police attempted to engage business owners and citizens in antidrug efforts, including the aggressive enforcement of municipal codes. The evaluators found a significant decline in drug complaints and arrests in the enhanced enforcement areas, but not in the standard enforcement areas.

Green (1996) analyzed a problem-solving approach to neighborhood drug enforcement in Oakland, California, which emphasized the establishment of working relationships between police, residents, property owners, and proprietors. Like the Jersey City experiment, the Oakland program combined traditional law enforcement antidrug strategies with the targeting of drug hot spots, aggressive enforcement of building codes, and civil abatement actions. Green reports that areas targeted in this way experienced a reduction in signs of physical disorder, an increase in citizen reporting of drug activity, a decline in arrests, and a drop in field contacts relative to citywide trends.

In summary, when enforcement and problem-solving efforts are focused on drug hotspots and involve the community, the probability of preventing crime and drug abuse can be significantly increased. We should point out, however, that traditional reactive drug market arrests show mixed results, and most studies have found no effect on crime (Kleiman, 1988; Kleiman, Barnett, Bouza, & Burke 1988; Pate, 1984; Uchida, Forst, & Annan, 1992). Even a controlled experiment, which found that crack raids can lower crime rates, also revealed that the effects are short-lived—approximately one week (Sherman & Rogan, 1995).

EFFECTIVENESS OF COMMUNITY ANTIDRUG INITIATIVES

Community antidrug strategies can be understood through two basic theoretical models (see Chapter 3 for more detail). The first involves informal social control. This model suggests that reductions in crime and the fear of crime are by-products of various processes that include vigorous enforcement of social norms (Greenberg, Rohe, & Williams, 1982; Jacobs, 1961), clearer delineation of neighborhood boundaries and identities (Suttles, 1972), and establishment of a stronger sense of community and increased social interaction (Conklin, 1975; DuBow & Emmons, 1981).

Community antidrug initiatives also can be understood as opportunity reduction. This model emphasizes the deterrence value of designing or modifying the physical environment to enhance the security of commercial and residential settings (see Chapter 7) and of encouraging residents to adopt measures (both physical and social) to minimize the risk of victimization to themselves or their neighbors (see Chapters 2 through 5).

More recently, the opportunity reduction model has been elaborated in the "rational choice" and "situational crime prevention" formulations, which postulate that crime can be controlled by changing situations and environmental factors so that individuals perceive potential targets less favorably (see Chapter 8). Cornish and Clarke (1986) assume that offenders make rational choices about being involved in criminal behavior according to the expected gains and costs of committing crimes. For example, Reuter, MacCoun, and Murphy (1990) concluded that people sell drugs because the money they earn by doing so exceeds the money they could earn through legitimate means.

Situational crime prevention perspectives build on the rational choice model by assuming that crime can be controlled by altering situations and environmental factors so that potential criminals perceive the potential costs to outweigh the expected gains (Clarke, 1992). Clarke divides crime control tactics into three categories: those that increase the effort to be involved in criminal activity, those that increase the risks to potential offenders, and those that decrease the expected gains from criminal activities.

Antidrug rallies and vigils are consistent with the informal social control model. Antidrug marches build a sense of shared concern and neighborhood cohesion. They promote informal social control by conveying a message to drug dealers that they do not own the streets and that residents care about what goes on there.

Block watches and citizen patrols, as noted in Chapter 3, directly promote informal social control: Citizens surveil the streets and, through their presence, discourage drug buying and selling. Block watches and patrols can also be thought of in situational crime prevention terms as (a) increasing the effort involved in drug selling and buying (because sellers might be forced to change locations and therefore be more difficult for buyers to find), (b) increasing the risk to drug buyers and sellers (because the police might be summoned) and (c) decreasing the expected gains from selling drugs (because buyers and sellers might find it harder to find each other and complete a transaction).

Code enforcement, environmental modification, and abatement actions are best thought of in situational crime prevention terms. These actions make it more difficult to sell drugs by denying potential sellers an hospitable environment. Sellers are forced to move to new locations where buyers might have more difficulty finding them. Sales might suffer as a result, and expected gains can be reduced.

With these concepts in mind, we turn our attention to empirical studies of the effectiveness of community antidrug efforts. Gauging the success of community antidrug initiatives is difficult. If the initiatives studied are truly indigenous, then no one knows ahead of time where they will start. This precludes collecting baseline data on important social variables for pre-post comparisons. It also precludes selecting a priori matched pairs of neighborhoods and randomly implementing the antidrug initiative in half of the neighborhoods. Usually, the best that can be done in making concurrent comparisons is to select the best available comparison area after the initiative has sprung up.

Police data on drug complaints and arrests are one type of indicator of success of community antidrug initiatives. Police data have some advantages as outcome measures. They are inexpensive to collect. Also, complaints and arrests are available historically so they can be used in pre-post comparisons in the neighborhood where antidrug initiatives begin. There are, however, serious drawbacks to using police data to gauge drug activity. First, police data are inherently limited because they do not include those incidents that residents fail to report. Davis, Smith, and Hillenbrand (1991) found that reported drug activity represents only a small proportion of all activity witnessed by citizens. Second, the intended effect of a block-watch initiative is to increase crime reports as a result of enhanced surveillance of the streets. Therefore, an increase in complaints and arrests suggests that the initiatives are successful even though, typically, increases in these indicators are taken to mean that drug activity is on the rise. A third problem with using police data to evaluate community initiatives is that many police departments do not aggregate data on complaints of drug activity and few departments can produce data on complaints or arrests for particular neighborhoods within their districts (Davis, Smith, & Hillenbrand, 1991).

The level of drug activity in an area can also be gauged by interviewing residents. Surveys avoid some of the problems of using police data. Most important, survey data provide an unbiased estimate of the extent of drug activity in an area if careful sampling is performed. But there are shortcomings to survey data as well. For reasons just discussed, researchers rarely have the opportunity to interview residents before the start of a community antidrug initiative. Therefore, they must be asked after the fact to reconstruct perceptions of drug activity, disorder, and crime before the start of the antidrug initiatives. Such retrospective accounts lack the reliability of concurrent accounts. Moreover, some residents might underestimate the extent of neighborhood drug problems out of fear or involvement of themselves or acquaintances.

Davis, Smith, Lurigio, and Skogan (1991) evaluated the impact of community antidrug initiatives using patrol and block-watch strategies. In neighborhoods served by four exemplary citizen initiatives, Davis and colleagues conducted telephone surveys that compared residents' perceptions of current neighborhood conditions with their recollections of preprogram conditions and with the perceptions of residents of a comparison neighborhood in the same city. (Comparison neighborhoods were picked because of their similarity to the program areas on official crime statistics, residents' demographics, socioeconomic status, and housing stock.) The investigators assumed that a program effect was present if residents' perceptions in the program neighborhood changed for the better over time while residents' perceptions in the comparison neighborhood remained constant or became worse over time.

The survey data generally showed few preexisting differences between program and comparison neighborhoods in either residents' characteristics or residents' perceptions along the six dimensions described. Differences did emerge, however, after the antidrug initiatives began. All the areas with antidrug initiatives (but none of the comparison areas) showed reduced fear of crime; three of the four antidrug initiative areas showed enhanced social control and cohesion; and two of the four initiative areas showed increased resident empowerment and neighborhood satisfaction and reduced signs of physical decay.

Similar results on the effectiveness of community antidrug activities were obtained by Rosenbaum and his colleagues who reported data from three of the "best" CRDA sites (Rosenbaum, Lavrakas, Wilkinson, & Faggiani, 1997). Because the CRDA efforts were seeded, the researchers knew where the efforts would begin and conducted true baseline surveys with neighborhood residents in program and control sites. The three sites had the most intensive and successful program implementations—neighborhoods in Chicago, Hartford (Connecticut), and Waterloo (Iowa).

The CRDA program in these three intensive sites was effective at increasing target area residents' awareness of, and participation in, antidrug activities. Relative to residents in control areas, residents in the target areas also reported greater satisfaction with their neighborhoods as a place to live, less desire to move out, greater social interaction with neighbors, and more favorable attitudes about the police with whom they had formed a partnership. No differences were found, however, on fear of crime, feelings of empowerment, or use of the local environment (parks and stores). Although the results were somewhat mixed, overall they were more positive than those of previous evaluations of community anticrime programs. The evaluators reached the following conclusion: "community organizations, with limited federal funding and good technical assistance, *can* make a difference in the lives of neighborhood residents *if* they involve a well-planned, intensive, and persistent effort." (Rosenbaum et al., 1997, pp. x–xi).

Two studies have investigated the effectiveness of drug house abatement actions. One study examined abatement programs in five cities (Smith, Davis, Hillenbrand, & Goretsky, 1992) and the other in a single city (Lurigio, Davis, Regulus, Gwisada, Popkin, Dantzker, Smith, & Ouellet, 1993). The studies indicated that drug abatement actions are effective in achieving their immediate goal of eradicating drug activity. In all six cities, compliance was obtained from property owners, and no further drug problems were experienced on the premises in at least 85 percent of targeted properties.

The study by Lurigio, et al., also compared residents' perceptions of crime and disorder between 20 individual blocks where abatement actions had occurred and 20 similar comparison blocks in the same area. The survey results showed that few residents of targeted blocks were aware that abatement actions had occurred. The authors also reported no effects of the abatement actions on residents' perceptions of drug activity and other signs of social disorder on the block. Lurigio, et al., speculated that the failure to find an impact on residents' perceptions was due to how the abatement actions were handled. In contrast with some other cities in the Smith, et al., study, where abatement actions were accompanied by extensive media coverage, the abatement program investigated by Lurigio, et al., went about its business quietly without fanfare.

The findings from this small group of studies of citizen antidrug initiatives are generally quite positive. To say, however, that community efforts *can* make a difference is not the same as saying that they are *likely* to make a difference. By and large, researchers have studied the best programs they could find. The findings of the studies we have discussed say nothing about the effectiveness of more run-of-the-mill citizen initiatives. Also, the evaluation research to date has been limited in quantity and quality. More controlled evaluations are needed to increase our confidence in estimates regarding the effectiveness of these initiatives.

Moreover, we must remember that community antidrug initiatives are very limited in what they are trying to achieve. They are not concerned with reducing citywide drug activity. Rather, they are simply trying to reduce drug sales in their neighborhoods. Drug sales are sometimes displaced to other, less vigilant neighborhoods. We will shortly examine this issue in greater detail.

But, given these caveats, it appears that community antidrug initiatives can be effective—at least in a limited way. Surprisingly, they can do this even without widespread community participation. One program described by Davis, Smith, Lurigio, & Skogan (1991) was known by just 4 percent of local residents and comprised essentially just three individuals. This handful of individuals patrolled their neighborhood in their car. When they spotted drug dealers, they parked in front of them and took photographs of buyers and sellers. The intimidation tactics were highly effective, although the patrollers were involved in confrontations from time to time. This initiative was particularly small, but as Roehl, et al. (1995) observed, in general, participation in community antidrug efforts is low.

We speculate that small community antidrug initiatives can be effective because they work on the basis of opportunity reduction rather than by informal social control. Block-watch programs directed against street crimes such as robbery, burglary, and stranger assault were based on the social control model of crime prevention. To have an effect on these crimes, citizen programs had to elicit behavioral changes in large portions of the community:

Many people had to surveil and be willing to report crimes if relatively infrequent and unpredictable events like burglary and robbery were to be affected. Seldom was such participation achieved. Rosenbaum (1987) noted, "the typical levels of participation in watch programs are hardly sufficient to produce occasional surveillance" (p. 125). Rosenbaum further argued that there was little evidence that block-watch programs changed people's willingness to engage in social interaction, informal social control, or surveillance of the neighborhood. In addition, he continued, even if all these developments appeared as a result of block-watch organizing efforts, the changes would be insufficient to affect local street crime rates (see Chapter 3).

Citizen antidrug initiatives, however, do not need to bring about changes in social control to be effective. In sharp contrast with robberies, burglaries, and like crimes, drug sales are conducted from relatively stationary locations (a street corner, store, or dwelling), and sellers are not difficult to spot. Particular sellers change location from time to time, as dictated by police and community pressure, but sellers must be easy to locate by both established customers and passers-by looking for drugs. Drug sellers, in other words, operate retail businesses and therefore, must be semipublic and semi-visible figures.

Because drug sellers engaged in conducting business are not difficult to locate, they can be readily targeted by community members interested in curtailing their activity. Sellers and their clients can be harassed in a variety of ways: Police can be called, transactions can be photographed, license plates can be written down, and so forth. Each of these activities creates a climate unfavorable to conducting business. Opportunities for dealers are curtailed by increasing the effort involved in selling drugs, increasing the risk to buyers and sellers, and decreasing profits as potential buyers are driven off. These actions can be undertaken by small groups of concerned citizens. Thus, contrary to conventional wisdom and research on community crime prevention, large segments of the community do not necessarily have to cooperate in efforts to reduce opportunities to sell drugs.

WORDS OF CAUTION

Despite the potential for good to emerge from citizen antidrug initiatives, there are also potential harmful effects. In closing this chapter, we delineate some of these potential risks and express a few words of caution.

Erosion of Civil Liberties

Probably most widely discussed in the media is the potential for vigilantism and the erosion of civil liberties. Block-watch or patrol members can cross the line from surveillance to intimidation, encouraging escalation and violence. This has been a frequently expressed concern of law enforcement officials and one that was realized to a degree in successful actions by the Church of Islam in Washington, D.C., and Brooklyn, New York (Davis & Lurigio, 1996).

The aggressive pursuit of neighborhood drug enforcement needs to be balanced with a concern for individual constitutional rights. Police drug crackdowns often involve stop-and-frisk practices. Historically, the courts have permitted the police to use this tactic when they suspected the presence of weapons or potential for violence. But it is questionable whether transporting illegal drugs from one location to another constitutes a similar immediate danger (Rosenbaum, 1993).

A recent spate of anti-loitering laws have also attempted to make it easier to curb neighborhood drug sales. These laws have sometimes been directed against drug-dealing gangs by authorizing police to disperse groups of known gang members. Other times, laws have restricted loitering in certain areas labeled as high-drug activity locations (Davis, Smith, Lurigio, and Skogan, 1991).

Stop-and-frisk practices and anti-loitering laws cause concern because they circumscribe the rights of individuals for the greater welfare of the community. They are also troublesome because they are used disproportionately against minorities. According to Rosenbaum (1993, p. 68), "This approach to the drug war is likely to encourage prejudicial responses that are unfavorable to disadvantaged and minority communities, whereby skin color is too often associated with drug activity."

Drug house abatement and forfeiture laws can also erode civil liberties, especially when recklessly applied. Because abatement strategies hold property owners accountable for tenants' behaviors, these statutes might infringe on owners' rights to use and enjoy property (Smith et al., 1992). Furthermore, statutes that permit authorities to close properties without notifying owners might infringe on due process rights. Improperly applied abatement laws can injure innocent family members, who are evicted with drug dealers, and other tenants who are forced out with the closure of entire buildings.

Asset forfeiture laws have generated far more debate about civil liberties than abatement statutes because they ignore the fundamental presumption of innocence: Under many forfeiture statutes, authorities can seize property before trial, even if the owner is unaware that the property was used to store or distribute drugs (Rosenbaum, 1993). To obtain their seized property, defendants must prove that they are innocent or that their property was not used for drug activity.

Regardless of these dangers, residents living in neighborhoods with blatant drug sales want aggressive law enforcement. Rosenbaum (1993) found, through neighborhood surveys, that most inner-city residents were willing to accept infringements on individual rights (for example, round up suspected drug users even without sufficient evidence) to reduce drug trafficking. The same was not true for residents living in higher-income, lower-crime areas. He concluded that "residents of neighborhoods with visible drug markets have repeatedly called for police crackdowns on their own neighbors and their calls have been heard" (p. 77).

Problems Caused by Large Numbers of Arrests

The aggressive pursuit of low-level drug dealers and users produces large numbers of arrestees that the courts are poorly equipped to handle. Drug arrests in the United States increased 52 percent between 1980 and 1987, while the total number of arrests for nondrug cases increased by just 11 percent (Belenko, 1990). Drug arrests currently number more than one million each year. Some have wondered whether attention to enforcement of drug-related laws is diverting money and resources away from enforcing other laws (Blumstein, 1993). Others argue that strict enforcement of drug-related laws is a sensible strategy for reducing all types of crime because drug offenders commit a large proportion of all crimes (for example, Boyum & Kleiman, 1995).

The large increases in drug arrests have placed a serious strain on the courts and corrections. During the 1980s, time to disposition for drug felonies rose precipitously—in some cities to a year (Goerdt & Martin, 1989). When the courts become overwhelmed with drug cases, they typically respond by releasing defendants on a wholesale basis. For example, Press (1987) reports that a police crackdown in New York City drug markets between 1985 and 1987 resulted in a large backlog of pending cases: The combination of crowded court dockets and crowded jails put pressure on courts to plea bargain cases "cheaply," in effect neutralizing the value of mass arrests. Similarly, Smith and colleagues (1994) found that dramatic increases in drug case backlogs in Chicago preceded an increase in nonreporting probation as a sentencing option.

Tonry (1994) noted that the massive numbers of narcotics arrests have seriously affected a whole generation of African-American youth. This group—along with Hispanics—is caught disproportionately in drug efforts to curb local drug nuisances. Tonry demonstrated that drug arrests are responsible for worsening racial disparities in prisons across the country. In addition, research indicates that having a criminal history record reduces access to legitimate employment opportunities (Bushway, 1996), which only contributes to the cycle of illegal economies and violence that we want to prevent.

Displacement

Drug dealers driven from one neighborhood by zealous citizens or police can simply set up shop somewhere else. Lab (1992) reviewed evidence concerning the displacement of crime (primarily robbery and burglary) caused by citizen prevention programs and concludes that "displacement is a plausible concern in considering the impact of the [crime prevention] projects" (p. 81). Because drug dealing is more like a business than is robbing or breaking and entering, drug dealers might be expected to be especially recalcitrant: Chased from one location, they might have strong financial incentives to establish themselves elsewhere.

However, evidence from evaluations of neighborhood antidrug efforts have seldom found displacement effects. For example, displacement has been found only in a few studies of police crackdowns (see Sherman, 1990). Research on drug house abatement reviewed by Davis and Lurigio (1996) gives little indication that geographic displacement occurs when drug dealers are dislocated. Davis and Lurigio report on data from a pilot project in Milwaukee that tracked the activities of evicted drug sellers. The evidence suggested that only a small proportion continued to sell narcotics at their new locations. Green (1996) reported that not only did a code enforcement and police crackdown ant-drug effort in Oakland fail to generate displacement effects, but it diffused benefits to the surrounding area, confirming a phenomenon observed earlier by Clarke and Weisburd (1994). In other words, drug problems improved at targeted sites and in the area surrounding each individual target as well. More research is needed to determine the extent to which community antidrug efforts displace problems or diffuse benefits. The reality is that very few studies have examined displacement or diffusion effects, and of those that have, few have done so carefully enough—with sufficient scientific rigor—to rule out competing hypotheses.

Even if displacement is found to occur reliably, Barr and Pease (1990) argue that when drug activity travels from high- to low-crime areas, it has "benign" consequences because it evens out the geographic distribution of crime. Moreover, if motivated neighborhoods can displace their crime to other, less motivated areas, that could be regarded as a fair outcome, according to Barr and Pease. Indeed, an increase in crime in a less organized neighborhood might lead citizens there to organize as well, although this outcome is by no means assured. These are important policy issues beyond the scope of research proper.

REFERENCES

Barr, R. & Pease, K. (1992) A place for every crime and every crime in its place: An alternative perspective on crime displacement. In D. Evans, N. Fife, & D. Herbert (eds.), *Crime, policing, and place: Essays in environmental criminology.* London: Routledge.

Belenko, S. (1990) The impact of drug offenders on the criminal justice system. In R. A. Weisheit (ed.), *Drugs, crime, and the criminal justice system.* Cincinnati: Anderson.

Blumstein, A. (1993). Making rationality relevant: The American Society of Criminology 1992 Presidential Address. *Criminology* 31, 1–16.

Boyum, D., & Kleiman, M. A. R. (1995). Alcohol and other drugs. In J. Q. Wilson and J. Petersilia (eds.), *Crime* (pp. 295–326). San Francisco: ICS Press.

Bushway, S. (1996). *The impact of a criminal history record on access to legitimate employment.* Unpublished doctoral dissertation. H. John Heinz School of Public Policy and Management, Carnegie Mellon University.

Clarke, R. V. (ed.). (1992). *Situational crime prevention: Successful case studies.* New York: Harrow and Heston.

Clarke, R. V. & Weisburd, D. (1994) Diffusion of crime control benefits: Observations on the reverse of displacement. In R. V. Clarke (ed.) *Crime Prevention Series* (pp. 165–184, Number 2). Monsey, NY: Criminal Justice Press.

Conklin, J. (1975). *The impact of crime.* New York: Macmillan.

Cook, R., & Roehl, J. (1993). National evaluation of the community partnership program: Preliminary findings. In

R. C. Davis, A. Lurigio, & D. Rosenbaum (eds.), *Drugs and the community* (pp. 225–250). Springfield, IL: Charles C. Thomas.

Cornish, D. B. & Clarke, R. R. (1986)(Eds.). *The reasoning criminal.* New York: Springer-Verlag.

Davis, R. C. & Lurigio, A. J. (1996) *Fighting back: Neighborhood anti-drug strategies.* Thousand Oaks, CA: Sage.

Davis, R. C., Smith, B. E., & Hillenbrand, S. W. (1991). *Reporting of drug-related crimes: Resident and police perspectives.* Washington, DC: American Bar Association.

Davis, R. C., Smith, B. E., Lurigio, A. J., & Skogan, W. G. (1991). *Community response to crack: Grassroots anti-drug programs.* Report of the Victim Services Agency, New York, to the National Institute of Justice.

DuBow, F. & Emmons, D. (1981). The community hypothesis. In D. A. Lewis (Ed.), *Reactions to crime* (pp. 167–182). Beverly Hills, CA: Sage.

Eck, J., & Spelman, W. (1987). Who ya gonna call?: The police as problem busters. *Crime and Delinquency* 33, 31–52.

Fagan, J. & Chin, K. (1990) Violence as regulation and social control in the distribution of crack. In M. De la Rosa, E. Y. Lambert, and B. Gropper (eds.) *Drugs and violence: Causes, correlates, and consequences* (NIDA Research Monograph 103). Washington, DC: U.S. Government Printing Office.

Goerdt, J. & Martin, J. A. (1989) The impact of drug cases on case processing in urban trial courts. *State Court Journal* Fall, 4–12.

Goldstein, H. (1990). *Problem-oriented policing.* New York: McGraw-Hill.

Garofalo, J. & McLeod, M. (1988). *Improving the effectiveness of neighborhood watch programs.* Washington, DC: National Institute of Justice, U.S. Department of Justice.

Green L. A. (1996) *Policing places with drug problems.* Newbury Park, CA: Sage.

Greenberg, S., Rohe, W. M., & Williams, J. R. (1982). *Safe and secure neighborhoods: Physical characteristics and informal territorial control in high and low crime neighborhoods.* Washington, DC: National Institute of Justice.

Jacobs, J. (1961). *Death and life of great American cities.* New York: Vintage.

Kelling, G. L., & Coles, C. M. (1996). *Fixing broken windows.* New York: Free Press.

Kleiman, M. A. R. (1988). Crackdowns: The effects of intensive enforcement on retail heroin dealing. In M. A. R. Kleiman, A. Barnett, A. V. Bouza, & K. M. Burke (eds.) *Street-level drug enforcement: Examining the issues.* Washington, DC: U. S. Department of Justice, National Institute of Justice.

Kleiman, M. A. R., Barnett, A, Bouza, A. V., & Burke, K. M. (eds.). (1988). *Street-level drug enforcement: Examining the issues.* Washington, DC: U. S. Department of Justice, National Institute of Justice.

Lab, S. P. (1992). *Crime prevention: Approaches, practices, and evaluations.* Cincinnati: Anderson.

Lurigio, A., Davis, R., Regulus, T., Gwisada, V., Popkin, S., Dantzker, M., Smith, B., & Ouellet, A. (1993) *An evaluation of the Cook County State's Attorney's Office Narcotics Nuisance Abatement Program.* Chicago: Loyola University Department of Criminal Justice.

McPherson, M. & Silloway, G. (1987). The implementation process: Effort and response. In A. Pate, M. McPherson, & G. Solloway (eds.), *The Minneapolis community crime prevention experiment.* Washington, DC: Police Foundation.

Newman, O. (1973) *Defensible space: Crime prevention through urban design.* New York: Collier.

Pate, A. (1984). *An evaluation of the Urban Initiatives Anti-Crime Program: Final report.* Washington, DC: Department of Housing and Urban Development.

Press, A. (1987) *Piecing together New York's criminal justice system: The response to crack.* New York: New York Bar Association.

Rengert, G. F. (1990). *Drug marketing, property crime, and neighborhood viability: Organized crime connections.* Report to the Pennsylvania Commission by the Department of Criminal Justice, Temple University.

Reuter, P., MacCoun, R., & Murphy, P. (1990). *Money from crime: A study of the economics of drug dealing in Washington, DC.* Santa Monica, CA: RAND.

Roehl. J. A. (1995) *National process evaluation of the weed and seed initiative* (Draft report). Washington, DC: National Institute of Justice.

Roehl, J. A., Wong, H., Huitt, R., & Capowich, G. E. (1995). *A national assessment of community-based anti-drug initiatives: Final report.* Pacific Grove, CA: Institute for Social Analysis.

Rosenbaum, D. P. (1987). The theory and research behind Neighborhood Watch: Is it a sound fear and crime reduction strategy? *Crime and Delinquency* 33, 103–134.

Rosenbaum. D. P. (1991). The pursuit of "justice" in the United States: A policy lesson in the war on crime and drugs. *Canadian Police College Journal* 15, 239–255.

Rosenbaum, D. P. (1993). Civil liberties and aggressive enforcement: Balancing the rights of individuals and society in the drug war. In R. C. Davis, A. J. Lurigio, & D. P. Rosenbaum (eds.), *Drugs and the community* (pp. 55–84). Springfield, IL: Charles C. Thomas.

Rosenbaum, D. P. (ed.). (1994). *The challenge of community policing: Testing the promises.* Newbury Park, CA: Sage.

Rosenbaum, D. P., Bennett, S. F., Lindsay, B., & Wilkinson, D. L. (1994). *Community responses to drug abuse: A program evaluation.* Washington, DC: National Institute of Justice.

Rosenbaum, D. P., Lavrakas, P. J., Wilkinson, D. L., & Faggiani, D. (1997). *Community Responses to Drug Abuse National Demonstration Program:* *An impact evaluation.* Final report to the National Institute of Justice. Chicago: Center for Research in Law and Justice, Department of Criminal Justice, University of Illinois at Chicago.

Rosenbaum. D. P., Lewis, D. A., & Grant, J. (1986). Neighborhood-based crime prevention: Assessing the efficacy of community organizing in Chicago. In D. P. Rosenbaum (ed.), *Community crime prevention: Does it work?* (pp. 109–136). Newbury Park, CA: Sage.

Schneider, A. L. (1986). Neighborhood-based anti-burglary strategies: An analysis of public and private benefits from the Portland program. In D. P. Rosenbaum (ed.), *Community crime prevention: Does it work?* (pp. 68–86). Beverly Hills, CA: Sage.

Sherman, L. W. (1990). Police crackdowns: Initial and residual deterrence. In M. Tonry and N. Morris (eds.), *Crime and justice: A review of research* (pp. 1–48). Chicago: University of Chicago Press.

Sherman, L., Gartin, P., & Buerger, M. (1989). Hot spots of predatory crime. *Criminology* 27, 27–56.

Sherman, L., & Rogan, D. P. (1995). Deterrent effects of police raids on crack houses: A randomized controlled experiment. *Justice Quarterly* 12, 755–781.

Skogan, W. G., & Hartnett, S. M. (1997). *Community policing, Chicago style.* New York: Oxford University Press.

Smith, B. E., Davis, R. C., Hillenbrand, S. W., & Goretsky, S. R. (1992). *Ridding neighborhoods of drug houses in the private sector.* Washington, DC: American Bar Association.

Smith, B. E., Lurigio, A., Davis, R. C., Goretsky-Elstein, S., & Popkin, S. (1994) Burning the midnight oil: An examination of Cook County's night drug court. *Justice System Journal* 17, 41–52.

Suttles, G. (1972). *The social construction of communities.* Chicago: University of Chicago Press.

Tonry, M. (1994). Racial politics, racial disparities, and the ward on crime. *Crime and Delinquency* 40, 475–494.

Uchida, C. D., Forst, B., & Annan, S. O. (1992). *Modern policing and the control of illegal drugs: Testing new strategies in two American cities.* Technical report. Washington, DC: U.S. Department of Justice, National Institute of Justice.

Weingart, S. (1993). A typology of community responses to drugs. In R. C. Davis, A. Lurigio, & D. P. Rosenbaum (eds.), *Drugs and the community* (pp. 85–105). Springfield, IL: Charles C. Thomas.

Weingart, S. N., Hartmann, F. X., & Osborne, D. (1992). *Lessons learned: Case studies of the initiation and maintenance of the community response to drugs.* Report of the J. F. Kennedy School of Government (Harvard University) to the National Institute of Justice.

Weingart, S. N., Hartmann, F. X., & Osborne, D. (1994). *Case studies of community anti-drug efforts* (National Institute of Justice Research in Brief, October, 1994 issue). Washington, DC: National Institute of Justice.

Weisburd, D. L. & Green, L. (1995). *Policing hot spots: The Jersey City DMA experiment.* Manuscript submitted for publication.

PART IV

Reducing Criminal Opportunities Through Environmental Modifications

p.124 = blank

7

❂

Crime Prevention and the Built Environment

During the late 1960s and early 1970s, crime soared to unprecedented levels. Government administrators, politicians, social scientists, and public policy experts began searching for affordable, practical, and immediate remedies to the crime problem. One set of solutions, proposed by urban planners and architects, seemed to meet all these criteria. Its rationale was quite simple: Changing the physical (built) environment and influencing the way people use it can prevent crime. Beginning in public housing, social scientists and criminal justice practitioners started to explore modifications in architectural design as a strategy for stemming urban crime.

Throughout the 1970s, several research and development projects were undertaken to test the relationship between crime and the built environment with the support of federal grants from the Law Enforcement Assistance Administration (LEAA), the National Science Foundation (NSF), and the Department of Housing and Urban Development (HUD) (Rubenstein, Murray, Motoyama, & Rouse, 1980). Although these projects differed in their theoretical frameworks and in their methods for manipulating or modifying the physical environment, they all shared one or more of the following assumptions (Fowler & Mangione, 1986; Rouse & Rubenstein, 1978):

1. The physical environment can prevent offenses by blocking opportunities for crime or can make crimes more difficult to commit by creating obstacles or barriers to targets.

2. The physical environment can impede the behavior of offenders by eliminating places for concealment and convenient escape routes.

3. The physical environment can change residents' behaviors to increase the likelihood that offenders will be observed, deterred, or apprehended.

4. The physical environment can be structured or used by citizens to reduce crime through a number of mechanisms, including surveillance enhancement, street control, and social interaction and cohesion among residents.

In this chapter we describe anticrime efforts that concentrate on people's surroundings. First, we provide an overview of the major theories that laid the groundwork for environmentally based approaches to crime prevention. Second, we review research findings addressing both the impact of specific anticrime measures and the effects of comprehensive, multifaceted interventions, known as crime prevention through environmental design.

THEORETICAL FOUNDATIONS

First Generation Defensible Space Theorists

Wood (1981) was the first to propose a relationship between crime and the physical environment. She discussed, for example, how the inherent physical characteristics of public housing developments inhibited communication and contact among residents, the building blocks of informal social control. Jacobs (1961), an urban scientist and a contemporary of Wood's, wrote *The Death and Life of Great American Cities*, presenting a more elaborate perspective on crime and physical design. Drawing on anecdotal and observational evidence, she suggested that crime and the physical environment are related in a systematic, measurable, and ultimately controllable manner. Furthermore, she recommended improving the environment's natural surveillance capacities as a means to deter offenders and to increase their risk of apprehension. Another early theorist who emphasized the importance of the built environment in crime prevention efforts was Angel (1969):

> The physical environment exerts a direct influence on crime settings by delineating territories, reducing or increasing accessibility by the creation or elimination of boundaries and circulation networks, and by facilitating surveillance by the citizenry and the police. (p. 162)

The sketchy theoretical formulations of Wood (1981), Jacobs (1961), and Angel (1969) were fleshed out by the field's most prominent advocate: Oscar Newman. Newman's (1972) initial writings focused on architectural solutions to crime in and around public housing developments and spawned numerous studies on defensible space theory (for example, Gwaltney, 1978; Gwaltney & Yin, 1978; Reppetto, 1974; Taylor, Gottfredson, & Brower, 1980). Newman found that crime in housing projects most often occurred in areas where offenders' activities were difficult to observe. By the same token, he found that crime was reduced when buildings were restructured to permit residents to view doorways and other public places; that is, crime decreases when public housing residents are encouraged to assume responsibility for public areas, thereby exercising their normal "territorial" instincts to preclude predatory offenders (Clarke, 1992).

Newman (1973) argued that physical design changes could "release latent attitudes in tenants which allow them to assume behavior necessary to the protection of their rights and property" (p. xii). These behaviors included "a significant police function, natural to their daily routine and activities," that would "act as important constraints against antisocial behavior" (p. xii). According to Newman (1972), crime deterrence is

> The capacity of the physical environment to create perceived zones of territorial influence . . . the capacity of physical design to provide surveillance opportunities for residents and their agents . . . the capacity of design to influence the perception of a project's (housing development) uniqueness, isolation, and stigma . . . the influence of geographic juxtaposition with "safe zones" on the security of adjacent areas. (p. 50)

Although Newman's propositions were influenced by those of Jacobs, their work differed from each other's in a few basic respects (Greenberg, Rohe, & Williams, 1985). For example, Jacobs, an urban planner, applied her concepts to entire neighborhoods whereas Newman, an architect, concentrated on smaller units of analysis such as individual buildings and their immediate surroundings. Unlike Jacobs, Newman "moved beyond description to undertake quantitative analyses of the relationship between specific design features and crime" and "provided a wealth of detailed design suggestions for creating 'defensible space' through reducing anonymity, increasing surveillance, and reducing escape routes for offenders" (Clarke, 1992, p. 6).

Jacobs focused on surveillance in a more general sense, whereas Newman based his ideas about surveillance and about environmental use and maintenance on a hierarchy of physical space involving four zones demarcated by real and symbolic barriers (Newman, 1973):

- Public space. An area that is open to anyone and serves a variety of uses.
- Semi-public space. An area that is open to the general public but has a limited number of uses (for example, an apartment lobby).
- Semi-private space. An area that is restricted to a few persons from the public and is mainly occupied and used by residents of a building (for example, an apartment hallway).
- Private space. An area reserved for residents only (for example, within an apartment).

Newman (1973) tested his model of defensible space using archival data from the New York City Housing Authority. He compared two adjacent housing projects: one with defensible space characteristics (Brownsville) and one without them (Van Dyke). Newman reported that the less safely designed project experienced more crimes and higher maintenance costs that could not "be explained away by variations in tenant characteristics in the two projects" (p. 49). He extended his research in a series of analyses on the physical and social factors affecting crime in more than 100 New York City housing projects and concluded that "relationships between physical design features and crime patterns have been established" (1973, p. 234).

Additional support for defensible space theory was found in Boston and London, England. For example, Reppetto (1974) reported that physical site characteristics were strong predictors of residential burglary. In a study of London's public housing projects, Wilson (1978) indicated that vandalism was more prevalent in areas where certain aspects of the physical environment did not allow for defensible space. These design factors, however, were only important when the density of children in a project was low, which was the primary determinant of the vandalism rate.

More recently, Fisher and Nasar (1992) have recategorized defensible space features into three broad groupings, concentrating on victim-offender dynamics in specific settings. The first, *refuse,* refers to features that offer would-be offenders escape from detection (for example, tall bushes and dark corners). The second, *prospect,* refers to features that allow legitimate users to survey an area. The third, *escape,* gives legitimate users multiple paths for exiting an area. Fear of crime is highest in areas that offer high refuse to offenders, low prospects for surveillance, and few avenues for escape to legitimate users.

Newman's (1973) model is perhaps the most seminal of the so-called first generation defensible space theorists (Taylor, Gottfredson, & Brower, 1980); nonetheless, it has been subjected to the most serious criticisms (for example, Bottoms, 1974; Mayhew, 1979; Rubenstein et al., 1980), which he has attempted to address (for example, Newman & Franck, 1980). Although Newman's initial theory of defensible space was parsimonious (that is, the causes of and solutions to crime were boiled down to design factors), it has also been described as "overly restrictive" and deterministic (Taylor, Gottfredson, & Brower, 1980).

Newman has been attacked for ignoring how the social characteristics of residents in housing developments and in their adjoining neighborhoods affect crime rates. In replications of Newman's work on crime in public housing, for example, Wilson (1990) and others (Mawby, 1977; Taylor, Shumaker, & Gottfredson, 1985) found that the social status of building residents, building offender rates, and the number of children per building were better predictors of crime than were building height, building size, and other defensible space variables.

In a study of Baltimore neighborhoods, Taylor, Shumaker, and Gottfredson (1985) reported that the relationship between physical design features and crime was spurious; that is, it disappeared after they controlled for a neighborhood's social status. The primacy of social variables was confirmed again in a qualitative study of a multi-ethnic housing project in Boston. Merry (1981) found that the project had obvious defensible space features but that it still experienced high levels of crime and incivility, which she attributed to the project's ethnic fragmentation. Furthermore, Merry (1981) shed light on a crucial point: Although physical design can establish the conditions for citizens to exercise social control (that is, defensible space), it cannot guarantee that they will engage in such behaviors (that is, defended space). Other research evidence has also refuted Newman's assumption that physical design strategies are equally effective across social and cultural groups (for example, Scheflen, 1971; Suttles, 1968). More recent findings, however, suggest that physical design strategies work well across a wide range of settings (Crowe & Zahm, 1994).

Other critics have maintained that Newman's studies failed to account for larger neighborhood context, including a factor that investigators refer to as the "journey-to-crime" (Greenberg, Rohe, & Williams, 1985). Research on this factor has shown, for example, that African-Americans and youths tend to commit more crimes closer to home than do other demographic groups. Moreover, they generally commit more violent crimes closer to home than property crimes, and they commit more residential property crimes closer to home than commercial property crimes (Brantingham & Brantingham, 1981; Nichols, 1980; Titus, 1984). Thus, a community's crime rate (and the type of offending that occurs) can be predicted, to some extent, from demographic variables irrespective of the community's physical design features.

Finally, the most important omissions of Newman's research and of other studies done by the first generation defensible space theorists are their failure to define key concepts (for example, territoriality), to test basic assumptions regarding residents' behaviors (for example, their willingness to take advantage of surveillance opportunities), and to measure intervening or mediating variables (for example, residents' territorial behaviors and cognitions) (Taylor, Gottfredson, & Brower, 1980). These shortcomings of Newman's early work led Taylor and colleagues (1980) to conclude that defensible space theory has never been adequately conceptualized or tested (see also Greenberg, Rohe, & Williams, 1985). Nevertheless, Newman's ideas and research findings have influenced public housing designs in many parts of the world and were extremely influential in advancing crime prevention theory and practice (Coleman, 1985).

CPTED Theory

The second generation environmental theorists incorporated social and cultural variables in their crime prevention models and they made more realistic assumptions about peoples' thought processes and territorial behaviors (Taylor, Gottfredson, & Brower, 1980). From 1974 to 1978, LEAA and HUD awarded a total of 4 million dollars to test an extension of defensible space theory in a major initiative known as Crime Prevention Through Environmental Design (CPTED) (Jeffrey, 1971; Lavrakas, Normoyle, & Wagener, 1978). As Taylor and Harrell (1996) stated, "CPTED focuses on the settings in which crime occurs and on the techniques for reducing vulnerability in these settings" (p. 1). Jeffrey (1971), an early exponent of CPTED, is credited for ushering in "a new era in criminological thought that focused on the circumstances surrounding a crime incident rather than on the criminal offender" (Crowe & Zahm, 1994, p. 23).

Under the auspices of the Westinghouse Electric Corporation, a consortium of criminologists, social scientists, and urban planners initiated a number of changes in the physical and social environment, based on four crime prevention principles (Kaplan, O'Kane, Lavrakas, & Hoover, 1978; Lavrakas & Kushmuk, 1986):

1. *Access Control.* Preventing unauthorized persons from entering residences and businesses through anticrime devices such as locks, bars, and alarms and through psychological barriers such as crime prevention stickers, signs, street designs, and landscaping.

2. *Surveillance.* Strengthening the ability of legitimate users of the environment to observe suspicious persons, intruders, or events to deter crimes or detect crimes in progress.

3. *Activity Support.* Encouraging residents to use the built environment in ways that will render it less vulnerable to crime.

4. *Motivation Reinforcement.* Creating disincentives for offenders to commit crimes by increasing their perceived risk of apprehension and decreasing their perceived payoff.

The preceding principles are the proximate goals of CPTED programs. And, as Kushmuk and Whittemore (1981) noted, these goals are not mutually exclusive:

> Increased access control provides support for increased motivation reinforcement; increased surveillance serves to increase access control and motivation reinforcement; and increased activity support promotes increases in the other three. (p. 2)

Underlying CPTED principles is the notion of OTREP: Crime *o*pportunity is a function of *t*arget, *r*isk, *e*ffort, and *p*ayoff. Criminals are influenced by the inherent costs and benefits of criminal acts; crime is reduced when the risks outweigh the projected benefits (Lab, 1992). In short, a safe environment is one in which few easy targets exist, in which offenders perceive that their risk of being caught is high, in which considerable efforts are required to commit crimes, and in which criminals' payoffs are minimized (Kushmuk & Whittemore, 1981).

OTREP assumes a rational offender perspective (for example, Clarke, 1992). Criminals chose a target depending on whether there is a strong likelihood of their being seen and apprehended (that is, whether the potential crime site is watched by guardians who will act to prevent the crime), whether the site allows offenders easy entry and egress, and whether the site is vulnerable and attractive. In other words, offenders are opportunists, weighing the perceived benefits against the perceived difficulties in committing a crime and the risk of being apprehended (Cornish & Clarke, 1986). They consider the following factors in determining whether or not to commit a crime in a specific place (Taylor & Harrell, 1996, p. 2):

- How easy will it be to enter the area?

- How visible, attractive, or vulnerable do targets appear?

- What are the chances of being seen?

- If seen, will the people in the area do something about it?

- Is there a quick, direct route for leaving the location after the crime is committed?

CPTED's ultimate goals are to "reduce the incidence and fear of crime, thereby improving the quality of life" in a neighborhood (Crowe, 1991, p. 29) These goals, however, are not the endpoint of the CPTED model. For CPTED to really work, it must be "institutionalized" in a self-perpetuating process that sustains the favorable social and environmental conditions needed to achieve its ultimate goals on a continual basis (Kushmuk & Whittemore, 1981).

CPTED was clearly an advance over defensible space theories, but its own theories and studies have also been criticized. First, like defensible space theorists, early CPTED theorists assumed, without solid empirical support, that CPTED strategies are effective across socioeconomic strata (for example, Westinghouse, 1976). As it turns out, recent evidence has shown that CPTED strategies can work successfully in a variety of settings from luxury apartments to public housing developments (Feins & Epstein, 1996). Second, CPTED researchers have not fully described those components of the social environment that interact with design features to produce intended outcomes. In general, researchers have failed to specify the linkages among predictor, mediating, and outcome variables, making it difficult to interpret the results of CPTED studies. According to Taylor, Gottfredson, and Brower (1980), "in a typical (CPTED) study, several predictors and several mediating processes are examined, and the relationship between these two clusters of variables is only vaguely outlined" (p. 36). (For exceptions, see Fowler, McCalla, and Mangione, 1979, and Newman and Franck, 1980.)

Feins and Epstein (1996) nicely summarize several other criticisms leveled against CPTED and defensible space theorists:

> The assumption that people are naturally territorial may be naive, particularly in contemporary urban settings. Racial, ethnic, language, and class divisions may make a sense of neighborhood identity difficult to establish. Further, defensible space and territoriality are very difficult to quantify, making conclusive evaluations difficult . . . [A] sense of informal territoriality among residents is not sufficient to affect crime rates. Finally, users' and potential users' fear of victimization or retaliation, whether or not they are closely related to the realities of crime in the area, also have a

notable dampening effect on both individual and collective behavior. Thus, strategies to address and reduce fear may need to be implemented before the crime prevention benefits of spatial design/redesign can be realized. (p. B-6)

THE NATURE AND EFFECTS OF ENVIRONMENTAL STRATEGIES

In the next section, we review a variety of investigations into the specific components of defensible space and CPTED strategies. Our review is organized according to four basic and closely related crime prevention activities: target hardening, access control, surveillance enhancement, and community-building measures (see also Rubenstein et al., 1980). We first discuss findings regarding the individual effects of these four measures, then we describe major CPTED initiatives that, by definition, involve multiple anticrime strategies.

TARGET HARDENING

Description of Efforts

Target hardening or hardware measures employ physical barriers to prevent crime. Target hardening techniques, including locks, bars, grills, alarms, fences, meshes, immobilizing devices, and reinforced materials, are based on the simple notion that physical obstacles protect property by making it more impenetrable and less susceptible to criminal actions. Specifically, by increasing the level of difficulty or potential hazards associated with reaching a target, these measures deter would-be offenders in two general ways: Offenders will reject a target that they would have pursued if the target were not hardened, or they will fail to overcome the target-hardening device while attempting to commit a crime (Stanley, 1976).

Another form of target hardening, which takes an indirect approach to controlling crime, is property marking. Operation Identification (OI) is a collective term describing crime prevention efforts that instruct citizens to mark permanently their personal property as a means to diminish their risk of being burglarized.

The typical OI program involves enrolling residents in the project, providing them with materials to mark their valuables, and asking them to place signs in their windows and communities warning potential burglars about the program, as a psychological deterrent to crime (Heller, Stenzel, & Gill, 1975). In addition, participants register their identification numbers with local police departments, enabling the return of stolen goods more quickly and reliably. The value of OI projects lies in their potential to prevent burglaries (that is, burglars are presumably dissuaded when they learn that valuables are inscribed with a traceable serial number) and to assist police officers in tracking the source of stolen goods (that is, a unique, personal identifier provides a crucial link between stolen property and burglary victims) (Lurigio & Rosenbaum, 1986).

Target-hardening measures are certainly not foolproof. In apartment buildings and housing complexes, vandals frequently destroy locks, meshes, and other reinforcing materials. And offenders always seem to possess enough ingenuity to circumvent the most sophisticated locks, bars, and alarm systems. Also, if they are deterred in one location, offenders can seek less protected or unprotected property or environments; hence, target-hardening techniques might only displace and not eradicate some percentage of crime (Clarke & Mayhew, 1980).

Research Findings

Hardware.   The impact of target hardening devices has been examined in numerous studies. Notwithstanding our caveats regarding their shortcomings, these measures appear to be very effective across different circumstances and settings. For example, Clarke (1983) reported that thefts from public telephones were dramatically reduced in the late 1960s when the British Post Office replaced aluminum coin boxes with steel ones. In public housing, target hardening has been shown to be useful in preventing burglaries. According to the Seattle Law and Justice Planning Office (1975), the installation of deadbolt locks, solid-case doors, short walls, and window restrictions significantly reduced burglaries at three of four public housing sites (see also Brill and Associates, 1975, 1977). Similarly, Pease (1991) reported that upgrades in door and window security reduced burglaries on a British public housing estate from 526 in the year before the intervention to 132 three years after the intervention.

Clarke (1992) presented a variety of successful case studies of target hardening initiatives: Decker's (1972) study showing that a slug rejection device reduced the use of slugs in New York City parking meters; Mayhew and colleagues' (1976) study showing that the placement of steering column locks on all cars (old and new) in West Germany produced a 60 percent decline in the country's auto theft rate; Ekblom's (1987) study showing that the installation of anti-bandit screens on London's post office counters cut robbery by 40 percent; and Challinger's (1991) study showing that fortified coin boxes decreased public telephone vandalism in Australia.

Several investigations have demonstrated that residential burglary victims were less likely to have been protected by hardware than were nonvictims (Reppetto, 1974; Walsh, 1980). Specifically, Pope (1977) and Scarr (1972) both reported that poorly secured dwelling units in residential areas were burglarized more frequently than were units with secure locks, doors, and window frames. Furthermore, as Mayhew (1982) noted, the sizable numbers of unsuccessful burglary attempts are evidence of the effectiveness of household security efforts—although they are probably also a function of other preventive factors (Rosenbaum, 1988). Finally, burglars report that they are deterred when faced with locks that are difficult to pick or break (Bennett & Wright, 1984).

Alarms and Security Cameras.   Despite their widespread use, few valid studies of alarms and security cameras have been conducted. One of the most conclusive studies of alarms was done in the schools and businesses of Cedar Rapids, Iowa (Cedar Rapids Police Department, 1975). Schools that received alarm systems experienced a 75 percent reduction in burglaries compared with a 25 percent reduction in matched schools without alarms. Although businesses did not show a similar reduction in burglaries, alarms in these locations were associated with a significant reduction in attempted burglaries (55 percent [alarm group] versus 8 percent [control group]) and with significant increases in the rates of arrest (31 percent [alarm group] versus 6 percent [control group]) and clearance (46 percent [alarm group] versus 27 percent [control group]). When break-ins did occur at buildings with alarms, they took place at entries where the alarms were not hooked up (Cedar Rapids Police Department, 1975). The effectiveness of alarms is further supported by studies of known burglars. Interviews with samples of burglars indicated that many of them considered whether an alarm was present when they planned their crimes (Reppetto, 1974) and that the presence of an alarm influenced their choice of targets (Bennett & Wright, 1984).

Surette (1985) studied the impact of cameras on businesses in Florida. He found that cameras had no effect on reported crime, but that they did lead to increases in feelings of security among business owners. Two other major studies examined the effectiveness of cameras as a crime prevention tool. The first evaluated the Hidden Cameras Project in Seattle (Whitcomb, 1978). A total of 150 businesses were chosen for the study. Half were randomly selected to be equipped with concealed cameras; the other half served as the control group. Robberies occurring at businesses with cameras were more likely to be cleared and more likely to result in convictions of offenders.

The second study evaluated the impact of closed-circuit cameras in three buildings of the Bronxdale Housing Project in New York City (Musheno, Levine, & Palumbo, 1978). Television cameras were placed in elevators and public lobbies, and residents could simultaneously view these areas by tuning in to Channel 3 (the bottom half of the screen showed the elevator, the top half showed the lobby). The buildings with cameras were compared with matched buildings without them. At three-months follow-up, no effects were found on crime rates or fear of crime. The investigators attributed this disappointing result to the fact that very few residents watched channel 3 every day and that the crime rate was fairly low in these buildings at the start of the project.

Three studies conducted in England found that the installation of closed circuit television cameras reduced thefts from automobiles parked in a university's parking lot from 92 in the year before the cameras were installed to 31 in the year after (Poyner, 1981); curtailed the vandalism of seats in double–decker buses by two-thirds (Poyner, 1993); and lowered the number of muggings and thefts at high-risk stations on the London Underground—these crimes, however, appeared to be displaced to stations without cameras (Mayhew, Clarke, Burrows, Hough, & Winchester, 1979; see also Burrows, 1980).

Property Marking.   Heller, Stenzel, and Gill (1975) surveyed nearly 100 property-marking projects (that is, OI programs) across the country. They found that, in general, the burglary rates of OI participants were significantly reduced after they enrolled in the project. For example, participants in OI programs in Seattle and in St. Louis (Heller, Stenzel, & Gill, 1975) experienced 33 percent and 25 percent reductions in burglary, respectively. Other studies also found that displaying property-marking stickers in windows significantly lowered burglary victims' risk of future burglary (Laycock, 1985; Schneider, 1986)—although in the Laycock study, previous nonvictims of burglary who did not participate in the program had a lower risk of future victimization than did OI participants.

In South Wales, Laycock (1986, 1991) reported that a highly-publicized property-marking campaign, involving three villages, reduced burglary 40 percent with little or no displacement to nonparticipating homes. Reductions in burglary rates continued during the second year following program implementation. Laycock (1991) noted, however, that the vast publicity associated with the program, including massive television coverage and door-to-door visits by police officers, might have affected burglary rates more than did the property-marking component of the intervention. Based on this research, Laycock (1991) made the following statements about crime prevention programs:

1. Areas with high crime rates, including burglary, might welcome crime prevention initiatives even if the areas have a reputation for poor relations with the police.

2. The easier it is for members of the public to participate in crime prevention schemes, the more likely they will be to do so.

3. It is probably as important to tell the burglars about the scheme as it is to tell the general public. It might be worth contemplating how this can be achieved.

4. The evidence suggests that the use of a window or door label, indicating marked property, is effective in reducing burglary. The public can be reassured, therefore, that any anxieties that decals increase the chances of victimization are unfounded (p. 72).

On the negative side, OI projects do not appear to affect burglaries citywide, even in small towns. For example, Mattick and colleagues (1974) reported that 255 cities in Illinois with property-marking programs did not experience reductions in citywide burglary rates when compared with 389 cities without such programs (for an exception, see Schneider, 1986). There is also no evidence that OI programs lead to increases in the numbers of apprehended or convicted burglars or that they facilitate the recovery or return of stolen property (Lurigio & Rosenbaum, 1986; Rosenbaum, 1988). Furthermore, reductions in burglary rates, reported by individual OI projects, may be attributable to the tendency of program participants to employ other crime prevention strategies in conjunction with property engraving (for example, target hardening), suggesting that they were more security conscious to begin with or that they had a lower risk of victimization before they participated in the program. Hence, burglary reductions might actually have been caused by other security measures (Lurigio & Rosenbaum, 1986). The null effects of OI projects at the community level can also be explained by low participation levels. Heller, Stenzel, and Gill (1975), for example, indicated that 85 percent of surveyed property-marking programs were able to recruit only 10 percent of their targeted populations.

ACCESS CONTROL

Description of Efforts

Access control measures involve erecting boundaries to restrict the use of nonpublic space to "legitimate" or intended users (Crowe & Zahm, 1994). Such boundaries can be symbolic (low walls or landscaping) or real (gates, high fences) and can apply to single family residences or to entire neighborhoods; for example, in the case of the latter, they might reduce criminal activity by limiting the flow of traffic with cul-de-sacs or one-way streets. In reference to access control in apartment complexes, Newman (1976) has recommended that only a few residents share the same entry or space outside the entry to a building; this strategy is called clustering. Clustering divides a large housing complex into several semi-public areas to increase offenders' perceived risk of detection and apprehension (Rouse & Rubenstein, 1978). In short, areas that allow offenders unrestricted paths for ingress and egress (that is, those with a lot of unassigned public space) are believed to be more vulnerable to crime (for example, Dingemans & Schinzel, 1977; Jacobs, 1961; Newman, 1976).

Related to access control is the elimination of ill-defined areas where residents and nonresidents can engage in unstructured and unmonitored activities (Rouse & Rubenstein, 1978). In other words, areas should be clearly designed according to specific use purposes. Jacobs (1961), Newman (1976), and Brill and Associates (1975) all hypothesized that "unassigned" public space fosters crime. Similarly, Newman (1976) argued that placing conflicting groups (teenager versus senior) and land use purposes (recreational versus commercial) in adjacent areas prevents people from developing territorial attitudes toward their surroundings and from engaging in protective measures (Rouse & Rubenstein, 1978).

From a defensible space perspective, the argument is that street use should be restricted mainly to neighborhood residents. Streets designed to accommodate large numbers of nonresidents increase the number of both offenders and potential victims in a community. Furthermore, these unrestricted streets are difficult to surveil because residents cannot distinguish their neighbors from strangers. Hence, Gardiner (1978) maintained that the presence of major arterial streets in a residential neighborhood encourages criminal activity.

Access control has a definite downside. For example, fences or shrubbery can interfere with surveillance strategies; that is, various types of landscaping for controlling access can become unintended hiding places for offenders. In addition, severe access control can create a "fortress mentality" that fuels fear of crime, isolates people from their neighbors, and undermines community building strategies (Clarke & Mayhew, 1980; Rouse & Rubenstein, 1978).

Research Findings

Street Layout, Accessibility, Automobile Traffic, and Area Use. Studies have shown that the location of a busy street in a residential area is related to increases in residential burglaries (Dietrick, 1977; Fowler, McCalla, & Mangione, 1979; Newman & Wayne, 1974) and fear of crime (Fowler, McCalla, & Mangione, 1979). Greenberg, Rohe, and Williams (1985) reported that low-crime neighborhoods, when compared with adjacent and socially similar high-crime neighborhoods, had fewer major arteries and more boundary streets that restricted access to outsiders. In short, low-crime neighborhoods were less permeable because they had more one-way, narrower, and low-volume streets (White, 1990).

Newman and Wayne (1974) compared adjacent private and public streets in St. Louis. Private streets were those separated from connecting streets by cul-de-sacs, gates, blocked entrances, or other types of restrictions. They found that private streets experienced fewer crimes than public streets and that the residents of private streets were less fearful of crime than those living on public streets. Bevis and Nutter (1977) reported that the accessibility of a street was related to its burglary rate: Streets with cul-de-sacs and streets that formed "T" or "L" intersections (that is, less accessible streets) had lower rates of residential burglary than streets with cross intersections (that is, more accessible streets). The relationship between street accessibility and crime remained after the investigators controlled for the age, race, and income of block residents. Similarly, White (1990) found that the number of streets in a neighborhood that were accessible from major, outside traffic arteries was a more powerful indicator of the area's burglary rate than its stability, housing density, or economic status.

Additional support for the relationship between accessibility and crime is provided in the following research findings:

- Commercial establishments located in areas with heavy automobile traffic were more likely to be victimized (Duffala, 1976).

- The higher the percentage of lots in an area that is zoned for commercial use, the higher the risk of robbery (Harrell & Gouvis, 1994).

- Heavy automobile traffic on surrounding streets was associated with higher victimization rates in single-family homes, apartments, and duplexes (Dietrick, 1977).

- Incidences of burglary and robbery in luxury high rises were positively correlated with levels of street traffic (Reppetto, 1974).

- Public housing apartments near streets or recreational areas where escape routes were available had higher crime rates (Brill and Associates, 1975).

- Stores located on corners had higher burglary rates than did those located in the interior of blocks (Luedtke & Associates, 1970).

- A road-closure scheme, severely restricting opportunities for cruising, reduced prostitution, auto theft, and burglary in north London's red light district (Matthews, 1990).

Pedestrian Traffic.   In an analysis of crimes in Detroit, Luedtke and Associates (1970) reported that two-thirds of the major crime sites in that city had either light or sporadic pedestrian traffic in their vicinities. Pablant and Baxter (1975) found that schools surrounded by higher levels of pedestrian activity had lower vandalism rates. Baumer and Hunter (1978) found that residents in Hartford, Connecticut, who perceived a greater density of people on the streets were more fearful of crime than residents who perceived fewer pedestrians.

Baum, Davis, and Aiello (1978) found that a high level of foot traffic emanating from nonresidential land use caused residents to use their front lawns less often and to withdraw from their neighbors, a phenomenon called social cocooning. Residents on blocks with higher levels of commercial or institutional land use were also more fearful of crime, had a harder time recognizing their neighbors, were more likely to call the police, experienced higher victimization rates, and were less likely to intervene when seeing suspicious activities (see also, Kurtz, Koons, & Taylor, 1995; Roncek & Faggiani, 1985).

In a review of studies on pedestrian traffic and crime, Rubenstein and colleagues (1980) concluded that both high and low levels of pedestrian traffic are associated with more crimes: High levels have more potential victims whereas low levels have a paucity of potential witnesses. In their words, "the best summary statement of the relationship between pedestrian traffic activity and crime is that it depends on who the pedestrians are as well as how many of them there are" (p. 35).

Taylor and Harrell (1996) emphasize the importance of social and organizational factors in determining the success of changes in land use to prevent crime. They suggest that community involvement of residents, neighborhood organizations, and businesspersons is necessary to avoid any adverse repercussions on the interests of these major groups. Taylor and Harrell (1996) further suggest that the ultimate crime reduction benefits of land use changes depend on community mobilization and support.

SURVEILLANCE ENHANCEMENT

Description of Efforts

Surveillance approaches to crime prevention consist of two general types. The first involves placing more illumination (for example, street lights) or people (for example, security guards) in strategic locations to observe criminal activity. These are usually referred to as formal surveillance measures (Clarke & Mayhew, 1980). The second involves changing the physical environment to facilitate observations of suspicious behavior or actual crimes (for example, building an apartment complex so that windows face a common pathway or courtyard). These activities are called natural surveillance measures and are exemplified best by Newman's (1972) architectural solutions that design housing to give residents an unobstructed view of vulnerable targets (Clarke & Mayhew, 1980). Natural surveillance opportunities increase with the growth of pedestrian traffic and outdoor activity and are consistent with Rubenstein and colleagues' (1980) social surveillance rationale.

According to Jacobs (1961), diversity in land use and street design is the key to crime prevention through enhanced surveillance. Neighborhoods and blocks that combine residential, commercial, institutional, and leisure functions promote the continual use of streets and provide what she calls "a basic supply of activities and eyes" (p. 40). In contrast, single land use areas are likely to be deserted for long periods of time, increasing criminal activity because there are fewer opportunities for observation (Greenberg, Rohe, & Williams, 1985). Angel (1968) modified Jacob's (1961) theory by suggesting that crime is expected to be high in a "critical intensity zone" in which the number of people on the street are large enough to supply a steady stream of potential victims but not large enough to produce adequate surveillance.

Enhanced surveillance is purported to have several benefits: increases in the number of arrests and crimes halted in progress, decreases in citizens' fear of crime, and improvements in the quality of evidence available for investigations and prosecutions (Rubenstein et al., 1980). Surveillance is supposed to work by deterring potential offenders from committing crimes because they perceive that others will witness and therefore respond to their illicit activities. These two assumptions—that offenders' perceived risk of detection deters them from committing crimes and that citizens will act after they witness offenses—are indispensable for the surveillance approach, but they remain largely untested.

Research Findings

Land Use.   Jacob's (1961) hypothesis about the preventive effects of mixed land use has received little empirical support. For example, Dietrick (1977) reported that homes located near commercial areas were *more* likely to be burglarized. Furthermore, certain commercial establishments (for example, liquor stores, pawn shops, adult book stores, bars) and service agencies (for example, halfway houses, drug treatment clinics) can facilitate crime by attracting offenders to residential neighborhoods (Greenberg, Rohe, & Williams, 1982). In addition, Brantingham and Brantingham (1978) indicated that blocks with less housing variation, on the basis of housing type and value, had higher burglary rates than did blocks with more heterogeneous housing. Finally, Greenberg, Rohe, and Williams (1982) found that neighborhoods with low crime rates were more likely to be homogeneous in their land use when compared with adjacent high crime neighborhoods similar in their social composition. The researchers concluded that land use diversity, by itself, is not sufficient to reduce crime and that both the nature and extent of such diversity must be considered in any analysis of crime.

Street Lighting.   In 1967, the President's Commission on Law Enforcement and Administration of Justice stated that "there are strong intuitive reasons to believe that improved street lighting may reduce some types of crime in some areas" (p. 51). During the decade following this observation, street lighting projects proliferated, and street lighting has become one of the most thoroughly studied anticrime measures in America (Lab, 1992). The basic logic of street lighting is that greater illumination will improve surveillance, will increase the number of crimes observed, will lead to more crimes being reported, and will ultimately reduce the crime rate (Rubenstein et al., 1980).

The theoretical basis underlying the use of street lighting to combat crime is linked to situational crime prevention approaches that seek to reduce opportunities for crime and to increase offender risk through environmental modifications. For example, enhanced street lighting eliminates areas where offenders can conceal themselves and alerts pedestrians to potential offenders so that pedestrians can evade offenders before a crime can occur. Increased illumination as a crime reduction strategy is also grounded in perspectives that focus on strengthening community cohesion and informal social control through more effective use of streets and greater investment in neighborhood improvement. For example, good street lighting can encourage greater use of pedestrian streets at night, thereby increasing the number of potential guardians and witnesses in an area and discouraging the number of would-be criminals (Painter & Farrington, 1997).

Several cities, including Atlanta, Boston, Fort Worth (Texas), and New Orleans employed street lighting to reduce crime, but each found that, overall, increased illumination had no impact on crime (Lewis & Sullivan, 1979; Reppetto, 1974). There are exceptions, however. For example, Wright (1974) found that increased street lighting in Kansas City was associated with significant reductions in violent crime and with modest reductions in property crime in both residential and commercial areas of the city. In an extensive study of burglars, Bennett and Wright (1984) reported that offenders tended to select targets with minimal illumination.

Tien, Reppetto, and Hanes (1977) conducted an extensive review of street light projects and their effects on crime. These researchers concluded that street lighting does not decrease crime. Nonetheless, it does appear to reduce residents' fear of crime and to enhance their feelings of security. Tien and colleagues also noted that improved street lighting, by itself, cannot be effective against crime without the active support of both citizens (in reporting what they observe) and police (in responding to citizens' reports and in conducting patrols). Tien and colleagues called for more carefully controlled studies to assess the effect of varying light intensities on peoples' perceptions of safety (micro-level analysis) and on area-wide crime statistics (macro-level analysis).

Painter and Farrington (1997) contended that the Tien, Reppetto, and Hanes (1977) review was "too negative and dismissive of the available evidence" (p. 210) and that its pessimistic conclusions about street lighting's crime reduction capacity essentially foreclosed studies on the topic in the United States. In Great Britain, however, there was a renascence of interest in street lighting research in the late 1980s. These studies were summarized by Painter and Farrington (1997). As they reported, the evidence is mixed regarding street lighting's effects on crime, fear of crime, disorder, and pedestrian land use. But Painter and Farrington (1997) argued that these studies are difficult to interpret because the research, in general, was poorly designed (for example, the investigations lacked control areas). In a controlled study, conducted in two adjacent public housing estates in the English town of Dudley, Painter and Farrington (1997) found that improved street lighting in the experimental area increased the number of female pedestrians on the street after dark, increased residents' satisfaction with their estates, and decreased their fear of crime. Improved lighting did not reduce the number of crimes committed after dark or the number of crimes reported to the police.

COMMUNITY-BUILDING MEASURES

Description of Efforts

Community-building or activity support measures are part of the most complex causal chain linking environmental design to crime and crime prevention behaviors. These strategies are designed "to bring people together in open or public places, or to guide the movements of persons and the placement of activities, or to restrict the people in a given area to 'legitimate' users or residents of the area" (Rubenstein et al., 1980, p. 12).

The proper housing structures or arrangements will purportedly improve the ability of neighbors to recognize one another, build a greater sense of community and territoriality, and encourage the number of legitimate users of the environment. Having an investment in their surroundings gives residents the motivation to protect property and to respond to crime and suspicious behavior by calling the police or directly intervening before or during the commission of criminal acts. The technique of clustering serves community building by instilling among residents a sense of neighborhood, territoriality, and social cohesion (Rouse & Rubenstein, 1980). In addition, placing benches and picnic tables along well-kept city sidewalks or in housing developments puts more "eyes on the streets" and promotes surveillance opportunities (Lavrakas, 1992).

Research Findings

The rationale for community building contains many of the elements found in other crime-reduction measures such as access control and surveillance enhancement. Hence, few investigations have examined the effects of community activities alone. In their review of studies regarding the relationships among community building activities, crime, and the built environment, Rubenstein and colleagues (1980) divided empirical evidence into two broad categories, which we adopt for our description of these studies: correlational evidence based on natural variation in the environment, and empirical evidence derived from a manipulation of the built environment and the collection of pre- and post-intervention data. This latter set of studies contains research that falls under the rubric of crime prevention through environmental design. Because of the extensiveness and importance of CPTED research, we review these investigations in a separate section.

Correlational Evidence.   Newman (1973) conducted the first exploratory research on the topic of environmental design and community building. As we discussed earlier, Newman hypothesized that large housing developments engendered in residents feelings of anonymity, isolation, and alienation from their neighbors. These feelings interfere with residents' abilities to exercise "potent territorial prerogatives" and to engage in natural surveillance activities, which are important means to deter crime and to alleviate fear of crime. Newman reported results that supported his contentions. Specifically, he found that larger housing projects had higher crime rates and that their residents were more fearful of crime and felt less safe. Although Newman did not expound on the social constructs that mediated these effects, his results related certain physical characteristics with social constructs that were hypothesized to affect crime rates.

Franck's (1978) study of public housing advanced Newman's work by exploring the mediators between environmental variables and fear of crime. She found that the larger the number of apartments forming a discrete group of tenants, the stronger the social cohesion is among residents and the greater the likelihood is that the tenants will work together to solve problems. In addition, the number of apartments per floor was negatively related to community building (that is, residents' attachment and sense of cohesion) but positively related to residents' perceived personal safety. Furthermore, the level of acquaintanceships had a negative impact on personal safety. Thus, Franck's data were only partially supportive of the community-building rationale.

Newman and Franck (1980) collaborated to study factors influencing crime and instability in 63 housing developments in three cities. Their research employed archival analyses and interviews with residents, building managers, and police officers. Some of their findings were quite consistent with the community building model of crime prevention: higher levels of control of space (that is, residents' perceptions that tenants will intervene if suspicious or criminal activity occurs outside their apartments) are related to lower levels of crime (personal and property) and fear of crime; building size is negatively related to control of space; building size affects crime and fear of crime indirectly through control of space; and the more residents use shared outdoor areas, the lower the crime rate and fear of crime are. Other findings were inconsistent with the community-building rationale: the larger the building, the less frequently residents interact and the *lower* the rate of personal crime, and the greater the level of social interaction, the higher the crime rate is.

Rubenstein and colleagues (1980) attribute these contradictory results to methodological artifacts present in the Newman and Franck (1980) study, which they also criticize for its measurement problems and its failure to specify the correct ordering of variables in cause-effect relationships. Despite these shortcomings, the research of Newman and his associates has made an important contribution to the field by highlighting the contribution of social variables in the built environment.

Empirical Evidence from Environmental Manipulations. Rubenstein and colleagues (1980) described three evaluations of programs that implemented environmental changes relevant to the community-building rationale. The first involved a partial test of defensible space theory in three public housing developments in a small midwestern city (Chenoweth, 1978). The study used surveys of residents before and after several modifications were made in the physical environment, including installing fences to provide private, enclosed spaces for residents and rerouting pathways to control pedestrian traffic. These changes had no effects on residents' proprietary attitudes, control of space, territorial behaviors, social cohesion, or their perceptions of crime and fear of crime.

The second evaluation involved another test of defensible space theory. In this study, Kohn, Franck, & Fox (1975) collected data on two housing developments in Washington, D.C. (Clason Point) and Baltimore (Markham Gardens). They explored residents' behaviors and attitudes and measured crime levels following physical design modifications in both locations, such as the creation of semi-private zones and small recreational areas. Few findings supported the hypothesized crime-reduction impact of these changes. For example, at Clason Point, burglary, robbery, and theft declined but vandalism doubled; residents' reported sense of safety there increased, but one-third thought the crime problem had gotten worse. At Markham Gardens, only one respondent thought that the crime situation improved because of the physical changes, and at Clason Point, neither "neighboring" behaviors nor the number of acquaintances per resident increased following the modifications.

The third evaluation involved a crime reduction program in a Cincinnati housing project. Half of the residences were renovated, half were not. The renovations, designed to increase neighborliness, social cohesion, and territoriality, included adding sitting areas where surveillance was fostered, creating individual yards, installing lights, and building a playground. Hand (1971) reported that the renovated areas, when compared with the nonrenovated areas, experienced less fear of crime and fewer criminal victimizations.

CPTED PROJECTS

As we discussed earlier, CPTED research and demonstration projects were implemented during the 1970s with the aid of federal grants. The multiyear evaluations we describe next represent the most extensive investigations ever conducted of the CPTED model. One was in a residential area, the other in a commercial area.

CPTED in a Residential Community

In 1973, an interdisciplinary team of specialists, sponsored by the National Institute of Justice (NIJ), assessed the street crime problem in the once thriving and fashionable area known as North Asylum Hill, located near the business center of Hartford, Connecticut. The housing stock had been declining and long-time residents were moving out because of the growing unsavoriness of the community. The specialists proposed a three-pronged approach to reduce crime and fear of crime: changing the physical environment, stimulating community organizing efforts, and improving police-community relations. Physical design modifications involved restricting vehicular traffic and defining the boundaries of the neighborhood by building cul-de-sacs, narrowing entrances to streets, and making streets one-way.

The initiative started in the fall of 1974 with the work of community groups staffed by residents and police; these groups launched a block watch program and a recreational project for youths, and they brought about improvements in a large neighborhood park. In early 1975, the police began instituting a team policing strategy resulting in officers permanently assigned to the area and prioritizing the needs and concerns of Asylum Hill residents.

The Hartford Experiment, as it came to be known, was evaluated in five waves of data collection. The first three waves provided preprogram data (1973, 1975, 1976) and the last two waves provided impact data (1977, 1979). The study, funded by NIJ, used surveys of Asylum Hill residents and police, official crime data, pedestrian and traffic counts, and interviews with community leaders. Investigators also collected data in the rest of the city, which served as the study's control area.

Fowler and Mangione (1986) reported several significant changes in the evaluation's key variables. Specifically, territorial behavior became more frequent (that is, residents were more likely to intervene in suspicious activities), and residents were more likely to look out for one another's homes and to perceive their neighbors as resources. Moreover, residents' fears of burglary and robbery were lower than expected, and they were more likely than expected to view crime as declining.

Fowler and Mangione (1974, 1982) made the following observations and recommendations about CPTED programs: First, changes in the physical environment can act as catalysts in improving the character of neighborhoods. Second, helping residents gain control of their community is an effective mechanism for reducing their fear of crime. Third, CPTED programs must be implemented on a realistic timeline—at least five years is needed for the institutionalization of a CPTED project. Fourth, visible changes in physical design are more expensive to institute than are changes in the social environment, but they are much easier to achieve; social cohesiveness and activity support are more elusive concepts than surveillance and access control. Fifth, CPTED strategies are more likely to be effective if they involve a small number of agencies, special interests, and community groups. Finally, CPTED can be successful with existing community resources and support.

CPTED in a Commercial Setting

CPTED in a commercial setting was implemented in the Union Avenue Corridor (UAC) of Portland, Oregon—a site that was chosen because of its particular vulnerability to crime. The UAC strip occupied an area approximately four miles long and four blocks wide. Its surrounding residents were mostly middle-to-low income African-Americans and its surrounding crime rate was three times higher than the crime rate in the rest of the city (Kushmuk & Whittemore, 1981). By the early 1960s, UAC had become a blighted area with many vacant lots, boarded-over buildings, and adult businesses. Crime and fear of crime kept business investors away from UAC, which also suffered because of the civil unrest that erupted in Portland in the late 1960s.

The Westinghouse consortium and Portland officials developed a plan for rejuvenating UAC. The program they recommended was based on the theories and principles of CPTED and was implemented from 1974 to 1979. It contained seven elements: (a) security surveys were conducted by a police-appointed security advisor; (b) two "Safe Streets for People" were constructed by redesigning streets and intersections, intensifying street lighting, and improving the conditions of roads along Union Avenue: (c) a Residential Activity Center and miniplaza was created along Union Avenue; (d) a "Cash Off the Streets" program was developed to encourage citizens (especially older residents) not to carry substantial amounts of cash in UAC; (e) law enforcement support was enhanced by improving police patrols and proposing a UAC storefront police precinct; (f) UAC businesses were promoted through planned community events and general economic development; and (g) UAC was made more accessible by improving transportation into and out of the corridor.

Two evaluations of the UAC CPTED effort were performed. Lavrakas, Normoyle, & Wagener (1978) conducted the first. They employed post-hoc evaluative techniques to determine whether the UAC project was a valid implementation of CPTED theory and whether the UAC project was responsible for attaining any of CPTED's proximate goals (for example, improving the physical security of the built environment, increasing territoriality, developing positive social networks) and its ultimate goals, namely, reducing crime, alleviating fear of crime, and improving the quality of life in the community. To answer these questions, they interviewed UAC residents, business proprietors, and other key persons with knowledge about UAC; they observed UAC pedestrian activity; and they analyzed crime and economic data.

Business proprietors in Portland significantly improved their levels of physical security and instituted a number of crime prevention measures whereas residents did not. Consequently, commercial burglaries dropped 48 percent and robberies 17 percent whereas residential burglaries dropped only 14 percent. Efforts to increase pedestrians' use of the UAC environment appeared to fail, and there was little evidence that the residential community became more cohesive. However, the cohesiveness of the business community did increase and a local business association was revitalized. In the words of the evaluators (Lavrakas, Normoyle, & Wagener, 1978)

> It is beyond the scope and resources of this evaluation to carefully document whether more should have been accomplished, [but] there are many reasons to state that a good start has been made to implement the CPTED concept in UAC. (p. 55)

Kushmuk and Whittemore (1981) performed the second evaluation of the UAC project in 1980. They replicated the evaluation design and methods of Lavrakas, Normoyle, & Wagener (1978), and they attempted to document the "institutionalization" of CPTED, a long-term outcome of the Westinghouse CPTED initiative (Kaplan et al., 1978). Results of the reevaluation again showed that businesses, but not nearby residents, engaged in a variety of anticrime behaviors, which they maintained since 1977. There was also a significant reduction in commercial burglaries. The most successful CPTED strategies were security services, organization and support of the business community, and street lighting.

Kushmuk and Whittemore (1981) offered three major lessons for other communities intending to implement CPTED programs. First, successful implementation requires several years, strong political support, and consistent leadership. Second, complicated and coordinated anticrime efforts are difficult to put into place; those that involved only a few groups and piggybacked onto existing efforts were easier to initiate and sustain. Third, changes in the physical environment were much easier to achieve than were those in the social environment.

SUMMARY AND CONCLUSIONS

In this chapter we described several anticrime efforts that focus on changing the physical environment to reduce offenders' opportunities for crime, to increase the likelihood that offenders will be apprehended, and to encourage citizens to engage in activities that promote territoriality, surveillance, and social cohesion.

Oscar Newman, an architect, was one of the most influential proponents of defensible space theory, linking crime—mostly in public housing developments—to environmental factors and suggesting strategies for altering building structures and layouts to make residents safer. CPTED advanced defensible space theory by incorporating social variables into formulas for combating crime. Both defensible space and CPTED theories provided a broad foundation for environmentally based crime prevention programs and spawned a substantial body of research. They have been criticized, however, for failing to specify their constructs more clearly and to explain fully the interactions between the social and physical environment that influence communality, fear of crime, and crime rates.

Numerous studies have tested the effectiveness of particular components of defensible space and CPTED strategies. We categorized these strategies into four crime prevention activities: target hardening (that is, employing physical barriers, such as locks, bars, and alarms), access control (that is, restricting the use of nonpublic space to "legitimate citizens" by erecting real or symbolic boundaries), surveillance enhancement (that is, placing more illumination or people in strategic locations to observe criminal activity), and community building measures (that is, bringing people together to increase social cohesion and to put more "eyes on the streets"). CPTED projects have been evaluated in extensive multiyears studies in a residential area of Hartford, Connecticut, and in a commercial area of Portland, Oregon. These evaluations have yielded promising results and important lessons for developing and implementing such programs.

Taylor and Harrell (1996) enumerated several unanswered research questions that have theoretical and practical importance to the field. For example, what is the temporal or causal relationships between physical decay and residents' perceptions of crime and actual crime rates? How do social, economic, and cultural factors influence the success of crime reduction strategies employing physical environmental modifications? Are different physical environmental strategies for reducing crime more or less effective as a function of crime type? These questions provide directions for future investigators.

REFERENCES

Angel, S. (1968). *Discouraging crime through city planning*. Berkeley: University of California Press.

Baum, A., Davis, A. G., & Aiello, J. R. (1978). Crowding and neighborhood mediation of urban density. *Journal of Population* 1, 266–279.

Baumer, T. L., & Hunter, A. (1978). *Street traffic, social integration, and fear of crime*. Evanston, IL: Northwestern University.

Bennett, T., & Wright, R. (1984). *Burglars on burglary: Prevention and the offender*. Aldershot, England: Gower.

Bevis, C., & Nutter, J. G. (1977). *Changing street layouts to reduce residential burglary*. St. Paul, MN: Governor's Commission of Crime Prevention and Control.

Bottoms, A. E. (1974). Review of O. Newman's *Defensible space*. *British Journal of Criminology* 14, 204–206.

Brantingham, P. L., & Brantingham, P. J. (1981). Notes on the geometry of crime. In P. J. Brantingham & P. L. Brantingham (eds.), *Environmental criminology* (pp. 27–54). Beverly Hills, CA: Sage.

Brill and Associates. (1975). *Victimization, fear of crime, and altered behavior: A profile of four housing projects in Boston*. Washington, DC.

Brill and Associates. (1977). *Comprehensive security planning: A program for Capper Dwellings, Washington, DC*. Washington, DC: Department of Housing and Urban Development, Office of Policy Development and Research.

Burrows, J. (1980). Closed circuit television and crime on the London underground. In R. V. G. Clarke & P. Mayhew (eds.), *Designing out crime* (pp. 75-83). London: Her Majesty's Stationary Office.

Cedar Rapids Police Department. (1975). *Installation, testing, and evaluation of a large-scale burglar alarm system for a municipal police department—A second phase completion report*. Cedar Rapids, IA.

Challinger, D. (1991). Less telephone vandalism: How did it happen? *Security Journal* 2, 111–119.

Chenoweth, R. E. (1978). *The effects of territorial markings on residents of two multifamily housing developments: A partial test of Newman's theory of defensible space*. Dissertation Abstracts International 38, 5088.

Clarke, R. V. (1983). Situational crime prevention: Its theoretical basis and practical scope. In M. Tonry & N. Morris (eds.), *An annual review of research* (pp. 225–256). Chicago: University of Chicago Press.

Clarke, R. V. (1992). *Situational crime prevention: Successful case studies*. New York: Harrow & Heston.

Clarke, R. V., & Mayhew, P. (eds.). (1980). *Designing out crime*. London: Her Majesty's Stationary Office.

Coleman, A. (1985). *Utopia on trial: Vision and reality in planned housing*. London: Hilary Shipman.

Cornish, D. & Clarke, R. V. (1986). *The reasoning criminal: Rationale choice perspectives on offending*. New York: Springer-Verlag.

Crowe, T. D. (1991). *Crime prevention through environmental design*. Boston: Butterworth-Heinemann.

Crowe, T. D. & Zahm, D. L. (1994). Crime prevention through environmental design. *Land Development* 14, 22–27.

Decker, J. F. (1972). Curbside deterrence: An analysis of the effect of a slug rejectory device, coin view window and warning labels on slug usage in New York City parking meters. *Criminology* 12, 127–142.

Dietrick, B. (1977). *The neighborhood and burglary victimization in metropolitan suburbs*. Paper presented at the annual meeting of the Society for the Study of Social Problems, Chicago.

Dingemans, D. J., & Schinzel, R. H. (1977). Defensible space design of housing for crime prevention. *Police Chief* 44, 34–36.

Duffala, D. C. (1976). Convenience stores, armed robberies, and physical environmental features. *American Behavioral Scientist* 20, 227–246.

Ekblom, P. (1987). *Preventing robberies at sub-post offices: An evaluation of a security initiative.* London: Home Office, Crime Prevention Unit.

Feins, J. D. & Epstein, J. C. (1996). *Solving crime problems in residential neighborhoods: Comprehensive changes in design, management, and use.* Cambridge MA: Abt Associates.

Fisher, B., & Nasar, J. L. (1992). Fear of crime in relation to three exterior site features: Prospect, refuge, and escape. *Environment and Behavior* 24, 35–65.

Fowler, F., & Mangione, T. W. (1974). *Implications of map and fear data for crime control design.* Boston: Center for Survey Research, University of Massachusetts, Boston, and the Joint Center for Urban Studies of MIT and Harvard University.

Fowler, F. J., & Mangione, T. W. (1982). *Neighborhood crime, fear, and social control: A second look at the Hartford program.* Washington, DC: Department of Justice.

Fowler, F. J., & Mangione, T. W. (1986). A three-pronged effort to reduce crime and fear of crime: The Hartford Experiment. In D. P. Rosenbaum (ed.), *Community crime prevention: Does it work?* (pp. 87–108). Beverly Hills, CA: Sage.

Fowler, F. J., McCalla, M. E., & Mangione, T. W. (1979). *Reducing residential crime and fear: The Hartford neighborhood crime prevention program.* Washington, DC: Department of Justice.

Franck, K. A. (1978). *Community by design: A study of moderate-income, federally assisted housing developments.* Unpublished doctoral dissertation, City University of New York.

Gardiner, R. A. (1978). *Design for safe neighborhoods: The environmental security planning and design process.* Washington, DC: Department of Justice.

Greenberg, S. W., Rohe, W. M., & Williams, J. R. (1982). *Safe and secure neighborhoods: Physical characteristics and informal territorial control in high and low crime neighborhoods.* Washington, DC: U.S. Department of Justice, National Institute of Justice.

Greenberg, S., Rohe, W., & Williams, J. (1985). Neighborhood conditions and community control. In *Community crime prevention* (pp. 47–63). Washington, DC: Center for Responsive Governance.

Gwaltney, M. K. (1978). *Designing safe environments: What is a feature?* Santa Monica, CA: Rand.

Gwaltney, M. K., & Yin, R. K. (1978). *Designing safe environments: Bibliography.* Santa Monica, CA: Rand.

Hand, J. (1971). Your home: Lock it or don't leave it. *Living Now* 10, 108–113.

Harrell, A. & Gouvis, C. (1994). *Community decay and crime.* Washington, DC: Urban Institute.

Heller, N. B., Stenzel, W. E., & Gill, A. (1975). *National Evaluation Program—Phase 1 summary report: Operation Identification Projects.* Washington, DC: Law Enforcement Assistance Administration.

Jacobs, J. (1961). *The death and life of great American cities.* New York: Random House.

Jeffrey, C. R. (1971). *Crime prevention through environmental design.* Beverly Hills, CA: Sage.

Kaplan, H., O'Kane, K., Lavrakas, P. J., & Hoover, S. (1978). *CPTED final report on commercial demonstration in Portland, Oregon* (mimeo). Arlington, VA: Westinghouse Electric Corp.

Kohn, I., Franck, K. A., & Fox, S. A. (1975). *Defensible space modification in row house communities.* New York: Institute for Community Design Analysis.

Kurtz, E., Koons, B., & Taylor, R. B. (1995). *Nonresidential land use, informal, resident-based control, physical deterioration, calls for police service.* Paper presented at the annual meeting of the Academy for Criminal Justice Sciences, Boston.

Kushmuk, J., Whittemore, S. (1981). *A re-evaluation of crime prevention through environmental design in Portland Oregon.* Arlington, VA: Westinghouse Electric Corp.

Lab, S. P. (1992). *Crime prevention: Approaches, practices, and evaluations.* Cincinnati: Anderson.

Lavrakas, P. J. (1992). Community-based crime prevention: Citizens, community organizations, and the police. In L. B. Joseph (ed.), *Crime, communities, and public policy* (pp. 85–122). Chicago: University of Chicago Press.

Lavrakas, P. J., & Kushmuk, J. W. (1986). Evaluating crime prevention through environmental design: The Portland Commercial Demonstration Project. In D. P. Rosenbaum (ed.), *Community crime prevention: Does it work?* (pp. 202–227). Beverly Hills: Sage.

Lavrakas, P. J., Normoyle, J., & Wagener, J. (1978). *CPTED commercial demonstration evaluation report.* Evanston, IL: Westinghouse Electric Corp.

Laycock, G. (1985). *Property marking: A deterrent to domestic burglary?* London: Home Office, Crime Prevention Unit.

Laycock, G. K. (1986). Property marking as a deterrent to domestic burglary. In K. Heal & G. Laycock (eds.). *Situation crime prevention: From theory with practice* (pp. 49–62). London: Her Majesty's Stationary Office.

Laycock, G. K. (1991). Operation identification or the power of publicity? *Security Journal* 2, 67–72.

Lewis, E. G., Sullivan, T. T. (1979). Combating crime and citizen attitudes: A study of corresponding reality. *Journal of Criminal Justice* 7, 71–79.

Luedtke, G., & Associates. (1970). *Crime and the physical city: Neighborhood design techniques for crime reduction.* Spring-field, VA: National Technical Information Council.

Lurigio, A. J., Rosenbaum, D. F. (1986). Evaluating research in community crime prevention: A critical look at the field. In D. P. Rosenbaum (ed.), *Community crime prevention: Does it work?* (pp. 19–45). Beverly Hills, CA: Sage.

Matthews, R. (1990). Developing more effective strategies for curbing prostitution. *Security Journal* 1, 182–187.

Mattick, H. W. et al. (1974). *An evaluation of Operation Identification as implemented in Illinois.* Chicago: University of Illinois Press.

Mawby, R. I. (1977). Kiosk vandalism: A Sheffield study. *British Journal of Criminology* 17, 30–46.

Mayhew, P. (1979). Defensible space: The current status of crime prevention theory. *Howard Journal of Criminal Justice* 18, 150–159.

Mayhew, P. (1982). Situational crime prevention: Two proposals for research in the context of public housing. In M. Hough & P. Mayhew (eds.), *Crime and public housing: Proceedings of a workshop held in September 1980.* London: Home Office, Research and Planning Unit, Paper 6.

Mayhew, P., Clarke, R. V. G., Sturman, A., & Hough, J. M. (1976). *Crime as opportunity.* Home Office Research Study No. 34. London: Her Majesty's Stationary Office.

Mayhew, P., Clarke, R. V. G., Burrows, J., Hough, J. M., & Winchester, S. W. C. (1979). *Crime in public view.* Home Office Research Study No. 49. London: Her Majesty's Stationary Office.

Merry, S. E. (1981). *Urban danger: Life in a neighborhood of strangers.* Springfield, IL: Mombiosse.

Musheno, M., Levine, J. P., & Palumbo, D. J. (1978). Television surveillance and crime prevention: Evaluating an attempt to create defensible space in public housing. *Social Science Quarterly* 58, 647–656.

Newman, O. (1972). *Defensible space.* New York: Macmillan.

Newman, O. (1973). *Architectural design for crime prevention.* Washington, DC: National Institute of Law Enforcement and Criminal Justice.

Newman, O. (1976). *Designing guidelines for creating defensible space.* Washington, DC: Department of Justice.

Newman, O., & Franck, K. A. (1980). *Factors influencing crime and instability in urban housing developments.* Washington, DC: National Institute of Justice.

Newman, O., & Wayne, F. (1974). *The private street system in St. Louis.* New York: Institute for Community Design Analysis.

Nichols, W. W. (1980). Mental maps, spatial characteristics and criminal mobility. In D. E. Georges-Abeyie & K. D. Harries (eds.), *Crime: A spatial perspective* (pp. 17–29). New York: Columbia University Press.

Pablant, P., & Baxter, J. C. (1975). Environmental correlates of school vandalism. *Journal of the American Institute of Planners* 3, 270–277.

Painter, K. & Farrington, D. P. (1997). The crime reducing effect of improved street lighting: The Dudley Project. In R. V. Clarke (ed.), *Situational crime prevention: Successful case studies* (2nd ed., pp. 209–226). Albany, NY: Harrow and Heston.

Pease, K. (1991). The Kirkholt project: Preventing burglary on a British public housing estate. *Security Journal* 2, 73–77.

Pope, C. E. (1977). *Crime specific analyses: The characteristics of burglary incidents.* Washington, DC: Department of Justice.

Poyner, B. (1981). Crime prevention and the environment: Street attacks in city centres. *Police Research Bulletin* 37, 10–18.

Poyner, B. (1993). *Design against crime: Beyond defensible space.* Toronto: Butterworth.

President's Commission on Law Enforcement and Administration of Justice (1978). *Task force report: Crime and its impact—An assessment.* Washington, DC: U.S. Government Printing Office.

Reppetto, T. (1974). *Residential crime.* Cambridge, MA: Ballinger.

Roncek, D. W., & Faggiani, D. (1985). High schools and crime: A replication. *Sociological Quarterly* 26, 491–505.

Rosenbaum, D. P. (1988). Community crime prevention: A review and synthesis of the literature. *Justice Quarterly* 5, 323–395.

Rouse, V. W., & Rubenstein, H. (1978). *Crime in public housing: A review of major issues and selected crime reduction strategies.* Washington, DC: Department of Housing and Urban Development.

Rubenstein, H., Murray, C., Motoyama, T., & Rouse, W. V. (1980). *The link between crime and the built environment: The current state of knowledge.* Washington, DC: National Institute of Justice.

Scarr, H. A. (1972). *Patterns of burglary.* Washington, DC: Government Printing Office.

Scheflen, A. E. (1971). Living space in an urban ghetto. *Family Process* 10, 429–450.

Schneider, A. L. (1986). Neighborhood-based antiburglary strategies: An analysis of public and private benefits from the Portland Program. In D. P. Rosenbaum (ed.) *Community crime prevention: Does it work?* Beverly Hills, CA: Sage.

Seattle Law and Planning Office. (1975). *Burglary reduction program.* Final report prepared for the Law Enforcement Assistance Administration. Seattle.

Stanley, R. (1976). *Crime prevention through environmental design.* Ottawa: Ministry of the Solicitor General.

Surette, R. (1985). Video street patrol: Media technology and street crime. *Journal of Police Science and Administration* 13, 78–85.

Suttles, G. O. (1968). *The social order of the slum.* Chicago: University of Chicago Press.

Taylor, R. B., Gottfredson, S. D., & Brower, S. (1980). The defensibility of defensible space. In T. Hirsche & M. Gottfredson (eds.), *Understanding crime* (pp. 17–36). Beverly Hills, CA: Sage.

Taylor, R. B., & Harrell, A. V. (1996). *Physical environment and crime.* Washington, DC: National Institute of Justice.

Taylor, R. B., Shumaker, S. A., & Gottfredson, S. D. (1985). Neighborhood links between physical features and local sentiments: Deterioration, fear of crime, and confidence. *Journal of Architectural and Planning Research* 2, 261–275.

Tien, J., Reppetto, T., & Hanes, J. (1977). *Elements of CPTED.* Arlington, VA: Westinghouse.

Titus, R. M. (1984). Residential burglary and the community response. In R. V. G. Clarke & T. Hope (eds.), *Coping with burglary* (pp. 89–113). Boston: Kluwer-Nijhoff.

Walsh, D. (1980). *Break-in: Burglary from private homes.* London: Constable.

Westinghouse Electric Corporation. (1976). *Crime prevention through environmental design: Residential demonstration plan.* Minneapolis.

Whitcomb, D. (1978). *Focus on robbery: The hidden cameras project—Seattle, Washington.* Cambridge, MA: Abt Associates.

White, G. F. (1990). Neighborhood permeability and burglary rates. *Justice Quarterly* 7, 57–68.

Wilson, S. (1978). Vandalism and defensible space on London housing estates. In R. V. Clarke (ed.), *Tackling vandalism* (pp. 14–26). London: Her Majesty's Stationary Office.

Wilson, S. (1990). Reduction of telephone vandalism: An Australian case study. *Security Journal* 1, 149–154.

Wood, E. (1981). *Housing design: A social theory.* New York: Citizens' Housing and Planning Council.

Wright, R. (1974). *Study to determine the impact of street lightning on street crime: Phase I, Final report.* Ann Arbor: University of Michigan.

8

𝕫

Situational Crime Prevention

Situational crime prevention was first introduced by Clarke (1983, p. 225) as "comprising measures directed at highly specific forms of crime that involve the management, design, or manipulation of the immediate environment in as systematic and permanent way as possible so as to reduce the opportunities for crime and increase its risks as perceived by a wide range of offenders." This is a very inclusive definition. Certainly, by this definition, situational crime prevention was being practiced long before it was labeled as such. All the efforts funded by the Justice Department to mark property to thwart burglars, to design buildings that encourage surveillance of public areas, or to organize neighbors into block-watch committees would fall under what Clarke terms "situational crime prevention." In one sense, situational crime prevention seems to be a new way of referring to what police or the public would call simply "crime prevention."

But the concept of situational crime prevention has led to new insights and new successes in fighting crime. Situational crime prevention is significant in two respects. First, it shifts the emphasis away from the criminal to the environment. Situational crime prevention differs from what Fattah (1993) refers to as the positivist approach to criminology. Positivist criminology contends that criminals—by virtue of genetics or developmental environment—possess psychological traits that differ from the rest of the population (Wilson & Hernstein, 1985). In essence, people are time bombs waiting to go off. Under this model, the way to reduce crime is to alter (through punishment, therapy, or rehabilitation) the potential criminal's motivational set.

The notion of criminal dispositions in criminology lost favor at the same time as the idea that behavior was determined by fixed personality traits lost ground in psychology (Mischel, 1968).[1] In psychology, theories of behavior rooted in the construct of internal motivation or drives lost ground to theories that emphasized situational inducements or incentives (Shaver and Tarpy, 1993). Operant conditioning proponents such as Skinner (1963) and others spoke of behavior as being under "stimulus control." They did not deny the existence of internal stimuli such as hunger, thirst, or sex as a precondition of behavior, but focused instead on the extent to which behavior can be elicited through manipulation of aspects of the environment.

A parallel change occurred in criminology. Criminologists began to speak about criminal behavior from a "rational choice" (Clarke and Cornish, 1985) or "routine activities" (Cohen and Felson, 1979) perspective. These perspectives posit that the likelihood of a crime being committed depends on how potential criminals perceive various elements in the environment (for example, Felson, 1986). Situational crime prevention is analogous to the operant psychologist's notion of stimulus control: Crime is encouraged or discouraged by how stimuli are arrayed in the environment—stimuli that can be altered through management, design, or manipulation of the environment by crime prevention planners.

The other respect in which situational crime prevention represents an innovation is in its crime-specific focus. It targets very specific crimes, based on the assumption that the situational determinants of each type of crime are different. Clarke (1992) cites an example based on research by Poyner and Webb (1991) that showed that residential burglaries in two British communities were committed by two different groups of offenders with quite different modus operandi. Thus, the authors concluded, steps taken to stop burglary of electrical appliances (committed by professional burglars in cars) would be quite different than steps taken to prevent burglary of cash and jewelry (committed by opportunistic thieves on foot). The focus of situational crime prevention on incentives and deterrents for specific behaviors distinguish it from previous approaches to crime prevention that tended to lump together prevention steps for large categories of crimes (for example, residential burglaries).

Situational crime prevention is also based on the idea that situations are more predictable than individuals (Weisburd, 1997). Consistent with this assumption, research indicates that a large percentage of criminal events are clustered at specific addresses or locations—referred to by criminologists as "hot spots" (Sherman, Gartin, & Buerger, 1989; Weisburd & Green, 1994; Weisburd, Maher, & Sherman, 1992). Thus, situational crime prevention measures can be designed to reduce the higher-than-normal opportunities for criminal behavior that are provided by such environments.

---

1. We should note, however, that offender-focused criminology has made a resurgence in the 1990s under the auspices of "developmental criminology" (see Tremblay & Craig, 1995, for a review).

THE ROOTS AND CONTEXT OF
SITUATIONAL CRIME PREVENTION

According to Clarke (1995), situational crime prevention was a term coined within the British government's Home Office Research Unit. The idea originated from Home Office studies of rehabilitation of prisoners within the British correctional system. One lesson learned from those studies was that the likelihood of absconding or reoffending for juveniles residing in halfway houses was more closely linked to the institutional environment than to personality or background factors. The researchers concluded that opportunities for misbehaving could be "designed out" (Tizard, Sinclair, & Clarke, 1975; Clarke and Cornish, 1983).

The concept of situational crime prevention was compatible with other ideas that developed at about the same time in the United States. The notion that crime could be controlled through alteration of the physical environment had attained popularity through the work of Newman (1972) and Jeffrey (1971). These theorists argued that crimes could be prevented by changing the designs of residential and commercial spaces. Newman believed that design of residential buildings ought to limit public access and encourage residents to take responsibility for public areas through surveillance and territorial behavior. Newman's notion of "defensible space" and Jeffrey's notion of "CPTED" (crime prevention through environmental design) were quite consistent with the approach of situational crime prevention. (For details, see Chapter 7.)

Clarke, along with Cornish, was also the creator of the "rational choice" approach to criminology (Clarke and Cornish, 1985; Cornish and Clarke, 1986). This perspective assumes that potential offenders are (imperfect) rational decision makers who seek to benefit themselves economically and otherwise through the commission of crimes. The approach emphasizes the difference in decision processes involved in different offenses. The rational choice model thus allows researchers a framework to guide empirical scrutiny of these decision processes (for studies of offender decision making, see, for example, Feeney, 1986; Cromwell, Olson, & Avary, 1991). Situational crime prevention capitalizes on this knowledge to reduce opportunities for crime.

Situational crime prevention also is bolstered by routine activity and lifestyle perspectives on crime. Routine activity theory focuses on the convergence in space and time of three elements considered essential for crimes to occur: a potential offender, an attractive target, and the absence of capable guardians (Cohen and Felson, 1979). The routine activity perspective, growing out of social ecology (Hawley, 1950), explains crime through the movement of people in time and space. Closely related to the routine activity conceptualization of crime is the lifestyle perspective (Hindelang, Gottfredson, and Garofalo, 1978). Lifestyle theory asserts that the odds of falling victim to crime vary according to an individual's degree of exposure to high-risk situations—those that include potential offenders. Because the key variable in both routine activity and lifestyle perspectives is exposure, both imply an opportunity reduction approach to crime that is consistent with situational crime prevention.

Clarke's (1992) extension of the routine activity model makes the links to situational crime prevention even clearer. He proposes adding an additional element to the necessary ingredients for crime, namely, crime facilitators. Crime facilitators are defined as tools (for example, cars, weapons) that are essential to committing particular forms of crime. Making explicit the tools necessary to commit crimes encourages consideration of how to reduce potential criminals' access to such instruments.

SITUATIONAL CRIME PREVENTION STRATEGIES

Clarke (1992) defines 12 strategies available to situational crime prevention planners. Each strategy addresses one of three motivational concerns assumed to influence the behavior of potential offenders:

1. *Increasing the effort.* One set of strategies seeks to affect the amount of effort required for criminal acts. *Target hardening* techniques obstruct potential criminals by erecting physical barriers. Examples of target hardening are door locks, window bars, steering column locks, safes, and plastic screens to separate service workers (for example, bank tellers, liquor store clerks) from the public.

   Access control measures make it more difficult for potential criminals to gain entry to physical or virtual spaces. Access control has been widely used in urban design to reduce the number of outsiders entering particular spaces (for example, by blocking off streets to prevent outsiders from penetrating an area by car). It can also be used within buildings (for example, a reception desk in private or public housing). Passwords and account codes restrict access to files in electronic media.

   Some situational crime prevention applications try to *deflect offenders.* That is, they attempt to prevent potential criminals from being confronted with the chance to commit a crime. Examples of this technique include "graffiti boards" where people are encouraged to leave public messages and designing soccer stadiums to separate rival fans, thereby reducing the potential for violence.

   A final method identified by Clarke (1992) for increasing the effort involved in offending is to *control facilitators,* or paraphernalia that encourages or is essential to the commission of crimes. Gun control laws seek to limit the availability of certain types of weapons that might be used to commit crimes. Some cities have removed public telephones from locations where they are apt to be used by persons engaged in selling narcotics.

2. *Increasing the risks.* Another set of techniques described by Clarke seek to increase the risks to potential offenders. *Entry/exit screening* is designed to make it more difficult to bring in or remove certain objects to or from designated areas. For example, airport metal detectors are intended to increase the risks of attempting to bring guns or bombs onto airplanes. Theft detection screens are designed to prevent persons from improperly removing goods from stores or books from libraries.

   Formal surveillance is probably the best known situational crime prevention technique. Formal surveillance includes the use of uniformed officers or monitoring devices to deter would-be criminals. Security cameras and other electronic security devices extend the surveillance capabilities of the police. Technology advances will continue to expand the surveillance options available (for example, the "LoJack" device being marketed to prevent auto theft is believed an effective method of increasing the risk of detection. The device is placed inside the engine of the car and, when activated, allows the police to determine the car's exact location).

   Employees who work in areas open to the public can also act to deter potential crimes through *employee surveillance.* Subway station ticket sellers, hotel doormen, and others enhance surveillance in the areas they work and make it more risky to commit crimes.

   Natural surveillance is a collection of ways to increase the ability of humans or machines to surveil an area. Street lights make it possible for residents and passers-by to keep watch over activities on the street. Similarly, removing a hedge shielding the front of a house may increase the exposure of potential burglars to surveillance from passers-by.

3. *Reducing the rewards.* The goal of the last set of techniques discussed by Clarke (1992) is taking the profit out of crime. *Target removal* takes potential gains from crime out of reach of potential criminals. Examples include requiring exact fare on public transportation (so that drivers do not have access to cash) and timed lock boxes in convenience stores, which reduce the amount of cash available through robbing register clerks.

   Potential rewards can also be reduced by *marking property* targeted by burglars, thereby rendering the property useless to anyone other than the owners. Cattle branding, property marking programs, and vehicle identification numbers etched on auto parts are all examples of identifying property.

   Rewards can also be reduced by *removing inducements* for people to commit crimes. For example, immediate clean-up of graffiti takes away the offender's chance to see his or her work publicly displayed.

   The last situational crime prevention technique that Clarke defines is *rule setting.* Rules make it clear to offenders that they will incur high costs if they engage in proscribed behavior. For example, rules set by organizations concerning sexual harassment make it harder for potential offenders to excuse themselves.

APPLICATIONS OF SITUATIONAL CRIME PREVENTION

As we have seen, situational crime prevention covers a wide range of anti-crime activities. This diversity is reflected in the following case studies. These studies provide concrete representation of how practitioners of situational crime prevention approach problems.

Preventing Post Office Robberies

Ekblom (1992) evaluated a program to discourage a rash of post-office robberies in London in the early 1980s. Robberies had increased 400 percent in just one year, leading the government to analyze the methods used by the robbers and develop an appropriate deterrent. The deterrent selected was upgrading counter security screens that were already in use in post offices.

The old screens had not proved much of a deterrent, but the new ones did. Ekblom notes that post-office robberies dropped dramatically after the security screens were upgraded (although never to baseline levels). Because no comparison group had been identified as part of the antirobbery project, Ekblom went to significant lengths to ensure that the drop in post-office robberies he witnessed over time was not simply a drop in robberies in general. He examined trends in robbery of non post-office businesses and of robberies of postal employees or customers outside the secure areas where the screens were installed during the same period for which he examined the substation robberies. Pooling the three estimates, Ekblom concluded that the security screens reduced robberies by 40 percent.

The picture of the screen effects that emerged was complex. Ekblom found some evidence that robberies of staff and customers in nonsecure areas of the postal substations dropped along with robberies in secure areas. However, he also found that robbers escalated the methods in their attacks. Following upgrades of the counter screens, physical attacks against the screens declined. Instead, robbers more frequently threatened clerks with guns—fortunately firearms proved to be a relatively unsuccessful means of attempting robberies, with two failures for each success. Ekblom also suggests that it is likely that displacement occurred from robberies of secure areas inside postal substations to robberies on deliveries of stamps and cash to the substations.

This example is not wholly compatible with the premise of situational crime prevention that crimes are purely opportunistic. Although Ekblom concludes that the robbers of postal substations tend to be amateurs, his data provide some support for the notion of acts committed by persons *driven* to commit crimes and willing to seek alternative methods when their original plans are thwarted.

Preventing Bus Robberies

During the late 1960s, many cities stopped the practice of bus drivers giving change in favor of an exact change system. Evaluations showed dramatic drops in bus robberies coincident with the exact fare policies (Stanford Research Institute, 1970). For example, Chaiken, Lawless, and Stevenson (1992) report that bus robberies dropped from 67 to 7 per month after adoption of an exact fare policy. It would be hard to argue that this magnitude of decline, when replicated in several places, was not attributable to the policy change.

Chaiken, Lawless, and Stevenson's work is significant because the researchers made a serious effort to examine unintended effects of the crime prevention strategy, including an attempt to assess displacement. The authors reasoned (and local police suggested) that individuals thwarted from holding up buses might resort to robbing subway token clerks. After a careful analysis, they found evidence that such displacement occurred, but concluded that the increase in subway robberies was less than the reduction in bus robberies.

Chaiken and colleagues' work, like that of Ekblom discussed earlier, suggests (in part) a profile of criminals as individuals determined to break the law whose energies are channeled in different ways when they are blocked from their goal by situational crime prevention measures. Again, crime seems to have some dispositional element as well as an opportunistic one.

Reducing Bus Vandalism

Poyner (1992) describes an application of situational crime prevention that attempted to reduce vandalism on double-decker buses. Damage to buses was costing a transportation company a quarter million pounds annually. Most of the vandalism was occurring on the buses' upper decks and was perpetrated by school-age children.

The solution selected was to install closed circuit television cameras. Because of the large expense involved, the bus company decided to install live cameras in two buses and dummy cameras in three additional buses of the 80 that ran from a particular depot. Coincident with installation of the cameras, the bus company initiated an antivandalism public education campaign in the media and in the schools.

Video evidence of acts of vandalism proved useful in isolating and neutralizing perpetrators of vandalism. During the months after installation of the cameras, seat cushion repairs and the cost of cleaning bus interiors both declined dramatically. These declines were observed not only on the buses equipped with cameras, but on all buses. Whether the benefits were because of the cameras, the public education campaign, or both was unclear in this study.

Eliminating Undesirable "Cruising" by Teens in Cars

Bell and Burke (1992) report on an application of situational crime prevention to a nuisance problem in Arlington, Texas. On weekend evenings, 4,000 teens "cruised" a busy commercial street, making the street impassable to emergency vehicles. Crowds of teens often engaged in fighting, substance abuse, littering, and theft.

Initial efforts to solve the problem included stepped up traffic enforcement and barricades positioned to divert and break up the flow of traffic. Neither tactic made a substantial dent in the problem. Worse, both had unintended negative consequences. The increased traffic enforcement angered the parents of ticketed teens who paid the citations. Barricades reduced cruising traffic on the targeted street but diverted the teens to residential areas, provoking complaints from residents.

Like the failed traffic barrier strategy, the solution that ultimately worked was based on the idea of deflecting potential offenders. Teens were provided with a place (a large parking lot) where they could cruise with the blessing of the city. Costs (for rental of the lot, traffic enforcement, portable toilets, and clean-up) were high, but deemed worth it because the solution eliminated the problem.

This example once again points out that situational crime prevention strategies can have unintended effects. In this situation, displacement of the problem to a surrounding area was immediately realized because residents protested vigorously. In other applications, displacement or other unintended consequences might be missed because they simply are not looked for.

Preventing Repeat Victimization

One of the most exciting applications of situational crime prevention has been in working with repeat victims. A fundamental questions in crime prevention is deciding where and how to deploy crime prevention resources: In other words, how to ration crime prevention (Farrell & Pease, 1993). Logically, limited resources ought to be allocated to those persons most at risk. As it turns out, extensive literature shows that persons once victimized are at far greater risk than others of future victimization (see, for example, Hindelang, Gottfredson, & Garofalo, 1978; Sorenson, Siegel, Golding, & Stein, 1991). This is not surprising for victims of domestic violence: It is common belief that repeat domestic victimization is not only possible, but indeed likely if the victim remains in the situation. Yet, research has shown that robbery victims stand a 9 times greater chance of revictimization than do others, and sexual assault victims have a 35 times greater risk (Canada Solicitor General, 1988).

Work on repeat victimization has been even more prevalent in Great Britain than in North America (for example, Anderson, Chenery, & Pease, 1995; Farrell & Pease, 1993; see Farrell, 1995, for a recent summary). Findings from the British studies have been quite consistent with the North American results. For example, a recent research summary by the National Board for Crime Prevention (1994) of British crime rates showed that households once burglarized are reburglarized at four times the rate of unburglarized houses and that 22 percent of motor vehicle thefts are accounted for by just 8 percent of the victims.

The risk of revictimization is greatest in the period soon after the previous victimization for crimes as diverse as school crime, residential burglary, bias crime, domestic violence, auto crimes, neighbor disputes, and retail crimes (Farrell & Pease, 1993). In domestic violence cases, for example, the risk of revictimization is highest within the first 11 days and declines thereafter (Lloyd, Farrell, & Pease, 1994). In residential burglary, 40 percent of repeat burglaries occur within one month of the previous burglary (Anderson, Chenery, & Pease, 1995); after about six months the likelihood of repeat burglary returns to the average levels for a given area (Polvi, Looman, Humphries, & Pease, 1991). These studies support the notion of event dependency in repeat victimization: Something about being victimized a first time increases the risk of another victimization. For example, burglars visiting a house for the first time might note additional items worth coming back for.

Neatly enough, people are not only at highest risk, but also most likely to be especially receptive to crime prevention opportunities immediately following victimization. There is a "window of opportunity" during the first weeks after a crime during which victims feel vulnerable and are willing to consider seriously behavioral and lifestyle changes (Davis & Smith, 1994; Anderson, Chenery, & Pease, 1995).

The British have been leaders in working with victims to prevent revictimization. In a crime prevention program for victims of residential burglary in a housing estate, situational crime prevention strategies included replacement of coin operated gas and electricity meters (a frequent target), security upgrades, property marking, victim support and information, and "cocoon" neighborhood watch (involving the victim's six nearest neighbors). An evaluation showed a substantial reduction in burglary for the entire estate over the next three years, compared with an earlier period and also compared with the remainder of the police subdivision (Pease, 1992). Similar programs for burglary victims in three housing estates showed a decrease in repeat victimization; although there was no apparent diffusion of benefits to other residents, neither was there any clear evidence of displacement (Tilley & Webb, 1994).

In a West Yorkshire project, victims of burglary or automobile theft received an increasing level of police response based on the number of victimizations suffered in the previous year. Strategies included (as appropriate to a particular victim) security upgrades, property/vehicle marking, "cocoon" watch, focused patrol, offender targeting, priority fingerprinting, and the loan of burglar alarms and vehicle location devices. Evaluation results are not yet available (Anderson, Chenery, & Pease, 1995). In a domestic violence reduction project, victims received wearable alarms linked to the police by cellular phone, responding officers receive en route information on prior calls and on current court orders, victim service workers offered support and developed an action plan with the victim, and lecture and discussion sessions were held with the police to raise their awareness of the issue of domestic violence and the police role. Early evidence from victim interviews indicated that the pendant alarms have greatly increased the recipients' sense of security (Lloyd, Farrell, & Pease, 1994).

In the United States, Davis and Smith (1994) reported the results of a field test of a crime prevention program administered to recent victims. One group of victims of robbery, burglary, and assault received instruction in crime prevention and was offered free upgrades of home security hardware. Another group received traditional crisis counseling, but no crime prevention instruction. Relative to the crisis counseling group, victims assigned to the crime prevention training were significantly more likely to believe that the crime could have been avoided, had greater knowledge of crime prevention principles, and were more likely to engage in precautionary behaviors. Victims who had experienced the crime prevention training had a 33 percent lower rate of revictimization than controls over the next twelve months. However, the sample was small, and the victimization difference only attained marginal statistical significance.

The work with repeat victims is at an early stage of development and (with few exceptions) has not yet been evaluated extensively. Nonetheless, the British work appears to have major implications for crime control and for situational crime prevention.

IS SITUATIONAL CRIME PREVENTION ETHICAL?

Felson and Clarke (in press) discuss reservations that have been expressed about situational crime prevention by critics on the right and on the left, including that it unfairly places the burden for preventing crimes on victims, that it ignores the moral culpability of criminals; and that it neglects the role of social and economic inequities in causing crime. Felson and Clarke defend situational crime prevention on the basis that it is compatible with the three principles that ought to govern crime prevention in a liberal democracy: (a) providing crime prevention equally to all social strata, (b) showing respect for individual rights, and (c) sharing responsibility for crime prevention with all segments of society. Felson and Clarke further argue (p. 20) that situational crime prevention is ethically superior to other forms of crime prevention because "it is more defensible to arrange society so that people are not readily tempted into crime, rather than allowing temptations to abound and then visiting punishment on those who fall."

Nonetheless, reservations can be raised about the misapplication of situational crime prevention. We discuss two of the most compelling in the following sections.

Destructive Effects on Community

The concept of situational crime prevention is, in most respects, similar to the earlier notion of an opportunity reduction approach to crime prevention. The definition given by Rosenbaum (1988, p. 328) for opportunity reduction—

"removing or reducing specific opportunities for crime rather than attempting to change the offender's motivation to commit crime"—is compatible with the Clarke's definition of situational crime prevention given at the outset of this chapter. It is hard to criticize such approaches because they essentially are based on common sense. Few would argue that (in Clarke's terminology) opportunities for crime could not be reduced through managing, designing, or manipulating the environment. There are, however, at least two ways in which situational crime prevention is controversial: (a) It pushes us further down the path to a "big brother" society, and (b) it does not deter crime, but instead simply moves it around, that is, displaces it.

As we have seen through the examples of situational crime prevention discussed, one way in which situational crime prevention deters crime is through modifying the physical environment to convey a warning to potential criminals that crimes will be difficult to commit or easy to thwart once in progress. These alterations to the physical environment, however, convey information to the general public as well as to potential law breakers—information that can produce unintended effects. Skogan (1986, 1990) synthesizes evidence suggesting that cues in the physical environment (such as bars on windows or iron gates) are important determinants of fear of crime. Crime prevention practices can contribute to this problem. Rosenbaum and Bickman (1983), reporting on a randomized field test of a burglary prevention program, found that recipients of preventive services experienced an *increase* in fear of crime relative to controls. The same environmental manipulations that convey a warning to potential criminals might also convey to other citizens a message that the environment is dangerous. Clearly, if the proliferation of visible security measures causes ordinary citizens to avoid using the streets and sidewalks because of fear of victimization, this type of avoidance behavior undermines the neighborhood's capacity to exercise surveillance, intervention, and other activities to prevent crime on the streets (see Chapter 5). Additional research is needed to examine how environmental alterations designed to reduce crime influence the perceptions of criminals and ordinary citizens.

Another concern about situational crime prevention is its preoccupation with a single goal—reduction in crime. A lower crime rate is cold comfort if the price is a more fearful citizenry. Preventing bus robberies through exact change policies or closed circuit cameras is a laudable goal, but needs to be weighed against potential drops in ridership that might result from these crime prevention efforts. Practitioners and evaluators of situational crime prevention need to be aware not only of displacement of crime but other unintended effects as well.

Some situational crime prevention applications also run the risk of weakening rather than strengthening the social dynamics of neighborhoods. The informal social control approach to crime prevention seeks to establish a stronger sense of community and increased social interaction (Conklin, 1975; DuBow & Emmons, 1981). Some situational crime prevention strategies are compatible with the objectives of prevention through increased informal social control. Both approaches, for example, advocate the idea of architectural and urban designs that increase surveillance of public spaces by residents. How-ever, the closed circuit television used in several situational crime applications might reduce social interaction if used in residential areas where residents feared the authorities. Such a possibility is not unlikely in neighborhoods com-posed largely of poor minorities or recent immigrants fleeing oppressive gov-ernments in their countries of origin. If social interaction is reduced in public places, then the opportunities for crimes to be committed without conse-quences are increased.

Clarke (1992) is not oblivious to these criticisms and, indeed, acknowl-edges that situational crime prevention raises for some the specter of night-marish visions of the future. Overzealous, obtrusive, and unattractive applications of target hardening (for example, barbed wire, guard dogs, and the like) or formal surveillance (for example, closed circuit TV cameras) might, he admits, herald for some the existence of a "fortress society" or a society controlled by "big brother." Clarke, however, does not seem overly worried by these possibilities. He argues that most applications of situational crime prevention are unobtrusive; that people are frequently willing to surrender a degree of autonomy in exchange for increased security; and that, if people are sufficiently disturbed, they will choose not to do business with establishments that have overstepped the bounds of what is acceptable.

Attention to consumer preferences for privacy can be attained at small "Mom and Pop" establishments. But large corporations or government agen-cies are likely to be less responsive to the sensitivities of consumers. Further, although Clarke sees situational crime prevention as a grassroots kind of phe-nomenon, strategies such as closed circuit television surveillance of public areas could just as easily be applied on a massive scale by government. This is already happening in the private sector.

Clarke is certainly correct in believing that situational crime prevention does not necessarily imply armed fortresses or a destruction of community. But the potential is there if anticrime zealots adopt situational crime preven-tion measures without concern for other consequences.

Displacement

Situational crime prevention is based on the fundamental belief that criminal behavior can be thwarted by interrupting a triggering chain of events. If a crime is thwarted, according to this model, there is no reason to expect neces-sarily that the potential criminal will simply look for another opportunity elsewhere. Indeed, if crime were based on a drive toward criminal behavior in some individuals, there would be little reason to promote situational crime prevention as a public policy. The best it could do is dislocate criminal activity in time, space, method, or type of offense. That might be comforting to busi-ness owners or other citizens interested only in protecting *their* property or persons, but it would matter little to policy makers interested in reducing crime in the larger society. Thus, the issue of displacement of crimes is critical to proponents of situational crime prevention.

Clarke (1992) argues that displacement has not proven to be a serious concern. He acknowledges that evaluations of crime prevention programs from the 1970s often found displacement effects. But he argues that more recent research has suggested that, although displacement is always a possibility, it is seldom realized. In fact, Clarke and Weisburd (1994) believe that, instead of leading to displacement, situational crime prevention applications can lead to a "diffusion of benefits." That is, crimes not directly addressed by the application might nonetheless be reduced. This phenomenon has been observed occasionally over the years in a variety of evaluations of anticrime efforts (for example, Chaiken, Lawless, & Stevenson, 1974; Miethe, 1991; Pease, 1991).

In other words, Clarke has turned a potential serious criticism of situational crime prevention into a potential benefit. Do other experts tend to agree that displacement is seldom encountered in applying crime prevention techniques? Lab (1992) reviewed evidence concerning the displacement of crime (primarily robbery and burglary) caused by citizen prevention programs, and concluded that "displacement is a plausible concern in considering the impact of the [crime prevention] projects" (p. 81).

Other reviews came to similar conclusions, although interpretations vary. Hesseling (1994) conducted a comprehensive review of 55 crime prevention studies and found evidence of displacement in nearly two-thirds (33 studies). Six studies reportedly found diffusion of benefits effects. In support of Clarke's position, Hesseling noted that, when displacement does occur, the magnitude of displaced crime is less than the magnitude of the thwarted crime. He also concluded (1994, p. 220), "the demand for crime is more or less elastic," in contrast with the assertions of early discussions of displacement (for example, Reppetto, 1976). In other words, persons who commit crimes are not simply driven to offend in other circumstances when an opportunity is taken away.

Eck (1993) reviewed 33 studies and found less evidence of displacement than would have been previously expected. He found no evidence of displacement in 18 studies, mild effects in 12, and strong displacement effects in just 3 studies. Eck argued that the likelihood of displacement occurring can be predicted from a careful consideration of the availability of similar opportunities that is, those in which offenders can use familiar techniques or work in familiar circumstances. Unfortunately, the argument can be made that similar opportunities can be found by many offenders who are thwarted, until situational crime prevention measures are more widely employed in society.

Expectations of displacement have, perhaps, been highest for low-level street sellers of narcotics: Davis and Lurigio (1996) reported that drug dealing is a crime that is often believed to be likely to be displaced spatially if thwarted in one location. Police and local activists often perceive drug dealers to be especially recalcitrant: Chased from one location, they might have strong financial incentives to establish themselves elsewhere. However, according to Eck (1993), evidence from evaluations of neighborhood antidrug efforts have seldom yielded apparent displacement effects. For example, displacement has been found only in a few studies of police crackdowns (see Sherman, 1990). Research on drug house abatement actions—civil actions often resulting in the eviction of drug offenders—reviewed by Davis and Lurigio (1996) has given little indication that displacement occurs when drug dealers are dislocated.

Displacement is a complex issue. It can occur in a variety of ways (see Barr & Pease, 1990 for a discussion), and it can be very difficult or impossible to measure all the possible avenues that it can take (Barnes, 1995; Weisburd & Green, 1995). But, the consensus is that displacement is not an inevitable effect of situational crime prevention applications. Such findings are clearly opposed to a dispositional view of criminal activity. On the other hand, under the right circumstances, displacement can occur, and this documented fact is not easy for pure situational theorists to explain. More research is needed on this important subject, delineating the conditions under which displacement is likely to occur.

CONCLUSIONS

Situational approaches to crime prevention have scored many impressive successes during their short history. Situational advocates have clearly shown that reducing opportunities can be sufficient to deter crime without addressing underlying causes of crime and without re-creating a lost sense of community in neighborhoods. They have also shown that thwarted opportunities do not lead inevitably to displacement, although displacement is possible when the offender perceives similar opportunities with little additional effort. Obviously, there are limits to what can be done to deter crime without addressing underlying causes or rebuilding dysfunctional communities, and time will tell what those limits are. But, for the moment at least, it appears that many criminal incidents can be prevented through interceding at various points in the causal chain of events.

One important caveat should be noted: Although a substantial and growing number of empirical studies provide evidence to support the effectiveness of situational crime prevention strategies, unfortunately, the bulk of this evidence is rather weak. The research designs are generally short-term case studies characterized by the absence of good control groups and no follow-up measurement. Clarke (1995, p. 108) himself admits that "in most case studies the individual evaluations were comparatively rudimentary." Weisburd (1997, p. 17), despite his support for the theory, points out that "in many areas of situational crime prevention practice, the rhetoric of success has clearly outstripped the empirical evidence available." Clearly, researchers must design and implement more rigorous evaluations of situational crime prevention initiatives.

Although more empirical research is needed, the future of situational crime prevention looks promising and the implications for public policy are significant. The resemblance is striking to the rise of cognitive and behavioral therapies in psychology, which also intercede in causal sequences rather than addressing root causes of behavior and mood disorders. Over the long run, cognitive-behavioral therapies have shown that they can be effective. In fact, they have proven far more efficacious in dealing with a range of psychological disturbances than have therapies that address root causes of behavior (Beck & Freeman, 1993). From a policy standpoint, the message is that we don't always need to identify or understand the causes of behavior to prevent its occurrence.

We need to remember, however, that any action—including situational crime prevention—can have unintended consequences. It is not enough to examine only the issue of displacement of crime. The same environmental cues that discourage crime can signal citizens that the environment is dangerous. The sight of well-fortified houses, closed circuit cameras surveilling public spaces, or package goods passed through a bullet-proof screens in liquor stores can help define how we think about ourselves and how much trust we have in each other. Exact fares on buses might reduce robberies, but they can also lower ridership by making patronage more difficult. Reducing crime is an important goal, but we need to remind those who adopt situational crime prevention strategies that our sense of community and civility are important values as well in our society.

REFERENCES

Anderson, D., Chenery, S. & Pease, K. (1995). *Biting back, tackling repeat burglary and car crime.* Crime Detection & Prevention Series Paper 58. London: Home Office.

Barnes, G. (1995). Defining and optimizing displacement. In J. Eck & D. Weisburd (eds.), *Crime and place. Crime prevention studies* (Vol. 4, pp. 95–113). Monsey, NY: Criminal Justice Press.

Barr, R., & Pease, K. (1992)). A place for every crime and every crime in its place: An alternative perspective on crime displacement. In D. J. Evans, N. R. Fyfe, & D. T. Herbert (eds.). *Crime, policing, and place: Essays in environmental criminology.* London: Routledge.

Beck, A. & Freeman, A. (1993). *Cognitive therapy of personality disorders.* New York: Guilford.

Bell, J. & Burke, B. (1992). Cruising Cooper Street. In R. V. Clarke (ed.), *Situational crime prevention: Successful case studies* (pp. 108–112). New York: Harrow and Heston.

Canada Solicitor General (1988). *Multiple victimization, Canadian urban victimiza-tion survey bulletin* (No. 10). Ottawa: Ministry of the Solicitor General.

Chaiken, J., Lawless, M., & Stevenson, K. (1974). *The impact of police activity on crime: Robberies on the New York subway system.* Santa Monica: Rand.

Chaiken, J., Lawless, M., & Stevenson, K. (1992). Exact fare on buses. In R. V. Clarke (ed.), *Situational crime prevention: Successful case studies* (pp. 216–222). New York: Harrow and Heston.

Clarke, R. V. (1983). Situational crime prevention: Its theoretical basis and practical scope. In M. Tonry & N. Morris (eds.), *Crime and justice: An annual review of research* (Vol. 4). Chicago: University of Chicago Press.

Clarke, R. V. (1992). Introduction. In R. V. Clarke (ed.), *Situational crime prevention: Successful case studies* (pp. 3–36). New York: Harrow and Heston.

Clarke, R. V. (1995). Situational crime prevention. In M. Tonry & D. Farrington (eds.), *Building a safer society. Crime and justice: A review of research* (Vol. 19). Chicago: University of Chicago Press.

Clarke, R. V. & Cornish, D. B. (1983). *Crime control in Britain: A review of policy research.* Albany: State University of New York Press.

Clarke, R. V, & Cornish, D. B. (1985). Modeling offenders' decisions: A framework for research and policy. In M. Tonry & N. Morris (eds.), *Crime and Justice: An Annual Review of Research,* (Vol. 6). Chicago: University of Chicago Press.

Clarke, R. V. & Weisburd, D. (1994) Diffusion of crime control benefits: Observations on the reverse of displacement. In R. V. Clarke (ed.) *Crime prevention series* (pp. 165–184, Number 2). Monsey, NY: Criminal Justice Press.

Cohen, L. & Felson, M. (1979). Social change and crime rate trends: A routine activity approach. *American Sociological Review* 44, 588–608.

Conklin, J. (1975). *The Impact of Crime.* New York: Macmillan.

Cornish, D. B. & Clarke, R. V. (1986). *The reasoning criminal: Rational choice perspectives on offending.* New York: Springer-Verlag.

Cromwell, P., Olson, J., & Avary, D. (1991). *Breaking and entering: An ethnographic analysis of burglary.* Newbury Park, CA: Sage.

Davis, R. & Lurigio, A. (1996). *Fighting back: Neighborhood anti-drug initiatives.* Thousand Oaks, CA: Sage.

Davis, R. C. & Smith, B. (1994). Teaching victims crime prevention skills: Can individuals lower their risk of crime? *Criminal Justice Review* 19, 56–68.

DuBow, F. & Emmons, D. (1981). The community hypothesis. In D. A. Lewis (ed.), *Reactions to crime* (pp. 167–181). Beverly Hills: Sage.

Eck, J. (1993). The threat of crime displacement. *Criminal Justice Abstracts* 25, 527–546.

Ekblom, P. (1992). Preventing post office robberies in London: Effects and side effects. In R. V. Clarke (ed.), *Situational crime prevention: Successful case studies* (66–74). New York: Harrow and Heston.

Farrell, G. (1995). Preventing repeat victimization. In M. Tonry & D. P. Farrington (eds.), *Building a safer society: Strategic approaches to crime prevention* (Vol. 19, in *Crime and justice: An annual review of research*). Chicago: University of Chicago Press.

Farrell, G. & Pease, K. (1993). *Once bitten, twice bitten: Repeat victimization and its implications for crime prevention.* Crime Prevention Unit Paper 46. London: Home Office.

Fattah, E. A. (1993). The rational choice/opportunity perspectives as a vehicle for integrating criminological and victimological theories. In R. V. Clarke & M. Felson (eds.), *Routine activity and rational choice.* New Brunswick, NJ: Transaction.

Feeney, F. (1986). Robbers as decision-makers. In D. B. Cornish & R. V. Clarke (eds.), *The reasoning criminal: Rational choice perspectives on offending.* New York : Springer-Verlag.

Felson, M. (1986). Linking criminal choices, routine activities, informal control, and criminal outcomes. In D. B. Cornish & R. V. Clarke (eds.), *The reasoning criminal: Rational choice perspectives on offending.* New York: Springer-Verlag.

Felson, M. & Clarke, R. V. (in press). The ethics of situational crime prevention. In G. Newman, R. V. Clarke, & S. Shoham (eds.), *Situational crime prevention and rational choice.* Farnborough, England: Dartmouth.

Hawley, A. (1950). *Human ecology: A theory of community structure.* New York: Ronald.

Hesseling, R. (1994). Displacement: A review of the empirical literature. In R. V. Clarke (ed.), *Crime prevention studies* (vol. 3, pp. 197–227). Monsey, NY: Criminal Justice Press.

Hindelang, M., Gottfredson, M., & Garofalo, J. (1978). *Victims of personal crime: An empirical foundation for a theory of victimization.* Cambridge, MA: Ballinger.

Jeffrey, C. R. (1971). *Crime prevention through environmental design*. Beverly Hills, CA: Sage.

Lab, S. P. (1992). *Crime prevention: Approaches, practices, and evaluations*. Cincinnati: Anderson.

Lloyd, S., Farrell, G. & Pease, K. (1993). *Preventing repeated domestic violence: A demonstration project on Merseyside*. Crime Prevention Unit Paper 49. London: Home Office.

Lloyd, S., Farrell, G., & Pease, K. (1994). *Preventing repeat domestic violence: A demonstration project in Merseyside*. Crime Prevention Unit Paper 49. London: Home Office.

Miethe, T. (1991). Citizen-based crime control activity and victimization risks: An examination of displacement and free-rider effects. *Criminology 29*, 419–440.

Mischel, W. (1968). *Personality and assessment*. New York: Wiley.

National Board for Crime Prevention (1994). *Wise after the event: Tackling repeat victimization*. London: Home Office.

Newman, O. (1972). *Defensible space: Crime prevention through urban design*. New York: Macmillan.

Pease, K. (1991). The Kirkholt project: Preventing burglary on a British public housing estate. *Security Journal 2*, 73–77.

Pease, K. (1992). Preventing burglary on a British public housing estate. In R. V. Clarke. (ed.), *Situational crime prevention: Successful case studies* (pp. 223–229). New York: Harrow and Heston.

Polvi, N., Looman, T., Humphries, C. & Pease, K. (1991). The time course of repeat burglary victimization. *British Journal of Criminology 31*(4), 411–414.

Poyner, B. (1992). Video cameras and bus vandalism. In R. V. Clarke (ed.), *Situational crime prevention: Successful case studies* (pp. 185–193). New York: Harrow and Heston.

Poyner, B. & Webb, B. (1991). *Crime Free Housing*. Oxford: Butterworth Architect.

Reppetto, T. (1976). Crime prevention and the displacement phenomenon. *Crime and Delinquency 22*, 166–177.

Rosenbaum, D. P. (1988). Community crime prevention: A review and synthesis of the literature. *Justice Quarterly 5*, 323–395.

Rosenbaum, D. & Bickman, L. (1983). *Scaring people into crime prevention: The results of a randomized field experiment*. Paper presented at the 91st annual convention of the American Psychological Association, Anaheim.

Shaver, K. & Tarpy, R. (1993). *Psychology*. New York: Macmillan.

Sherman, L. W. (1990). Police crackdowns: Initial and residual deterrence. In M. Tonry and N. Morris (eds.), *Crime and justice: A review of research* (pp. 1–48). Chicago: University of Chicago Press.

Sherman, L. W., Gartin, P. R., & Buerger, M. E. (1989). Hot spots of predatory crime: Routine activities and the criminology of place. *Criminology 27*, 27–56.

Skinner, B. F. (1963). Behaviorism at fifty. *Science 140*, 951–958.

Skogan, W. G. (1986). Fear of crime and neighborhood change. In A. J. Reiss, Jr., & M. Tonry (eds.), *Communities and crime* (Vol. 8 in M. Tonry & N. Morris [eds.] *Crime and justice: An annual review of research*). Chicago: University of Chicago Press.

Skogan, W. G. (1990). *Disorder and decline: Crime and the spiral of decay in American cities*. New York: Free Press.

Sorenson, S. B., Siegel, J. M., Golding, J. M., & Stein, J. A. (1991). Repeat sexual victimization. *Violence and Victims 6*(4), 299–301.

Stanford Research Institute (1970). *Reduction of robbery and assaults of bus drivers, Vol. 3, Technological and operational methods*. Stanford, CA: Stanford Research Institute.

Tilley, N. & Webb, J. (1994). *Burglary reduction: Findings from safer cities schemes* (Crime Prevention Unit Paper 51). London: Home Office.

Tizard, J, Sinclair, I., & Clarke, R. (1975). *Varieties of Residential Experience*. London: Routledge and Kegan Paul.

Tremblay, R. E., & Craig, W. M. (1995). Developmental prevention of crime: From pre-birth to adolescence. In M. Tonry & D. P. Farrington (eds.) *Building a safer society: Strategic approaches to crime prevention*. (Vol. 19, *Crime and Justice*). Chicago: University of Chicago Press.

Weisburd, D. (1997). Reorienting crime prevention research and policy: From the causes of criminality to the context of crime. *Research Report*. Washington, DC: National Institute of Justice, U.S. Department of Justice.

Weisburd, D., & Green, L. (1994). Defining the drug market: The case of the Jersey City DMA system. In D. L. MacKenzie & C. D. Uchida (eds.) *Drugs and crime: Evaluating public policy initiatives*. Newbury Park, CA: Sage.

Weisburd, D. & Green, L. (1995). Measuring immediate spatial displacement: Methodological issues and problems. In J. Eck & D. Weisburd (eds.), *Crime and place. crime prevention studies* (Vol. 4, pp. 349–361). Monsey, NY: Criminal Justice Press.

Weisburd, D., Maher, L, & Sherman, L. (1992). Contrasting crime general and crime specific theory: The case of hot spots of crime. *Advances in Criminological Theory* 4, 45–70.

Wilson, J. Q. & Hernstein, R. J. (1985). *Crime and human nature*. New York: Simon & Schuster.

PART V

Resource Mobilization, Partnerships, and Social Prevention

p.172 = blank

9

✿

Community Policing
and the Co-Production
of Safety

A thorough analysis of community-based crime prevention initiatives must, by necessity, recognize the critical role of law enforcement agencies in these efforts. Until recently, virtually all federal, state, and local funding for neighborhood crime prevention programs was distributed to local police agencies rather than to community organizations or other community-based agencies. Even today, the police remain the primary trusted recipient of crime prevention funding and are expected to take the lead in program development. Fortunately, police organizations in North America are facing a sweeping reform movement that promises, among other things, to return some of the responsibility for crime prevention to the community (Rosenbaum, 1998). Hence, we have devoted this chapter to the changing role of police in American society and to the potential this holds for mobilizing additional community resources, building new partnerships, solving persistent neighborhood problems, and preventing crime.

The past 15 years have been exciting for the police field as law enforcement agencies find themselves deeply involved in what was initially described as a "quiet revolution" in policing—the transition from the reform era to the community problem solving era (Kelling, 1988; Kelling & Moore, 1988). Despite considerable pessimism about whether real police reform is possible and whether the current excitement is simply another case of hype or self-deception, many experts believe that long-term changes in policing are unfolding. Their optimism is based on fundamental changes in the values and philosophies of police management, which are supported by research and reflect a new understanding of how to control and prevent crime (Kelling & Coles, 1996; Skogan & Hartnett, 1997). At the core of this new understanding is a deep appreciation of the importance of nonpolice resources in fighting the war on crime, especially the community's role as "co-producers" of public safety. Criminal justice scholars, administrators, and historians now recognize that one of the biggest mistakes in modern policing was to place total responsibility and accountability for public safety on the shoulders of law enforcement.

In this chapter, we take a close look at the co-production of public safety by the police and the community. Producing or fostering public safety involves controlling and preventing crime, maintaining public order, and—of increasing importance—influencing public fears, perceptions, and concerns about crime. How the police pursue these objectives (that is, what programs, strategies, and policies they develop and promote) depends largely on their beliefs about the origins of crime-related problems and about the effectiveness of nontraditional approaches to policing.

The long-held assumption that preventive patrols, rapid responses, and follow-up investigations would significantly reduce crime was based on a limited understanding of what causes crime. If the goal is to reduce crime and disorder, then police administrators must pay attention to research findings that indicate that community crime rates are seriously affected by social forces (Reiss, 1986) and that community-based actions must play a central role in any crime prevention program (Rosenbaum, 1988). The words of Jacobs (1961) effectively summarize this orientation:

> The first thing to understand is that public peace . . . is not kept primarily
> by the police, necessary as police are. It is kept primarily by an intricate,
> almost unconscious network of voluntary controls and standards among the
> people themselves, and enforced by the people themselves. (pp. 31–32)

Successful crime prevention depends more on the community than on the police. In contrast with the conventional view that citizens are ancillary to the police, the co-production perspective (Yin, 1979) suggests the opposite (that is, that the police are ancillary to citizens). Because the government resources for preventing crime continue to rest primarily with the police, however, the argument can be made that the police are largely responsible for developing a working partnership with the community to promote public safety. Hence, police administrators should give considerable attention to how their employees can serve as catalysts and resources for community anti-crime initiatives.

Police responses to the public's fear of crime should be based on factors that contribute to citizens' perceptions of their risk of criminal victimization. Traditional preventive patrols, rapid responses to calls for services, and efforts to identify and apprehend offenders are not sufficient to reduce citizens' fears (Moore & Trojanowicz, 1988). These approaches rest on presuppositions about fear of crime that are not supported by research. Numerous studies have shown that fear of crime is not simply an objective response to the risk of being victimized; instead, it is determined by a host of other personal, social, and environmental factors (Rosenbaum & Heath, 1990). Police need to be cognizant of these facts when developing new programs to reduce fear.

The era of believing that more police officers and quicker response times will solve the problems of crime and fear is being replaced by the era of increasing police–community contact and joint, neighborhood-based problem solving. How this quiet revolution translates into practical, publicly acceptable, and cost-effective programs and policies remains unclear. Indeed, bringing the revolution to fruition might be the biggest challenge facing police executives in the twenty-first century.

COMMUNITY POLICING

Community policing represents the driving force behind the current efforts to reform law enforcement, providing both the rationale and the mechanisms for changing significantly the nature and goals of policing in America. The success of the revolution rests largely on the effectiveness of the community policing model, which includes basic tenets regarding the importance of citizen participation, problem solving, fear reduction, order maintenance, and quality-of-life issues.

Multiple Definitions

Community policing is a very trendy term with numerous definitions. The popularity and ambiguity of the concept is both a blessing and a curse. On the positive side, everyone can identify with the term (after all, who is opposed to the concept of "community," or "mother" and "apple pie" for that matter?). The nebulous nature of the concept allows people to read into it favorable attributes and unlimited possibilities for change and innovation. On the negative side, the concept has been abused by law enforcement executives who use it to justify their pet programs; the cachet of community policing can produce a "halo effect" around such programs and prevent outside observers from distinguishing true police innovation from traditional policing. In addition, the popularity of the community policing concept raises public expectations and "create[s] the impression that, somehow, on implementation, community policing will provide a panacea for not only crime, disorder, and racial tensions, but many of the other acute problems that plague our urban areas" (Goldstein, 1993, p. 1).

The challenge is to determine what community policing is (and is not) and to differentiate it from traditional policing. Is community policing, in practice, truly ground-breaking or simply "old wine in new bottles"? Such clarification will help us examine the merits and limitations of these programs. Criminal justice scholars and police administrators have yet to articulate the full theory behind community policing or to enumerate all its components and operations. Theoretical imprecision has contributed to the criticism of community policing (for example, Klockars, 1988; Manning, 1988; Mastrofski, 1988). As Bayley (1988) states,

> Although widely, almost universally, said to be important, [community policing] means different things to different people—public relations campaigns, shopfronts and mini-stations, rescaled patrol beats liaison with ethnic groups, permission for rank-and-file to speak to the press, Neighborhood Watch, foot patrols, patrol-detective teams, and door-to-door visits by police officers. Community policing on the ground often seems less a program than a set of aspirations wrapped in a slogan. (p. 225)

Although definitional problems abound, it would be a mistake to conclude that community policing is all rhetoric and no substance or that there is no agreement regarding its core elements. Community policing has been implemented through a variety of programs and practices but the concept appears to be supported by a common set of guiding principles and elements (Eck & Spelman, 1987; Goldstein, 1990; Greene & Mastrofski, 1988; McElroy, Cosgrove, & Sadd, 1993; Murphy & Muir, 1984; Rosenbaum, 1994; Skogan & Hartnett, 1997; Skolnick & Bayley, 1986; Sparrow, Moore, & Kennedy, 1990; Toch & Grant, 1991; Trojanowicz & Bucqueroux, 1989). The most frequently cited elements of community policing include the following:

- Defining police work more broadly
- Reordering police priorities
- Paying greater attention to neighborhood disorder and quality-of-life issues
- Shifting to shared decision making with citizens
- De-emphasizing bureaucratic processes in favor of results
- Focusing on problem solving and prevention rather than on incident-driven policing
- Recognizing that the community plays a critical role in solving neighborhood problems
- Restructuring and reorganizing police departments to encourage and reward a fresh set of police behaviors

These shared concepts and assumptions are being translated increasingly into concrete changes, such as decentralized organizational structures, permanent beat assignments, more avenues for community participation and problem solving, and revamped performance evaluation systems.

Community policing, however defined, has become an abundant source of police reform and police research (Eck & Spelman, 1987; Goldstein, 1990; Greene & Mastrofski, 1988; McElroy, Cosgrove, & Sadd, 1993; Murphy & Muir, 1984; Rosenbaum, 1994; Skogan & Hartnett, 1997; Skolnick & Bayley, 1986; Sparrow, Moore, & Kennedy, 1990; Toch & Grant, 1991; Trojanowicz & Bucqueroux, 1989). Despite many uncertainties, hundreds of communities across the United States are moving "full speed ahead" with implementation.

For example, between 1994 and 1997, the Justice Department's Office of Community Oriented Policing Services (COPS) funded approximately 50,000 new police officer positions nationwide (toward a goal of 100,000) to serve in community policing roles (Community Policing Consortium, 1997). Because of a shortage of clear definitions and accepted criteria for measuring success, however, a wide range of activities and programs were able to "pass" as "community policing." Furthermore, until very recently, few carefully designed studies have explored how this multifaceted concept has been defined in specific locations and whether such operations have achieved desired results (see Rosenbaum, 1994, for early evaluation studies).

THE ROLE OF COMMUNITY

In the early- to mid-1980s, the focus of community policing was on the community. Progressive police departments used a variety of strategies to reduce the physical and psychological distance between the police and the citizens they served. Experimental programs were typically designed to increase foot patrols, create local ministations, encourage more and better police contacts with citizens, and create or support community organizations interested in crime prevention. Evaluations of these initiatives showed that crime rates were reduced only inconsistently, but that residents' perceptions of crime and their evaluations of local police were often improved significantly (for reviews, see Rosenbaum, Hernandez, & Daughtry, 1991; Skogan, 1990, 1994).

Some of the more basic questions are these: Why should the police work hard to get citizens involved in public safety? What goals and objectives will be served? Even though the goals for community involvement were unclear at first ("participation for participation's sake"), they are much clearer today—to empower the community, to enhance participation in crime prevention activities, to facilitate order maintenance activities, and to solve neighborhood problems. Police are expected to play pivotal roles in each of these strategies.

Community Building

In response to the problems of social disorganization and the erosion of informal social control in crime-ridden neighborhoods, community experts believe that systematic efforts are needed to bolster social networks and strengthen residents' attachment to their neighborhoods (see Chapter 3). The options for citizen participation and empowerment within neighborhoods are numerous. Local residents can engage in many different actions to help prevent crime and disorder (DuBow, McCabe, & Kaplan, 1979; Lab, 1988; Lavrakas, 1985; Lewis & Salem, 1986; Rosenbaum, 1988). They can get involved in protecting themselves, their families, their properties, and their streets through individual or collective actions. They can get involved in helping at-risk youth and families, as well as working to supervise and rehabilitate known offenders.

The argument for the central role of "community" in community policing is based on research findings that demonstrate that crime-related outcomes are controlled more by the social and economic forces in a community than by the traditional activities of the police (see Bursik & Grasmick, 1993, for a review). This perspective is radically different from that implicit in the conventional crime fighting model. Thus, the challenge for police today and into the twenty-first century is to find creative ways to help communities help themselves.

Community policing officers can pursue numerous paths toward achieving self-regulated and self-defended neighborhoods, including working jointly and equally with citizens to define local problems, educating the community about the causes of crime and disorder, helping develop action plans that are responsive to these issues, and working with citizens to identify and mobilize resources—both inside and outside the community—to solve and prevent the target problems. The possibilities for citizen involvement are variegated but the outcomes of these activities are still uncertain.

At this point, unfortunately, the rhetoric about community involvement in community policing has far exceeded the reality. For a variety of reasons, community participation in community policing has been limited in many cities. For example, a Vera Institute study of the implementation of community policing in eight cities—most in poor neighborhoods—found that some programs floundered because of residents' fears of crime and retaliation from drug dealers, pent-up hostility between residents and police, and a lack of understanding concerning residents' role in community policing (Grinc, 1994; Sadd & Grinc, 1994). Others have argued that police organizations have yet to take the community seriously as a partner in the fight against crime. Buerger (1994) claims that the "community" is used simply to legitimize and support the police function (like cheer-leaders) rather than to make any real contribution to crime reduction. Friedman (1994), a community organizer, complains that community leaders are typically left out of the professional dialogue about the future of community policing and too often the community is assigned a passive role with little decision-making authority.

Notwithstanding these concerns, evidence of successful community engagement is now available in Chicago. A major evaluation by Skogan and his colleagues indicates that an intensive joint effort by the Chicago Police Department and community organizations can go a long way toward stimulating citizen involvement in community policing if residents are given structured and predictable opportunities for input and participation (Skogan & Hartnett, 1997).

The community policing model calls for police officers to take on new and unfamiliar roles, such as community facilitators, coordinators, and referral agents. Whether the typical police officer can do this remains uncertain. Also, whether successful community-oriented initiatives can be maintained over time is unknown. Many of the community outreach efforts were started as special police units grafted onto the police organization. Many of these are at risk of disappearing when funding dries up, and other programs are fighting to be expanded and institutionalized.

We might also be causing a problem by setting our expectations too high for volunteer-based citizens' groups, especially those facing serious neighborhood problems. In highly disorganized and disadvantaged neighborhoods, it might be too much to expect individual citizens or voluntary grassroots organizations to play a primary role in stopping crime, drug activity, and disorder, except in narrowly defined geographic areas. Perhaps the primary aim should be to mobilize local institutions and agencies that are invested in the neighborhood (for example, churches, schools, social service agencies) by appealing to a much broader definition of community. In theory, the coordinated and persistent application of additional resources should help empower local residents over time and help the community build a physical and social environment that provides fewer opportunities for antisocial and criminal behaviors.

Problem Solving

One unique characteristic of the community policing model is its focus on problem solving, which became a widely visible strategy after 1987 (Eck & Spelman, 1987; Goldstein, 1990). This orientation has clear implications for community participation. Nearly every definition of community policing includes the notion that the police and community must work together to identify and solve neighborhood problems (Skogan, 1994). As Eck and Rosenbaum (1994) have observed,

> Ideally, problem solving needs a high level of community engagement to identify problems, to develop an understanding of the particular circumstances that give rise to them, to craft enduring preventive remedies, and to evaluate the effectiveness of the remedies. (p. 9)

Community policing officers know first-hand that community residents' cooperation is instrumental in solving neighborhood problems. The new police role can involve seeking community input about local problems through door-to-door surveys, community meetings, citizen-generated police records, and data from other sources.

Given the overuse of a single problem solving tool—arrest—advocates of the problem-oriented approach have encouraged police officers, whenever possible, to solve community problems without resorting to criminal law (for example, Goldstein, 1990). Solutions can be as simple as calling the sanitation department to report a persistent garbage problem or as complex as developing a long-term education and job training program to prevent youth violence. In community policing, a wide range of situational crime prevention measures can be implemented to reduce opportunities for crime (see Chapters 3, 6, and 7). Also, social crime prevention measures can be developed to attack the root causes of crime (see Chapter 10). In any event, the appropriate choice(s) among these options will depend on how the problem is defined and what resources are available to solve it.

Fighting Disorder

One primary problem-solving approach within the community policing repertoire focuses on attempts to eliminate physical and social disorders. This "Broken Windows," or order maintenance approach, to policing derives its legitimacy from a core tenet of community policing philosophy, namely, police should be responsive to the concerns of community residents when defining neighborhood problems. To the surprise of many police agencies, average citizens are often more concerned about incivility and disorder (for example, abandoned vehicles, broken windows, kids hanging out, loud music, open-air drug markets) than they are about serious crime (Skogan, 1990). Furthermore, the Broken Windows theory suggests that social and physical disorder, if left unchecked, will lead to more serious crime and neighborhood decline (Kelling & Coles, 1996; Skogan, 1990; Wilson & Kelling, 1982).

In any event, community pressure to get rid of public incivilities has led police departments to revisit a variety of aggressive order maintenance activities, ranging from traditional street sweeps to code enforcement. Although a few experimental programs were introduced in the early 1980s, such as the Fear-Reduction experiments in Houston and Newark (Pate, Wycoff, Skogan, & Sherman, 1986), this form of policing did not become popular again until the late 1980s and early 1990s, after Skogan's (1990) seminal work, *Disorder and Decline*, was published and after a dramatic increase in public pressure to crack down on drug markets. Police organizations then had both a theory and a problem to justify this approach to policing.

Although there is empirical evidence to support the hypothesis that increased disorder is associated with increased crime (for example, Skogan, 1990), there is less compelling evidence that *reducing disorder* will *reduce crime*. In fact, evaluations of police-community initiatives to eliminate "hot spots" of disorder often find that levels of *disorder* can be reduced significantly, but that these efforts have only limited, and short-term, effects on levels of *crime* (see Taylor, 1997, for a review).

Partnerships

At the heart of the community policing model is the empirically supported idea that the police are more effective in solving neighborhood problems when they use the resources available in the community than when they try to complete the task alone. With the emergence of community policing, emphasis is now given to the "co-production" of public safety (Lavrakas, 1985; Murphy & Muir, 1984; Rosenbaum, 1988). In this framework, safety is viewed as a commodity that is produced by the joint efforts of the police and community, working together in ways that were not envisioned or encouraged in the past. As Kelling and Coles (1996) state,

> In fact, no efforts at restoring order in the community will be successful
> in the long run without the development of a full partnership between
> citizens in the community and the criminal justice institutions that affect

conditions in their neighborhoods. This partnership must be fully inclusive of all racial, ethnic, religious, and economic groups; it must be subject to continuous renewal and reaffirmation; and it must provide the basis for the development of any efforts by the city to restore order, including the authority of police to implement an order-restoration program. (p. 234)

In the most progressive cities, community policing initiatives are now reaching beyond the basic police-citizenry partnership to create linkages with other institutions and agencies to mobilize additional resources to combat crime. Not only does this co-production activity recognize the limitations of the police as a self-contained, self-sufficient service organization, but it also underscores the importance of community resources as key elements in a comprehensive crime control plan.

The theory underlying partnerships is that the problems being addressed are too complex and intractable for a single organization to solve. The process of accurately defining and effectively solving a problem requires the coordination and application of resources from multiple sources. Hence, partnerships are typically created for the purpose of developing and implementing comprehensive, coordinated strategies (see Cook & Roehl, 1993; Florin, Chavis, Wandersman, & Rich, 1992; Klitzner, 1993; Prestby & Wandersman, 1985).

In recent years, partnerships have been formed to combat violence and drug abuse and these activities are part of a broader movement to formulate communitywide strategies in response to a wide range of social problems. For example, promising evaluation results have been obtained from studies of partnerships in the areas of health promotion (Shea & Basch, 1990) and drug abuse prevention (Bernard, 1990; Johnson, Williams, Dei, & Sanabria 1990; Pentz et al., 1989) in which parents, schools, the mass media, and other agents of change have teamed up to prevent the onset of problems.

Neighborhood-based antidrug partnerships have also shown some signs of success, according to results from multisite assessments. Rosenbaum and his colleagues (1994a) evaluated the Justice Department's Community Responses to Drug Abuse Program in nine cities and found that police and community organizations were able to work together effectively with other agencies on community antidrug strategies. Two other projects—the Robert Wood Johnson Foundation's 15-site Fighting Back Project (Klitzner, 1993) and the 250-site Community Partnership Program (Cook & Roehl, 1993) funded by the Center for Substance Abuse Prevention—represent major efforts to build coalitions to fight neighborhood drug abuse. Finally, the Justice Department has funded the Comprehensive Communities Program in 12 cities to support the forging of multi-agency partnerships, designed to reduce gang activity and violence through community policing and other approaches. Preliminary results suggest that some promising partnership models have been created and sustained (Kelling, Rocheleau, Rosenbaum, Roth, Skogan, & Walsh, 1997).

Coalitions or partnerships can include representatives from government agencies such as criminal justice, health, welfare, and social services. They also can include elected officials, private businesses, voluntary organizations, community and grassroots organizations, churches, and other groups that have a vested interest in neighborhoods. In theory, the more resources that can be marshaled, the better the chances are of ameliorating the problem. Although larger coalitions seek to be all-inclusive, in reality, the number of agencies involved in them is often limited, and the coalitions are often located in and coordinated by one agency.

Partnerships can vary in size and type (for example, grassroots versus professional members), number of committees, ethnic diversity, number of staff, membership criteria, decision-making processes, and approaches or orientations to the target problem (Cook & Roehl, 1993). The dynamics among the members of the partnership can be especially important for determining the partnership's success. The levels of cooperation, conflict, and participation among coalition members can be important for determining whether the problems are properly addressed or solved. Success is often linked to the presence of a key individual who has a vision, believes in the importance of the initiative, is highly motivated to see it succeed, and has access to the resources and political influence needed to make things happen. A coalition must be able to achieve internal goals, such as planning interventions, securing resources, recruiting all key organizations, maintaining stability, and keeping members satisfied about the group's progress.

In the final analysis, holding partnership meetings is a desirable objective, but the "bottom line" is whether the group can develop and implement a plan of action that will effectively address the target problems. The door is currently open for the police to become key actors in community organizing by creating or facilitating partnerships to address neighborhood problems related to crime and disorder. As organizers, facilitators, coordinators, or service providers within the community policing model, police organizations are now expected to "step up to bat" in a multi-agency context. From command personnel to the officers on the street, partnerships can provide a role for everyone. Who gets involved will depend on the size of the initiative and how easily the problem can be solved. When the problem is relatively small, a less ambitious partnership with fewer members will be sufficient. Under these conditions, line officers should be able to represent the police organization with limited involvement from top management. When the problem is large, highly visible, or patently political, or requires substantial interagency cooperation, however, then the police organization (and the community) is best served by the participation of police management personnel.

Every neighborhood and every problem will have its own special features, which means that community policing officers will need considerable freedom to develop relationships with other agencies and to make decisions about appropriate courses of action. The concept of empowering individual officers is both exciting and troublesome, depending on your perspective, but it is a central component of the community policing model. Individual police officers are expected to use their talents to think creatively about ways to solve neighborhood problems, unlike the current state of affairs in many agencies in which officers are reluctant to do anything unusual for fear of punishment.

Coincidentally, in addition to helping solve problems, this new approach to police work should yield happier employees. Several studies indicate that police officers are more satisfied with their jobs under these arrangements (see Lurigio & Rosenbaum, 1994, for a review).

The idea of empowering police is troublesome to those who fear corruption and the abuse of police powers. Obviously, in agencies in which such problems are rampant, giving beat officers more freedom could be problematic. However, most police organizations do not suffer from widespread abuse of authority (this problem is most likely to occur in larger urban departments), and preventive measures can be instituted to discourage unethical conduct. The bigger concern for most agencies should be whether beat officers have the training and skills to function in these new capacities and whether supervisors are prepared to manage staff under these new arrangements.

A Big Test

The most ambitious attempt at urban police reform is currently underway in Chicago and involves a variety of strategies to enhance problem solving and community engagement while restructuring the police bureaucracy. The city's program, known as Chicago's Alternative Policing Strategy (CAPS), was first implemented in 1993 in five prototype districts chosen to reflect the diversity of Chicago's neighborhoods.

A major evaluation of CAPS has been underway since 1993, and the early results look very promising (Skogan et al., 1995; Skogan & Hartnett, 1997).[1] Using a pretest-posttest control group design in the five prototype police districts, Skogan and his colleagues (1995) reported significant improvements in crime rates, in neighborhood disorder and decay, and in citizens' assessments of police performance during the first 17 months of the program. Along with evidence of positive program impact, the research team encountered several implementation problems. For example, regular beat meetings were designed as the primary vehicle to encourage citizen participation, but the traditional police leadership often hindered the development of police-citizen partnerships and problem-solving efforts. Furthermore, low participation rates in Hispanic neighborhoods suggested that the program was unable to reach this segment of the population. Subsequent findings, however, have indicated that the participation base of CAPS has expanded to include more women, nonwhites, and persons with lower levels of education (Skogan, 1995).

Evaluations and Unanswered Questions

To date, few carefully planned demonstration projects have been linked to well-designed quantitative evaluations of community policing. With a handful

---

1. The evaluation was funded by the National Institute of Justice, the Illinois Criminal Justice Information Authority, and the MacArthur Foundation. This is a longitudinal study conducted by Northwestern University with assistance from the University of Illinois at Chicago, Loyola University, and DePaul University.

of exceptions, community policing has been studied primarily through qualitative field methods (for example, Capowich & Roehl, 1994; Greene, Bergman, & McLaughlin, 1994; Hope, 1994; McElroy, Cosgrove, & Sadd, 1993; Sadd & Grinc, 1994; Skogan et al., 1995; Wilkinson & Rosenbaum, 1994; Wilkinson, Rosenbaum, Hanson, Stemen, Allen, & Roussos, 1997; Wilkinson, Rosenbaum, Hanson, Stemen, Allen, & Kaminska-Costello, 1997). Community policing researchers have conducted case studies of organizational processes and problem-solving activities and have occasionally supplemented them with quantitative outcome measures.

The focus of qualitative evaluations has varied substantially from general assessments of multiple police organizations (for example, Sadd & Grinc, 1994) to detailed ethnographies of police-community dynamics in specific neighborhoods (for example, Lyons, 1995). Field studies have shown the wide range of police strategies being pursued under the rubric of community policing, the multitude of problems that emerge during program development and implementation, and the struggles to implement community policing that ensue within organizations and target communities and among partnership members (Grinc, 1994). In short, researchers have uncovered a host of *internal* factors that have limited the success of community policing, ranging from rigid bureaucratic policies and procedures to a police culture that is fearful of change. These problems have led, during the 1990s, to widespread efforts by police management to reform their organizations from top to bottom.

Less research exists on *external* obstacles to community policing, but studies suggest that developing working partnerships with the community is much harder than expected because of a history of poor relations between police and residents, low levels of citizen involvement, conflicting agendas in the community, and ignorance by both police and citizens regarding the processes inherent in problem solving and community engagement. Despite the litany of reservations about community policing described in the literature, well-documented cases of implementation success have been reported (for example, Rosenbaum, Yeh, & Wilkinson, 1994b; Skogan et al., 1995; Skogan & Hartnett, 1997; Wilkinson & Rosenbaum, 1994; Wilkinson, Rosenbaum, Hanson, Stemen, Allen, & Roussos, 1997; Wilkinson, Rosenbaum, Hanson, Stemen, Allen, & Kaminska-Costello, 1997; Wycoff & Skogan, 1994).

The body of research on community policing has grown, but basic questions about these reform efforts remain unanswered, leaving several major gaps in our current knowledge. Filling these gaps will significantly advance criminal justice policy and practice. Above all, we need long-term studies to investigate how community policing initiatives evolve over time and how they affect police, community residents, and neighborhoods. (Most research is short-term, rarely reaching beyond one or two years.) Important longitudinal studies are currently underway in Chicago, Aurora and Joliet, Illinois, Madison, Wisconsin, and Tempe, Arizona.

We need rigorous impact studies to estimate program effects on target audiences. Qualitative case studies, which are very popular, are not sufficiently powerful to address important outcome questions. Specifically, what are the effects of organizational change and community interventions on police performance, public perceptions, levels of crime and disorder, and other key outcome measures? Extremely rare are evaluations that include the repeated measurement of primary community policing constructs, indices with known reliability and validity, adequate sample sizes, and carefully selected control groups.

Although many types of communities have been studied, the vast majority of rigorous evaluations have been conducted in large cities. Can current knowledge about community policing be generalized to smaller cities throughout the country? Research findings from Baltimore, Chicago, Houston, Newark, New York, Oakland, Seattle, Portland, and Philadelphia would appear to have limited external validity for smaller cities in the United States or elsewhere. Most police departments are much smaller than those studied in major evaluations of community policing (Reaves, 1992).

Case studies have been used to explore organizational reforms within police agencies but less often to document the dynamics of police-community interactions, considered the linchpin of community policing in practice. A paucity of useful qualitative data is available about the nature of police-community partnerships, especially as they develop in the context of neighborhood- and block-level meetings (see Lyons, 1995, and Skogan & Hartnett, 1997, for exceptions). More generally, the ability of police personnel to facilitate and coordinate working partnerships with schools, businesses, churches, social service agencies, and community leaders should be carefully documented so that police (and other partners) know what to expect and how to face emerging challenges. In addition, the architects of community policing are presently struggling to develop new systems to evaluate police officers and to encourage innovative police responses. But virtually all these efforts have centered around the development of internal performance evaluation systems. Given the importance of community needs, perceptions, knowledge, and activities in the community policing model, more attention should be given to formalizing and standardizing measures of residents' perceptions of police performance.

Implementation Issues

Optimism about the future of community policing should be tempered by widespread problems with program implementation. Whether these difficulties can be overcome remains to be seen and, in the final analysis, will determine the future of this reform movement. The internal and external obstacles to successful planning and implementation have been well documented through the process evaluations cited in this chapter. Many problems within police organizations threaten to derail the reform process, including inadequate training and supervision; top-down, rule-driven bureaucracies that undermine officers' discretion; outdated performance evaluation systems that reward "bean counting" of enforcement activities; limited resources to carry out additional police functions; and, above all, employees' general resistance to change. In a nutshell, most police organizations are simply not ready for serious police reform, and even the most progressive administrators would prefer to develop special units or delimited programs within the department than to upset the status quo by introducing large-scale reform initiatives. "Organizational readiness," as Rosenbaum and colleagues (1994a) defined it, implies that the agency "has in place the structure, policies, procedures, knowledge, and officer skills needed to deliver a new set of police services and a new approach to crime prevention and control" (p. 350). Too often police organizations are not "ready" as a bureaucracy to support community policing at the street level.

In the relatively short history of community policing, one lesson not yet learned is that serious organizational changes are a prerequisite to sustaining community policing programs. The process of change can start without much money or internal support from police personnel but such reform efforts will not survive unless formal mechanisms are established to create a new working environment and, eventually, a new police culture. The behavior of police officers—like that of all human beings—is shaped and controlled by rewards and punishments in their immediate environments. Therefore, in the absence of a new reward structure and performance evaluation system—one that identifies and encourages community-oriented, problem-solving behaviors and discourages traditional responses—street-level police behavior is not likely to change. Police chiefs and academics can talk incessantly about community policing, but the day-to-day behaviors of the beat officers will continue along traditional lines until revamped reward systems (both formal and informal) are instituted.

Outside the organization, the problems with community participation are serious (Grinc, 1994). Public education through a professional marketing (and de-marketing) strategy will help build a more productive relationship between the police and the community; nevertheless, the problem of mobilizing local residents runs deeper. In the inner city, community policing officers must understand that a lack of citizen participation is caused by feelings of hopelessness and despair, fear of offender retaliation, and deep-seated distrust and anger toward police officers.

For these reasons, the future of community policing in disadvantaged neighborhoods should not be built entirely on lofty assumptions about citizen mobilization and empowerment. In this context, the primary thrust of the community-oriented approach might have to be resource mobilization and skills training rather than citizen mobilization. When neighborhoods reach a certain level of decline, community mobilization will need to go beyond traditional community organizing tactics to provide needed services and opportunities for neighborhood self-improvement.

Prevention is a critical characteristic of the community policing model. Beyond policing, comprehensive community-based programs have shown considerable promise for alleviating a wide range of social problems, especially when interventions are early and intensive. The victims and perpetrators of violence are becoming younger each year, and this fact should encourage police officers to play an active role in multi-agency partnerships. Other agencies would benefit greatly from police officers' first-hand knowledge of juvenile delinquency, juvenile justice, and various street-level youth problems.

SUCCESSFUL COMMUNITY POLICING MODELS

Innovative crime control programs and reform initiatives in policing do not have a proud history. Despite some notable success stories, new programs and initiatives typically experience difficulty achieving their goals, and they are usually short-lived. Why is this? In the area of community crime prevention, research and evaluation data have demonstrated repeatedly that poor planning and weak implementation are the major culprits (Rosenbaum, 1987). Consequently, in this section we discuss several collective observations from researchers and practitioners in the field who have identified the basic ingredients needed to develop and maintain successful community-based programs (Lavrakas & Bennett, 1988). These ingredients can be viewed as stages in the process of problem definition, and program development, implementation, and evaluation. With the growth in community policing efforts, more law enforcement agencies and community organizations are learning the importance of achieving success at each stage in the process.

Problem Definition

Co-production initiatives should not be developed until the nature and extent of the target problems are understood. One major reason that prepackaged programs do not work as often as expected is that, without modification, they are not directly applicable to the particular problems and concerns of a community. Thus, one early step is to define the problem, and this can be accomplished through a variety of information gathering strategies, including surveys, key-person interviews, community meetings, public hearings, analyses of police data, and other approaches.

The persons and organizations that should be involved in the process of problem definition and program development must be identified. To use an example from the area of drug abuse prevention, the International Association of Chiefs of Police (IACP) (1988) has recommended the formation of a Community Task Force that includes, but is not necessarily limited to the following:

> Local government officials representing all legitimate political parties
> (drug use is not a partisan issue), school superintendent(s), selected
> business leaders, medical and mental health practitioners, pharmacists,
> religious leaders, treatment providers, social services administrators,

media management, civic and service group representatives (Rotary, Kiwanis, Lions, and others), parent groups, and neighborhood organizations. (p. 38)

Groups of this type can serve as the primary program planning vehicle. Formal surveys of the entire community or specific target groups can be extremely informative for problem definition, and, often, the results can be used as baseline data for program evaluation. In the drug abuse example, survey data might be collected about drug use among school-age children and on community priorities relative to the drug problem. In the 1980s, police departments in Evanston, Illinois, and Albuquerque, New Mexico, were models of how law enforcement agencies can work with local universities to seek community input in planning community crime prevention programs. Today, the National Institute of Justice encourages police-university partnerships through a specially funded program.

When defining the problem, planners must be careful to seek the input of all interested parties and stakeholders. Planning a co-production initiative is, almost by definition, a political process in which different analyses of the problem and different proposed solutions are inevitable. Not only is the inclusive approach politically astute, but it offers a more complete picture of the nature and extent of the problem.

Program Development

After the problem has been clearly defined, program components can be developed. The problem definition phase should assist the planning team in setting priorities and identifying the target group (for example, low-income areas, drug users under 18, crime victims, females, older citizens). During the program development phase, planners should set program goals, establish objectives and formulate strategies to achieve those goals, and garner the resources to implement the program. As part of this process, planners must agree on the level of program intervention (for example, community versus block versus individual versus school versus workplace) and the type of intervention (for example, directed patrol versus school curriculum versus media campaign versus training programs). This effort should result in an action plan that specifies what the group is planning to do and who is assigned responsibility for completing each task. For example, the Regional Drug Initiative in Portland, Oregon, has been cited as an exemplary comprehensive antidrug program because the participants developed a five-year action plan with clearly stated program goals and objectives, first year priorities, implementation steps, and evaluation criteria.

Two points should be emphasized: First, comprehensive programs are more likely to have an impact on crime problems than are single-strategy interventions (Rosenbaum, 1986). Second, given this fact, one primary objective of the planning committee should be to identify the persons, agencies, and organizations that can carry out the various tasks identified in the action plan. An assessment of current resources and responses to the problem is an integral part of this activity.

Program Implementation and Maintenance

After roles and responsibilities have been assigned, the program components can be implemented. Programs or interventions in practice rarely look anything like programs or interventions on paper. Most programs are implemented with less intensity, consistency, and resources than originally planned. Planners should be aware of this problem in advance and make a special effort to monitor the implementation process and hold people accountable for their respective contributions.

In the field of community policing, one of the biggest problems is encouraging and sustaining adequate levels of citizen participation. Many strategies have been proposed to ensure the continuity of voluntary citizen action, including the use of existing grassroots organizations, consistent opportunities to participate, technical assistance, training, strong leadership, input into the planning process, links to outside resources, a comprehensive agenda, and rewards for individual contributions.

Evaluation and Feedback

The success of innovative co-production efforts will depend largely on whether the processes and effects of these initiatives can be carefully documented through evaluation research. Without this documentation, police executives and their co-production partners will be asking funding agencies and other interested parties to rely solely on anecdotal evidence when it comes to describing program success.

Evaluations can be useful at all stages of program development and implementation. They can help determine the problem, the target population or area, and the most appropriate interventions for creating changes. Evaluations can also help administrators document how the program was implemented and what resources were employed. Deviations from the original action plan can be noted, and feedback can be provided to program administrators so that modifications can be introduced if necessary. In addition, evaluations can help determine whether the program has been effective in meeting its goals and whether it was worth the cost.

Although evaluations of co-production initiatives are important, several caveats must be addressed. First, sound evaluations require special skills, and therefore, the individuals involved in planning and implementing programs should seek assistance from professional researchers. Second, all persons with an interest or stake in the results should have an opportunity to comment on the evaluation plans (for example, what goals and objectives are being used as the criteria for success?). Third, the planning team should establish realistic goals for the program; otherwise, they are inviting failure. Fourth, researchers should employ outcome measures and research designs that are consonant with the goals of the program and are methodologically sound. Finally, evaluators should be aware of the major issues and problems in conducting evaluations in this field (Lurigio & Rosenbaum, 1986). These include possible displacement of crime rather than actual crime prevention, overreliance on unreliable police data, overly narrow criteria for success, failure to select proper control groups, and an inability to examine program effects beyond 12 to 18 months. None of these issues, however, should dissuade program advocates from supporting evaluations that can yield valuable evidence about the costs and benefits of programs. Different types of evaluations can serve different purposes, and each can provide useful information about the co-production of public safety.

CURRENT TRENDS AND ISSUES IN COMMUNITY POLICING

Since 1994, with the passage of the new Crime Act, the implementation of community policing in the United States has rapidly accelerated in thousands of communities, large and small. Not only does the Crime Act include plans for adding 100,000 new police officers on the street but to do so within a community policing framework. Hence, community policing has now been around long enough for us to begin to see a fair amount of reexamination, redefinition, and, to some extent, retrenchment in law enforcement circles. The early 1990s was a period of optimism and hope regarding community policing. Although much of this sentiment has continued, the second half of the decade has been a period of challenges and a recognition of real obstacles to this reform process. Hence, we close this chapter with our own observations from the field that have unearthed a few trends and issues in community policing that deserve further attention.

Realistic Time Frames for Reform

We have already reviewed the obstacles to reengineering police organizations so that they are more responsive to the community policing model. What we have not mentioned is the problem of time frame and the reluctance of police executives to push the reform agenda. Introducing new programs and practices in policing can be done fairly quickly and with apparent success, but making the *organizational* changes needed to sustain and institutionalize these initiatives can require 5 to 10 years, depending on the size of the organization. This conclusion is based on solid, long-term observations of police agencies in which planning teams have been working intensively and consistently for at least 5 years and, despite considerable progress, feel there is much work yet to be done (Wilkinson, Rosenbaum, Hanson, Stemen, Allen, & Roussos, 1997; Wilkinson, Rosenbaum, Hanson, Stemen, Allen, & Kaminska-Costello,

1997). Combine this with the short tenure of most police chiefs, and the reader can understand why the current trend for many police departments is to make only *cosmetic changes* in the name of community policing, while leaving the more difficult tasks (which often involve challenging the status quo) to someone else. Until police executives are given more job security, and until police unions become either less powerful or more flexible, our expectations for real organizational reform should remain low.

A Concern with Labels

We have noticed that some police administrators are struggling to find labels other than "community policing" to describe what they are doing, believing that this terminology carries too much connotative baggage. For some police chiefs, community policing is a public relations gimmick with no real substance. Others, seeing themselves as trend setters, believe that community policing is a trend that is now "passé." The true motives behind these aversions to the label are diverse. Some police executives are genuinely committed to reforming the police role and believe that community policing is developing a bad reputation as "do nothing" or "public relations" policing. Many of these executives prefer a more active and less ambiguous label for police activity that includes the phrase "problem solving" or "problem oriented" policing. Others are inclined to attack the term "community policing" (and the entire movement) as a diversionary tactic to avoid change altogether. They are hoping that others will join their quiet efforts to maintain the status quo by criticizing this latest "fad."

Implicit in most of these recent attempts to avoid the "community policing" label is a shared recognition that the term "community," when used in the context of policing, is problematic. Regardless of their motives, there is little question about the truth of this assertion. Practitioners and researchers alike have discovered that the "community" cannot be easily defined as a single, unidimensional, or monolithic social group. More often, there are many "communities of interest" within a single neighborhood. This problem does not, however, justify abandoning the concept of engaging with the community and hiding behind police-driven "POP" projects.

We believe strongly that the concept of community must be retained in this dialogue about policing because it embodies the key obstacles to the reform process—obstacles that the community policing movement has yet to define or address adequately. Above all, there is the fundamental problem of poor police-community relations, especially in minority communities. Essentially, a long history of negative contacts between the police and local residents in high-crime neighborhoods has placed a firm upper limit on police capacity to build strong and lasting partnerships with the community in the battle against crime, disorder, and drug abuse. Whether community policing strategies will overcome this problem *or* be overcome by it remains to be seen.

Zero-Tolerance Policing

The second trend is a concerted effort to operationally define community policing by aggressive enforcement tactics. This new emphasis follows somewhat directly from the Broken Windows theory, articulated earlier, which provides a justification for the renewed attention to policing incivilities and disorders (Kelling & Coles, 1996; Rosenbaum, 1998; Skogan, 1990). Not only do local residents want more attention paid to the problems of physical and social disorder, but the Broken Windows model also suggests that such attention will help prevent more serious crimes. Furthermore, responding to critics who say that community policing is "soft on crime," advocates of community policing have endorsed these increasingly popular enforcement and prevention tactics as a means of solving neighborhood problems.

Unfortunately, the process of translating theory into practice has created some distortion and miscommunication. Under the auspices of community policing, American police agencies are adopting what is called "zero tolerance" policing whereby officers are encouraged to make arrests for minor violations of traffic laws, city ordinances, and misdemeanors, regardless of local public sentiment. The problem is that enforcement activities have escalated, and some officers on the street have taken this approach too far, seeing themselves as combatants in a warlike setting. Police administrators want zero-tolerance within reason and within the confines of the law but, by the time the message reaches the street, some officers have translated it to mean "do whatever it takes." New York City is a prime example of community policing gone awry. According to the New York City Police Department, the precipitous 34 percent drop in the crime rate between 1991 and 1995 is due to aggressive order maintenance activities by police officers. But critics argue that this policy is to blame for police brutality, including the widely publicized, alleged torture of a Haitian immigrant in August 1997 by two New York City police officers (Goozner, 1997).

Although the extent of police brutality nationwide cannot be documented because of inadequate statistics, critics argue that zero tolerance policing and popular code enforcement tactics are insensitive to the true needs of poor and minority communities (which are the primary targets of these actions) and create an "us-versus-them" mentality (see Autrey, 1997; Lacayo, 1997). Poor, minority communities are the most inclined (despite what experts might think) to demand aggressive enforcement in violation of civil liberties (see Rosenbaum, 1993), and they are also the most likely to complain about it and dislike the police as a result. Thus, enforcement is not a simple yes–no option. It requires careful planning, the consent of the public, solid working relationships built on trust, a role for the community whenever possible, and the thoughtful exercise of police discretion.

In our modern media-dominated environment, the public is very sensitive to the issue of police misconduct. Documented cases of gross abuses of authority are rare. There can be little doubt, however, that misconduct in any city, in any neighborhood, derails efforts to build partnerships between the police and the communities they serve. (We only need to look at the effect of the Rodney King incident to understand this point.) The persistent historical problem of police corruption or unethical behavior undermines attempts to create new relationships with community residents. Recently, crooked cops have been indicted in New Orleans, Philadelphia, Chicago, and other big cities. When police officers plant or sell drugs, order executions, beat and rob citizens, and lie on the witness stand, the public trust can be severely damaged for a long time. Although these bad cops are very much the exception rather than the rule, their unethical behavior casts a large shadow over the entire police force. Hence, we can begin to see why the "community" component of community policing involves more than simply "solving problems." The major problem to be solved is one of mutual trust and respect between the police and citizenry.

Historically, specially appointed commissions have found evidence of police misconduct and have called for the dismissal of culpable staff. However, community policing as a reform movement should recognize that police corruption and abuses of authority on the street are systemic and organizational in nature rather than the result of a few "rotten apples." Joseph D. McNamara described the problem this way as it applies to zero-tolerance for disorder:

> During my years as a police chief, I found that police misconduct often had its roots in subtle indications by supervisors to officers that the sort of "extralegal" tactics common to quality-of-life policing were acceptable. Cops in minority neighborhoods would detain, question and push around people on the street without reason. If a young man asserted his legal right to leave, cops "kicked ass." Inevitably a number of officers felt justified in using illegal and at times fatal force. It was constantly necessary to emphasize to the officers that we were peace officers, servants of the community—not soldiers in a war against crime and drugs. (*Time Magazine*, September 1, 1997, p. 29)

McNamara implies that organizational climate and leadership are critical determinants of police behavior on the street. The organization communicates the message of what is acceptable behavior. Furthermore, police personnel who are prone to abuse authority (and this is a small percentage) will feel the freedom to do so in the absence of good supervision. Thus, to the extent that community policing becomes operationally defined as zero-tolerance policing with maximum discretion and little supervision or training, we can expect more problems in the future.

The most unfortunate outcome of this scenario is that a *single* incident in the community (for example, a shooting or abuse by one officer) can completely destroy years of progress toward community policing. By the mid 1990s, we had learned the hard way that community policing is still a very fragile and easily frustrated experiment. This instability is primarily caused by a fundamentally weak partnership with the community, typically defined by a long history of antagonistic relationships between the police and minority communities.

Finally, the debate about zero-tolerance policing has another dimension: whether aggressive police and government intervention in poor neighborhoods is helpful or harmful in empowering the community. Can aggressive policing (including the popular code enforcement tactics) serve as a substitute for self-regulating, neighborhood-based problem solving, or is it the first (and necessary) step in putting a community back on its feet? More research is needed before this question can be answered properly.

Problem-Oriented Policing (POP) Projects

Some agencies are running away from community policing and into the open arms of problem-oriented policing (POP). Although the theoretical framework of problem solving is attractive, we are beginning to see the limitations of this approach as widespread implementation occurs. These limitations include (1) the tendency to identify and solve simple (and not terribly important) problems and to avoid larger or more complex issues that, if addressed, might produce lasting results; (2) the tendency to remove problem offenders from one location (for example, prostitutes, drug dealers) without accepting responsibility for whether they are being displaced into other neighborhoods; (3) the growing tendency to rely on directed patrol as the primary problem solving strategy; and (4) insensitivity to the community at different stages of a problem-solving initiative.

Certainly, nothing is inherently wrong with using directed patrol of specific areas as a problem solving strategy (indeed, in many cases it is highly effective), but this should not become the only or primary tool of the police. In many cities, we have observed very creative problem-solving initiatives that involve the community, social service agencies, and other government units in collaborative partnerships. POP projects can vary in size and complexity, including the amount of time, the levels of police expertise and authority, the number of agencies required to adequately address the problem, and the perceived importance or severity of the problem being attacked. To truly implement community policing, police organizations must be willing to invest the time, skills, and imagination of their employees to take problem solving to the next level.

Police will also need to become increasingly sophisticated about working with the community to identify and define problems properly before any intervention. POP, without community input at *all* stages, will be limited at best and problematic at worst. Chicago is a fine example of how things can go awry. Despite an exemplary record on community policing in recent years (see Skogan & Hartnett, 1997), the identification stage of a problem-solving model backfired in the Latino neighborhood of Pilsen when a well-intended police memo described the entire community as prone to domestic violence, public drinking, public urination, and other problems (for example, "Hispanic men still think that the way to control their family members and spouses is to strike the other person."). This unprofessional memo, lacking all the necessary qualifiers, created community outrage and produced an immediate apology from Mayor Daley (Mills & Puente, 1997). Community input in defining local problems and in crafting such documents can help prevent this type of damage to police-community relations.

The Limits of Police Responsibility

The community policing movement has forced a reexamination and expansion of the role of police in society. With the failure of other institutions to fulfill their roles as protective forces against crime and neighborhood decline, the police (not unlike public schools) are being asked to take on greater responsibilities under the umbrella of community policing. Some police agencies have willingly done so, defining virtually everything as police work; others have refused and have retrenched into more traditional policing; still others have accepted the role that we have outlined in this chapter, with police serving as facilitators and coordinators of reform, working to leverage a wide range of resources to address neighborhood problems, and educating others regarding their crime prevention responsibilities.

Regardless of the merits of adding new roles and responsibilities to the police, unless police organizations can do a better job of managing traditional calls for service, there will always be a crisis about inadequate police resources. Whether the hiring and redeployment under the federal COPS grants will make a difference has yet to be determined. In any case, this national program should be viewed as only a temporary solution to persistent problems. Police, with community input, must decide what is important and what is not, both short-term and long-term, to allocate more efficiently and effectively what will always be perceived as inadequate money and staffing.

Finally, the issue of rethinking and reprioritizing the roles and responsibilities of the police can be defined by who or what is truly responsible for community crime rates. As we discuss in the final chapter, it is unclear how much police (or community groups for that matter) can do to have a *lasting* impact on the quality of neighborhood life, given the complex social and macrolevel economic forces behind the crime problem. Nevertheless, we can predict that our society will try, with unusual intensity, to define the proper role of police in society over the next decade. Without a doubt, the community policing movement and the COPS program has turned the spotlight on this question.

In summary, many federal, state, and local governments have invested heavily in community policing. The road to full-scale implementation has been rocky in recent years as thousands of agencies have struggled to redefine and repackage community policing to make it acceptable to the rank-and-file officers and to local communities. With the rise of zero-tolerance policing and the continuation of an aggressive drug war, community policing has become trapped in the crossfire. We believe that the road to successful implementation lies not in running away from the concept of "community" but in embracing it, studying it, understanding it, and responding to it appropriately. Without community support and the formation of true partnerships, community policing and true problem solving will be "history." Ongoing training and education programs for police and community leaders are absolutely critical to the success of community policing. The regional community policing institutes funded by the COPS office should play an important role in the institutionalization of cutting-edge education and training.

REFERENCES

Autrey, J. (1997, September 21). Can tough love mend a faltering neighborhood? *The Fort Worth Star*, News Sec., p. 1, Sunday Arlington AM ed.

Bayley, D. H. (1988). Community policing: A report from the devil's advocate. In J. R. Greene & S. D. Mastrofski (eds.), *Community policing: Rhetoric or reality?* (pp. 225–238). New York: Praeger.

Bernard, B. (1990). An overview of community-based prevention. In K. H. Ref, C. L. Faegre, & P. Lowery (eds.), *Prevention research findings* (pp. 126–147). Office of Substance Abuse Prevention Monograph 3. DHHS Pub. No. (ADM) 89–1615. Washington, DC: Office of Substance Abuse.

Buerger, M. (1994). The limits of community. In D. P. Rosenbaum (ed.) *The challenge of community policing: Testing the promises.* (pp. 270–273). Newbury Park, CA: Sage.

Bursik, R. J., & Grasmick, H. G. (1993). *Neighborhoods and crime: The dimensions of effective community control.* New York: Lexington.

Capowich, G. E., & Roehl, J. A. (1994). Problem-oriented policing: Actions and effectiveness in San Diego. In D. P. Rosenbaum (ed.), *The challenge of community policing: Testing the promises* (pp. 127–146). Thousand Oaks, CA: Sage.

Clarke, R. (ed.). (1992). *Crime prevention studies* (Vol. 2). Monsey, NY: Criminal Justice Press.

Community Policing Consortium. (1997). *Community policing exchange—tactical programs II: Youth initiatives.* Washington, DC.

Cook, R. F., & Roehl, J. A. (1993). National evaluation of the Community Partnership Program: Preliminary findings. In R. C. Davis, A. J. Lurigio, & D. P. Rosenbaum (eds.), *Drugs and the Community* (pp. 225–250). Springfield, IL: Charles C. Thomas.

DuBow, F., McCabe, E., & Kaplan, G. (1979). *Reactions to crime: A critical review of the literature.* Washington, DC: U.S. Department of Justice, National Institute of Justice.

Eck, J. E., & Rosenbaum, D. P. (1994). The new police order: Effectiveness, equity, and efficiency in community policing. In D. P. Rosenbaum (ed.), *The challenge of community policing: Testing the promises* (pp. 2–23). Newbury Park, CA: Sage.

Eck, J. E., & Spelman, W. (1987). *Problem solving: Problem-oriented policing in Newport News.* Washington, DC: Police Executive Research Forum.

Florin, P., Chavis, D., Wandersman, A., & Rich, R. (1992). A systems approach to understanding and enhancing grassroots organizations: The Block Booster Project. In H. E. Levine & R. L. Fitzgerald (eds.), *Analysis of dynamic psychological systems* (pp. 215–243). New York: Plenum.

Friedman, W. (1994). The community role in community policing. In D. P. Rosenbaum (ed.) *The challenge of community policing: Testing the promises.* (pp. 263–269). Newbury Park, CA: Sage.

Goldstein, H. (1990). *Problem-oriented policing.* New York: McGraw Hill.

Goldstein, H. (1993, August 24). *The new policing: Confronting complexity.* Paper delivered at the Conference on Community Policing, National Institute of Justice, Washington, DC.

Goozner, M. (1997, August 16). NYC cut in crime has brutish side. *Chicago Tribune*, Sec. 1, p. 1.

Greene, J. R., Bergman, W. T., & McLaughlin, E. J. (1994). Implementing community policing: Cultural and structural change in police organizations. In D. P. Rosenbaum (ed.), *The challenge of community policing: Testing the promises* (pp. 92–109). Newbury Park, CA: Sage.

Greene, J. R., & Mastrofski, S. D. (eds.). (1988). *Community policing: Rhetoric or reality?* New York: Praeger.

Grinc, R. M. (1994). Angels in marble: Problems in stimulating community involvement in community policing. *Crime and Delinquency* 40, 437–468.

Hope, T. J. (1994). Problem-oriented policing and drug market locations: Three case studies. In R. V. Clarke (ed.), *Crime prevention studies* (pp. 5–31). Monsey, NY: Criminal Justice Press.

International Association of Chiefs of Police. (1988). *Reducing crime by reducing drug abuse: A manual for police chiefs and sheriffs*. Washington, DC.

Jacobs, J. (1961). *The death and life of great American cities*. New York: Vintage.

Johnson, B. D., Williams, T., Dei, K. A., & Sanabria, H. (1990). Drug abuse in the inner city: Impact on hard-core users and the community. In M. Tonry & J. Q. Wilson (eds.), *Drugs and crime* (pp. 9–67). Chicago: University of Chicago.

Kelling, G. L. (1988). Police and communities: The quiet revolution. *Perspectives on policing*. Washington, DC: National Institute of Justice.

Kelling, G. L., & Coles, C. M. (1996). *Fixing broken windows*. New York: Free Press.

Kelling, G. L., & Moore, M. H. (1988). From political to reform to community: The evolving strategy of police. In J. R. Greene & S. D. Mastrofski

(eds.), *Community policing: Rhetoric or reality?* (pp. 3–26). New York: Praeger.

Kelling, G. L., Rocheleau, A. M., Rosenbaum, D. P., Roth, J. A., Skogan, W. G., & Walsh, N. (1997). *Preliminary cross-site analysis of the Bureau of Justice Assistance Comprehensive Communities Program*. Final report to the National Institute of Justice. Cambridge, MA: BOTEC Analysis Corporation.

Klitzner, M. (1993). A public/dynamic systems approach to community-wide alcohol and other drug initiatives. In R. C. Davis, A. J. Lurigio, & D. P. Rosenbaum (eds.), *Drugs and the community* (pp. 201–224). Springfield, IL: Charles C. Thomas.

Klockars, C. B. (1988). The rhetoric of community policing. In J. R. Green & S. D. Mastrofski (eds.), *Community policing: Rhetoric or reality?* (pp. 239–258). New York: Praeger.

Lab, S. (1988). *Crime prevention: Approaches, practices and evaluations*. Cincinnati: Anderson.

Lacayo, R. (1997). Good cop, bad cop. *Time Magazine* (September 1).

Lavrakas, P. J. (1985). Citizen self-help and neighborhood crime prevention policy. In L. A. Curtis (ed.), *American violence and public policy* (pp. 94–113). New Haven, CT: Yale University Press.

Lavrakas, P. J., & Bennett, S. F. (1988). Thinking about the implementation of citizen and community anti-crime measures. In T. Hope & M. Shaw (eds.), *Communities and crime* (pp. 221–234). London: Her Majesty's Stationery Office.

Lewis, D. L., & Salem, G. (1986). *Fear of crime: Incivility and the production of a social problem*. New Brunswick, NJ: Transaction.

Lurigio, A. J., & Rosenbaum, D. P. (1984). The impact of community policing on police personnel: A review of the literature. In D. P. Rosenbaum (ed.), *The challenge of community policing: Testing the premises* (pp. 147–166). Thousand Oaks, CA: Sage.

Lurigio, A. J., & Rosenbaum, D. P. (1986). Evaluation research in community crime prevention: A critical look at the field. In D. P. Rosenbaum, *Community crime prevention: Does it work?* (pp. 19–45). Beverly Hills, CA: Sage.

Lyons, B. (1995, June 1–4). *Responsiveness and reciprocity: Community policing in southeast Seattle.* Paper presented at the 1995 Annual Meetings of the Law and Society Association, Toronto, Canada. Seattle, WA: University of Washington Department of Political Science.

Manning, P. K. (1988). Community policing as a drama of control. In J. R. Greene & S. D. Mastrofski (eds.), *Community policing: Rhetoric or reality?* (pp. 27–46). New York: Praeger.

Mastrofski, S. D. (1988). Community policing as reform: A cautionary tale. In J. R. Greene & S. D. Mastrofski (eds.), *Community policing: Rhetoric or reality?* (pp. 47–68). New York: Praeger.

McElroy, J. E., Cosgrove, C. A., & Sadd, S. (1993). *Community policing: The CPOP in New York.* Newbury Park, CA: Sage.

McNamara, J. D. (1997). A veteran chief: Too many cops think it's a war. *Time Magazine* (September 1), 28–29.

Mills, S., & Puente, T. (1997,). Policing strategy memo backfires in Pilsen. *Chicago Tribune* (September 18), Sec. 1, p. 1.

Moore, M. H., & Trojanowicz, R. C. (1988). *Policing and the fear of crime* (Perspectives on Policing, No. 3). Washington, DC: National Institute of Justice and Harvard University.

Murphy, C., & Muir, G. (1984). *Community-based policing: A review of the critical issues.* Ottawa: Solicitor General of Canada.

Pate, A. M., Wycoff, M. A., Skogan, W. G., & Sherman, L. W. (1986). *Reducing fear of crime in Houston and Newark: A summary report.* Washington, DC: Police Foundation.

Pentz, M. A., Dwyer, J. H., MacKinnon, D. P., Flay, B. R., Hansen, W. B., Wang, E. Y., & Johnson, C. A. (1989). A multicommunity trial for primary prevention of adolescent drug abuse. *Journal of the American Medical Association* 261, 3259–3266.

Prestby, J. E., & Wandersman, A. (1985). An empirical exploration of a framework of organizational viability: Maintaining block organizations. *Journal of Applied Behavior Science* 21, 287–305.

Reaves, B. A. (1992). *Law enforcement management and administrative statistics, 1990: Data for individual state and local agencies with 100 or more officers.* (NCJ-134436). Washington, DC: U.S. Department of Justice, Bureau of Justice Statistics.

Reiss, A. J. (1986). Why are communities important in understanding crime? In A. J. Reiss & M. Tonry (eds.), *Communities and crime* (pp. 1–34). Chicago: University of Chicago Press.

Rosenbaum, D. P. (ed.). (1986). *Community crime prevention: Does it work?* Beverly Hills, CA: Sage.

Rosenbaum, D. P. (1987). The theory and research beyond neighborhood watch: Is it a sound fear and crime reduction strategy? *Crime and Delinquency* 33, 103–134.

Rosenbaum, D. P. (1988). Community crime prevention: A review and synthesis of the literature. *Justice Quarterly* 5, 323–395.

Rosenbaum, D. P. (ed.). (1994). *The challenge of community policing: Testing the promises.* Newbury Park, CA: Sage.

Rosenbaum, D. P. (1993). Civil liberties and aggressive enforcement: Balancing the rights of individuals and society in the drug war. In R. C. Davis, A. J. Lurigio, & D. P. Rosenbaum (eds.), *Drugs and Community* (pp. 55–82). Springfield, IL: Charles C. Thomas.

Rosenbaum, D. P. (1998, in press). The changing role of the police in North America: Assessing the current transition to community policing. In J. P.

Brodeur & B. Leighton (eds.) *Evaluating the delivery of police services*. Newbury Park, CA: Sage.

Rosenbaum, D. P., & Heath, L. (1990). The psycho-logic of fear reduction and crime prevention programs. In J. Edwards, E. Posavac, S. Tindale, F. Bryant, & L. Heath (eds.), *Applied social psychology annual* (pp. 18–34). New York: Plenum.

Rosenbaum, D. P., Hernandez, E., & Daughtry, S., Jr. (1991). Crime prevention, fear reduction, and the community. In W. A. Geller (ed.), *Local government police management* (Golden Anniversary Ed., pp. 96–130). Washington, DC: International City Management Association.

Rosenbaum, D. P., Bennett, S., Lindsay, B., & Wilkinson, D. L. (1994a). *Community responses to drug abuse: A program evaluation*. Washington, DC: National Institute of Justice.

Rosenbaum, D. P., Yeh, S., & Wilkinson, D. L. (1994b). Impact of community policing on police personnel: A quasi-experimental test. *Crime and Delinquency* 40, 331–353.

Sadd, S., & Grinc, R. (1994). Innovative neighborhood oriented policing: An evaluation of community policing programs in eight cities. In D. P. Rosenbaum (ed.), *The challenge of community policing: Testing the promises* (pp. 27–52). Newbury Park, CA: Sage.

Shea, S., & Basch, C. E. (1990). A review of five major community-based cardiovascular disease prevention programs. Part I: Rationale, design, and theoretical framework. *American Journal of Health Promotion* 4, 202–213.

Skogan, W. G. (1990). *Disorder and community decline: Crime and the spiral of decay in American neighborhoods*. New York: Free Press.

Skogan, W. G. (1994). The impact of community policing on neighborhood residents: A cross-site analysis. In D. P. Rosenbaum (ed.), *The challenge of community policing: Testing the promises* (pp. 167–181). Newbury Park, CA: Sage.

Skogan, W. G. (1995). *Community participation and community policing*. Evanston, IL: Police Evaluation Consortium, Center for Urban Affairs and Policy Research, Northwestern University.

Skogan, W. G., & Hartnett, S. M. (1997). *Community policing, Chicago Style*. New York: Oxford University Press.

Skogan, W. G., Hartnett, S. M., Lovig, J. H., DuBois, J., Houmes, S., Davidsdottir, S., Van Stedum, R., Kaiser, M., Cole, D., Gonzalez, N., Bennett, S. F., Lavrakas, P. J., Lurigio, A. J., Block, R. L., Rosenbaum, D. P., Althaus, S., Whelan, D., Johnson, T. R., & Higgins, L. (1995). *Community policing in Chicago, year two: An interim report*. Chicago: Illinois Criminal Justice Information Authority.

Skolnick, J., & Bayley, D. H. (1986). *The new blue line: Police innovations in six American cities*. New York: Free Press.

Sparrow, M. K., Moore, M. H., & Kennedy, D. M. (1990). *Beyond 911: A new era for policing*. New York: Basic Books.

Taylor, R. B. (1997). *Crime and place: What we know, what we can prevent, and what else we need to know*. Paper presented at the National Institute of Justice's Annual Research and Evaluation Conference, Washington, DC, July.

Toch, H., & Grant, J. D. (1991). *Police as problem solvers*. New York: Plenum.

Trojanowicz, R. C., & Bucqueroux, B. (1989). *Community policing: A contemporary perspective*. Cincinnati: Anderson.

Wilkinson, D., & Rosenbaum, D. P. (1994). The effects of organizational structure on community policing: A comparison of two cities. In D. P. Rosenbaum (ed.), *The challenge of community policing: Testing the promises* (pp. 110–126). Newbury Park, CA: Sage.

Wilkinson, D. L., Rosenbaum, D. P., Hanson, G. S., Stemen, D. D., Allen, M. E., & Roussos, K. (1997). *Community policing in Aurora: Results of a longitudinal evaluation*. Draft final report. Chicago: Center for Research in Law and Justice, University of Illinois at Chicago.

Wilkinson, D. L., Rosenbaum, D. P., Hanson, G. S., Stemen, D. D., Allen, M. E., & Kaminska-Costello, S. (1997). *Community Policing in Joliet: Results of a Longitudinal Evaluation*. Draft final report. Chicago: Center for Research in Law and Justice, University of Illinois at Chicago.

Wilson, J. Q., & Kelling, G. (1982). Broken windows. *Atlantic Monthly* (March), 29–38.

Wycoff, M. A., & Skogan, W. G. (1994). The effect of a community policing management style on officers' attitudes. *Crime and Delinquency* 40, 371–383.

Yin, R. K. (1979). *What is citizen crime prevention?* In *Review of criminal justice evaluation: 1978*. Washington, DC: Law Enforcement Assistance Administration.

10

✪

Strengthening Community Through Youth and Family Initiatives

The Social Prevention Model

The field of crime prevention (both practice and research) has been domi-
nated by opportunity reduction and victimization prevention approaches,
as illustrated throughout this book. These strategies for reducing criminal opportunities and protecting oneself (and loved ones) from victimization do not
address the individual's predisposition to engage in criminal behavior, nor do
they consider the larger social and economic conditions that contribute indirectly to criminality and drug abuse.

The "missing perspective" in the United States has been the "social problems" or "social prevention" model (see Bennett & Lavrakas, 1988; 1989;
Bright, 1992; Curtis, 1987; Hope, 1995; Rosenbaum, 1988a). This approach
to crime prevention, grounded in the 1960s war on poverty, has been pushed
ahead by a history of social prevention initiatives in Europe and Canada (see
Graham, 1990; Waller, 1988) and by the growing magnitude of youth problems in the United States. The social crime prevention model gives much-
needed attention to the "root causes" of crime, especially the forces that
contribute to delinquency, drug abuse, and a host of related adolescent problems. Based on the premise that crime is caused by the social ills of society, the
social crime prevention model focuses on developing programs and policies to
improve the health, family life, education, housing, work opportunities, and
neighborhood activities of potential offenders. Furthermore, recognizing the
cost-effectiveness of early detection and intervention, most of these crime
prevention initiatives focus on youth, targeting those individuals, neighborhoods, and families with the greatest risk of offending.

In this chapter, we will review some key initiatives in the area of social crime prevention, but with the understanding that this is a vast, loosely defined terrain without clear-cut boundaries. Hence, we will focus on social interventions at the level of early family supports, preschool education, community organizing, and youth employment.

The practical importance of this perspective to the crime prevention field should be clearly established from the start. In her book *Adolescents at Risk*, Dryfoos (1990) estimated that approximately 1-in-4 American youth (that is, seven million "high-risk" kids) will reach adulthood without the necessary skills to function in the workplace, in family life, and in other areas of societal responsibility. Another seven million run a "moderate risk" of not leading productive lives. Although we could debate the accuracy of these figures, the important fact today is that, on the road of human development, "at-risk" individuals are likely to experience a number of problems, including a higher-than-average risk of delinquency, teen pregnancy, substance abuse, and school failure. These problems, in turn, are likely to be caused by a host of earlier factors associated with living in neighborhoods of concentrated poverty— poor nutrition, poor health services, lack of parental support and supervision, child abuse, family violence, inadequate preschool and primary education, negative peer influences, and lack of community supports.

Schorr articulates society's stake in correcting this situation:

> High rates of violent juvenile crime, school failure, and adolescent child-bearing add up to an enormous public burden, as well as widespread private pain. Our common stake in preventing these damaging outcomes of adolescence is immense. We all pay to support the unproductive and incarcerate the violent. We are all economically weakened by lost productivity. We all live with fear of crime in our homes and on the streets. We are all diminished when large numbers of parents are incapable of nurturing their dependent young, and when pervasive alienation erodes the national sense of community. (1988, p. xix)

THEORETICAL AND EMPIRICAL RATIONALE

The scholarly basis for the social crime prevention model can be extracted from extensive literatures on juvenile delinquency and gangs (for reviews, see Klein, 1995; Spergel, 1995). After many decades of empirical work, criminologists in the second half of this century began to construct individual, social-structural, and social-process theories to explain criminality and delinquency (for an introductory overview, see Bartollas, 1993; Reid, 1988). The social crime prevention approach is not grounded in a single theory of crime but is consistent with several approaches that have received heightened attention recently, including developmental and social control theories. The developmental and life-course approaches, which are supported by careful longitudinal research, attempt to understand how criminality and delinquency evolve from childhood to adulthood (see Loeber & LeBlanc, 1990; Tonry, Ohlin, & Farrington, 1991; Tremblay & Craig, 1995). These approaches bring needed attention to critical childhood events and decisions that shape antisocial behavior during adolescence and adulthood and underscore (indirectly) the importance of early intervention with high-risk youth before any contact with the criminal justice system. The developmental and life course studies, along with traditional research on juvenile delinquency, remind us that crime is largely a *youth* problem. Indeed, considerable data support the age-crime curve, which shows "on average, rates of offending rise rather rapidly during early adolescence, reach a peak in the late teenage years, and then begin a gradual but steady decline thereafter" (Nagin, Farrington, & Moffitt, 1995, p. 112).[1]

A wide range of delinquency studies over the years (especially those stemming from the social control paradigm) have been able to identify the precursors to individual delinquent behaviors (for example, Gottfredson & Hirschi, 1990; Hirschi, 1969). Similarly, neighborhood and community studies have identified social and structural variables that contribute to differences in community-level crime rates (see Bursik & Grasmick, 1993; Sampson, 1986; Wilson, 1987). Collectively, this work and that of developmental criminologists has allowed researchers to systematically inventory the risk factors associated with delinquency, which, in turn, has led to more scientific approaches to the development of risk-focused prevention programs that target individuals, families, schools, and communities (for example, Hawkins & Catalano, 1992). We review only a few of the relevant interventions, many of which were introduced before this theorizing and empirical research but that, on closer scrutiny, continue to hold promise for preventing crime.

FAMILY SUPPORT SERVICES

A broad range of research indicates that disadvantaged families run a high risk of having offspring with multiple problems. Teen pregnancy and childbearing are particularly acute problems in the United States; rates are substantially higher than those in other industrialized nations (Jones et al., 1987; McElroy & Moore, 1997). The consequences of early births are severe and long-lasting (Furstenberg, Brooks-Gunn, & Morgan, 1987; Schorr, 1988). Unwed adolescent mothers are more likely to drop out of school, have more children, take low paying jobs, or turn to public assistance. The consequences for their children are substantial. The cycle of poverty continues into the next generation, as the offspring of young single mothers and parents living in poverty are more

---

1. We should note that although this pattern is true for most offenders, there are clearly subgroup differences in patterns of offending, with different trends (see Nagin & Land, 1993; Nagin, Farrington, & Moffit, 1995).

likely to experience low birth weight and poor nutrition, parental neglect, inconsistent discipline, poor role modeling, and unusually high levels of family discord and distress. This has led researchers to hypothesize that such children are at greater risk of learning and behavioral disorders, poor school performance, early sexual activity, and delinquency. Indeed, research is beginning to confirm these suspicions. The body of research documenting the link between early risk factors and subsequent criminality continues to grow. For example, teen motherhood not only portends an increased probability of her offending but also an increased likelihood of criminality by her offspring, especially in larger families (see Nagin, Pogarsky, & Farrington, 1997, for a review). Other studies have documented a "cycle of violence," in which abused or neglected kids are more likely to become juvenile offenders themselves (Widom, 1992). Children who show signs of criminality at a young age are more likely to become repeat, serious offenders than are youth who begin offending in their mid-teens (Farrington, 1987), and such children are likely to come from families with multiple psycho-social problems (Rutter & Giller, 1983).

Although national policy has failed to adequately address the problems of the family or the underclass, growing evidence indicates that local programs can make small inroads into these family-related problems. We will briefly review two types of family programs here: (1) support services for young or disadvantaged parents, and (2) preschool education programs. Evaluations of these interventions rarely focus on delinquency prevention effects because of the difficulties and costs associated with longitudinal research of this nature (see Tonry, Ohlin, & Farrington, 1991). More often the focus is on intermediate variables that are measurable in a shorter time frame and are known to be associated with delinquency.

Support for Young or Disadvantaged Parents

A wide variety of support services have been provided to young parents and families that are at risk of raising delinquent children. Parenthetically, it should be stated that if teenage pregnancy could be prevented, this would be the most desirable outcome for young girls who are still children themselves and are not prepared, psychologically or financially, for parenthood. Although parents and schools have been reluctant to discuss birth control and safe sex with adolescents, model school-based clinics have been successful in reducing school-age childbearing, delaying sexual activity, and helping pregnant students finish school (Zabin, Streett, Hardy, & King, 1984; Zabin, Hirsch, Smith, Streett, & Hardy, 1986).

Once a woman becomes pregnant, model programs for prenatal and infant development are designed to reduce the risk of low birth weight babies and disabilities, enhance the infant's health, and improve parenting skills. Schorr (1988) describes three successful programs serving different populations: low-income women in 13 of California's poorest counties, high school students in a Baltimore neighborhood, and adolescents in a low-income rural area in South Carolina. Each program went far beyond "routine obstetrical services" to provide social support and education for expectant mothers regarding the risks to a healthy baby from poor nutrition and drug or alcohol abuse. These programs focus on the needs of the infant, as well as on the responsibilities of parenthood.

The evaluations of prenatal and infant development programs have shown both short-term and long-term gains for the children and their parents. (Bright, 1992; Ontario Ministry of Community and Social Services, 1990; Schorr, 1988; Unger & Wandersman, 1985). Infants have generally experienced better physical health and higher birth weight, as well as fewer feeding problems, accidents, and emergency hospital visits. In some cases, long-term gains have been observed in fewer learning and behavioral problems at school and less delinquency. For parents, improved parenting skills, greater confidence in parenting, and expanded social networks were observed, among other outcomes. As Bright (1992) notes, programs with multiple components, spread over several years, are likely to have the biggest impact.

Beyond Infancy

Producing a healthy infant does not guarantee that the child will experience a normal childhood or a problem-free adolescence. All too often, family life is disrupted by economic stress and a lack of social supports, which can result in a chaotic and conflictual environment for the child. Normal psycho-social development is easily jeopardized when a child does not experience a supportive, consistent, and loving environment. Research suggests that growing up with family discord and unpredictability is a predictor of subsequent delinquency and antisocial behavior (Rutter, 1979; Widom, 1995; Wilson & Hernstein, 1985). Although the factors that contribute directly to delinquency are poorly understood, good longitudinal evidence indicates that early conduct problems—including drug use, aggression, truancy, and low educational achievement—are precursors to general delinquency; moreover, some evidence suggests that these factors also contribute to serious delinquency and recidivism (see Loeber & Stouthamer-Loeber, 1986, 1987, for reviews).

In response to this set of problems, family support programs have emerged to restore some stability and predictability to the home environment and to keep children on a normal developmental path. Bright (1992) articulates the six major policy goals of family support programs: (1) assisting families in achieving self-sufficiency, (2) assuring school readiness and success for children, (3) assisting children with special needs, (4) strengthening young families, (5) preventing child abuse and neglect, and (6) promoting maternal and infant health.

One example of a comprehensive family support program is the Beethoven Project in Chicago, supported by businessman-philanthropist Irving R. Harris and a variety of state and federal agencies under the "Ounce of Prevention" partnership. This program is located in one of Chicago's public housing projects and provides a wide range of services for pregnant women, young mothers, and children from birth to the time they enter school. Services include prenatal care, home visits, counseling, nutrition education, assistance to mothers trying to complete school or find a job, and assistance in preparing children for school (at the local Beethoven Elementary School). Readiness for school means that a child has reached the necessary levels of social, cognitive, and emotional development and is prepared to interact (and compete) on a "level playing field" with other first graders. Although some informal assessments of the Beethoven project have been conducted, we are unaware of any major evaluation of the project's impact.

One early childhood program that has been evaluated is the Children's House of the Yale Child Study Center. This small program, started in 1968, provided a wide range of services similar to the those of Beethoven Project, but for only two years after birth. Home visits were made by a pediatrician during the baby's first week, and then by a social worker, psychologist, and staff nurse twice monthly. Follow-up evaluations were conducted at 5 and 10 years after completion of the program, although the sample sizes were small. (See Seitz, Rosenbaum, & Apfel, 1985; Trickett, Apfel, Rosenbaum, & Zigler, 1981). The results were encouraging: After 10 years, almost all mothers in the program were off welfare (versus half in the control families). At the age of 13, only 28 percent of the children in the program had experienced problems with school adjustment (that is, a combined measure of test performance, absenteeism, and special services), whereas 69 percent of the matched comparison group had school adjustment problems (Seitz, Rosenbaum, & Apfel, 1985). Given the known relationship between absenteeism and delinquency, it is especially noteworthy that students in the program were absent an average of 7.3 days per year, and students in the comparison group were absent 13.3 days on average. In addition, mothers in the program were more likely to be off welfare, to have completed additional education, to have waited longer before having a second child, and to have fewer children. The comparison group was carefully matched with program participants on a number of variables and, if anything, was slightly more advantaged at the start of the program. Although these early evaluations are not scientifically compelling, they are suggestive.

In recent years, several controlled evaluations of early childhood interventions have been completed, and the results are consistently strong (for reviews, see Tremblay & Craig, 1995; Yoshikawa, 1994). One key element of program success is the home visit by social workers, psychologists, nurses, or others who provide a range of services, from social support to health tips. These outreach efforts have produced a number of positive effects, including less abuse and neglect, more responsive and attached parents, less antisocial behavior in school, improved cognitive skills, and lower arrest rates.

Parent Training for Problem Children

Brief attention should be given to parent training programs designed to help parents recognize and respond appropriately to their children's aggressive and delinquent behavior. To help solve America's crime problem, Wilson (1983) encouraged parents to pursue "child management training" to control "bratty behavior." Parenting courses teach parents how to apply rewards and punishments more consistently and less harshly, communicate in a constructive (rather than destructive) manner, resolve problems, avoid unnecessary conflicts with their children, negotiate standards of conduct, and other skills. The most widely known initiative is the Oregon Social Learning Program for parents with delinquent and aggressive children. Evaluation results indicate that aggressive behavior can be reduced for as much as one year, but the effects then dissipate (Patterson, Chamberlain, & Reid, 1982). Furthermore, the dropout rate for parents was very high (approximately half after one year), indicating that it is difficult to sustain parental motivation. Overall, the evaluation literature is more encouraging: Tremblay and Craig (1995) cite numerous studies in which parent training in school settings has reduced children's disruptive or delinquent behavior. Whether these findings can be generalized to the most difficult families in inner-city neighborhoods is uncertain.

Preschool Programs

Young children living in low-income families and troubled neighborhoods are often ill-prepared for school. Their language is less well developed than that of middle-class kids, and their motivation to achieve and self-confidence about school is often lower (Kagan, 1984). Essentially, these children begin school at a huge disadvantage, and, as we know from the delinquency literature, school failure predisposes them to a host of problems later in life. In the 1960s, educators and researchers in the United States recognized this disadvantage and sought to correct it by creating developmentally focused preschool programs. These projects variously focused on improving IQ scores, learning skills, social skills, or home environments. Their focus on educational readiness laid the foundation for the highly touted Project Head Start.

The Perry Preschool Program in Ypsilanti, Michigan, is perhaps the best example of these early programs, and one of the few that was created specifically to prevent delinquency later in life. In 1962, David Weikart, a psychologist, recruited 123 black children (ages 3 and 4) from low-income families in Ypsilanti (all families were below the poverty line). Using a randomized experimental design, children were randomly assigned to either the experimental preschool program or to the control group. The Perry Preschool lasted two-and-a-half hours per day for two school years. Some distinguishing features included a high teacher-pupil ratio (1 to 5), team teaching, weekly home visits lasting approximately one-and-a-half hours, and student participation in planning classroom activities.

Longitudinal evaluations of the Perry program have revealed some impressive results (Schweinhart & Weikart, 1983; Berrueta-Clement, Schweinhart, Barnett, Epstein, & Weikart, 1984). At the age of 19, program participants were more likely than the control group to have graduated from high school, be working, be attending college, or be receiving further training. Furthermore, the rates of arrest and teen pregnancy for Perry participants were 40 and

42 percent lower, respectively, than the control group. A cost-benefit analysis of the Perry preschool revealed that the program costs about $5,000 per child; a one-year initiative will yield $6 for every $1 invested, and a two-year program will yield approximately $3 for every $1 invested (Schweinhart, 1987).

The Perry Preschool Program and other early education initiatives provided the foundation for Project Head Start, which evolved into one of the most successful national antipoverty programs in U.S. history. Starting with the 300 poorest counties in the nation in 1965, Head Start was designed as a comprehensive program to eliminate the physical, intellectual, and social barriers to success in school. Schorr describes the Head Start model:

> When three- to five-year-old children are systematically helped to think, reason, and speak clearly; when they are provided hot meals, social services, health evaluations, and health care; when families become partners in their children's learning experiences, are helped toward self-sufficiency, and gain greater confidence in themselves as parents and as contributing members of the community, the results are measurable and dramatic. (1988, p. 192)

The initial evaluation of Head Start by the Westinghouse Learning Corporation showed mixed results (Richmond, Stipek, & Zigler, 1979). The evaluation focused heavily on cognitive variables and IQ scores and found that early gains produced by Head Start were often lost by the third or fourth grade. However, some positive long-term effects of Head Start and other preschool programs have been documented in subsequent evaluations (see Lazar & Darlington, 1982). Students in these programs were less likely than comparison students to be held back a grade or placed in special education during elementary and junior high school. (Students who experience such problems are more likely to drop out and have problems with employment and law violation.) Yoshikawa (1994) has reviewed several controlled evaluations of preschool programs and concludes that such programs can be very effective: Their effects include helping parents find employment and increasing the spacing of births.

Experts in the field claim that the most effective preschool programs are those with professional staff who are knowledgeable in early childhood development, a curriculum based on child development principles that is adequately supported, managed, and evaluated; high teacher-pupil ratios; small classes; close collaboration between teachers and parents; and integration with local resources and services (Graham, 1990; Schweinhart, 1987). The latest studies suggest that home visitation plays a critical role in enhancing the effectiveness of preschool programs (Tremblay & Craig, 1995; Yoshikawa, 1994).

In the late 1980s and early 1990s, a growing appreciation developed among national policy makers in this country for the importance and cost-effectiveness of preschool education. Congress agreed to expand Head Start funding so that the program could reach 100 percent of those in need (in 1990, it served only about 20 percent of the high-risk population). Policy analysts and researchers questioned, however, whether the typical Head Start program will have the resources needed to be effective. Unlike the Perry Preschool, most Head Start programs spend about 60 percent less per child and do not employ professional staff (Bright, 1992).

Home Care and Family Preservation

If good early intervention is not possible, then family support can be provided for older children who find themselves in abusive or neglectful family environments. Out-of-family placement (such as, foster care and group care) is often unavailable and, when provided, can have adverse consequences for the child (research on the advantages and disadvantages of foster care is weak—see National Research Council, 1993). Furthermore, leaving children in abusive and neglectful family environments can be equally damaging (Reiss & Roth, 1993). An alternative model is to provide professional intervention at home to help improve family functioning and preserve the family. Such an approach was initiated in 1974 in Tacoma, Washington, and came to be known as the Tacoma Homebuilders program (Kinney, Madsen, Fleming, & Haapala, 1977; Schorr, 1988). Seeking to prevent out-of-family placement for children living in difficult families, a team of professional social workers, psychologists, and counselors responded to family crises within 24 hours. They provided a wide range of services in the home rather than in offices (everything from help with household chores to family therapy), and they were prepared to draw on and coordinate with other community services as needed. For the first six years, placement was unnecessary for 92 percent of the families, and, in most of those cases, placement had seemed imminent because of the program's emphasis on crisis cases. These data leave many questions unanswered regarding the program's impact (for example, what would be the rate of placement without the program? What is the magnitude of the abuse problem in "successful" families?). Nevertheless, the apparent success of the Tacoma Homebuilders program led to widespread funding for replication programs, and several states have experimented with large-scale implementation. Unfortunately, evaluations of family preservation programs have produced only mixed results (see National Research Council, 1993). Positive results appear to be easier to achieve with white rural families than with African-American and Hispanic families living in inner-city neighborhoods and facing additional drug and crime problems.

In the late 1990s, with media attention focused on cases of extreme child abuse and neglect, we began to see a shift in emphasis from family preservation to child protection. As Swarns (1997, p. A1) observes in the *New York Times,* this change means "spending fewer dollars on family counseling, sending more children into foster care, and turning increasingly to law enforcement for assistance in serious cases of physical abuse." Unfortunately, insufficient research has been done to document the conditions under which home visitation programs are effective with abusive or dysfunctional families. After examining several support programs for high-risk families, Schorr (1988, p. 176) identified what she believes are some common elements of success:

"All of them offer services that are comprehensive and intensive. All have highly professional staffs (some of whom work closely with paraprofessionals). All use insights and skills from psychiatry and child development in working with families to establish an atmosphere of trust and confidence." This suggests that there are no short cuts to solving our social problems. Low-budget, short-term projects with poorly trained staff are not likely to succeed, but better research is needed to test these hypotheses.

In addition to a paucity of good research on this subject, we see many politicians who are afraid to invest in prevention programs because they are expensive and cannot promise short-term results (that is, successful outcomes before the next election). Historically, our society has been unwilling to fully endorse the idea of flexible, individualized, intensive, and professional services because of the cost and time implications. In the long run, however, effective prevention programs should be substantially cheaper than what we have now, namely, expensive criminal justice and welfare bureaucracies that are over-burdened, inefficient, ineffective, and discriminatory.

COMMUNITY-BASED PROGRAMS

The model prevention programs described can be characterized as service de-livery interventions provided by professionals that focus on young children, young single parents, and low-income families. As high-risk children grow older, the influence of schools, peers, and the neighborhood in general play an increasingly important role in shaping youths' behavior, especially in single-parent, low-income environments. Community context is very important for sustaining and reinforcing appropriate social behavior. Hence, we devote the remainder of this chapter to community-based programs, which tend to rely more on volunteers than on professionals, give more attention to delinquent adolescents than to young families, and often seek to help both the neighbor-hood and high-risk individuals.

Early Programs

The history of community-based, youth-oriented crime prevention programs in the United States is often traced to the Chicago Area Project, an innovative program started in 1931 by Clifford Shaw to encourage community self-help in crime-ridden Chicago neighborhoods. The Chicago Area Project emerged from the ecological approach developed by researchers at the University of Chicago. Shaw and McKay (1931; 1942) studied the spatial (geographic) dis-tribution of juvenile crime in Chicago and concluded that the highest levels of delinquency occurred in the poorest areas of the inner city—areas they de-scribed as "socially disorganized." These neighborhoods were largely defined by three structural factors: low economic status, ethnic heterogeneity, and res-idential mobility. Lacking stability, these neighborhoods were unable to nur-ture the informal social control processes needed to regulate deviant behavior and prevent other types of social problems. The conclusions reached by Shaw and McKay have been confirmed by other researchers using more sophisticated methods. Lack of neighborhood stability does seem to encourage delinquency, and neighborhoods that experience the fastest social change also experience the highest delinquency rates (Bursik, 1986; Schuerman & Kobrin, 1986). To better explain the relationship between social disorganization and delinquency, Byrne and Sampson (1986) have expanded the model to include other critical variables such as friendship ties, organizational participation, the opportunity structure for crime, and the adequacy of local services.

Based on early social disorganization theory, the Chicago Area Project was designed to organize community residents and to restore the social processes needed to generate a self-sufficient, self-regulating community (for more about the theory behind community organization, see Chapter 3). The professionals initiated a community committee that would plan and implement the Chicago Area Project, relying on support from community leaders and local institutions (for example, churches). Three major programs were developed: youth recreation, neighborhood renewal, and youth counseling (see Ludman, 1993; Schlossman & Sedlak, 1983; Schlossman, Zellman, & Shavelson, 1984). Several sports leagues were started to encourage delinquent youth and gang members to become involved in positive activities and outlets for physical aggression. To get more community residents involved, vacant lots were transformed into playgrounds, boys' clubs were started, and a summer camp was developed. Along with other activities, community self-renewal was an important goal of the Chicago Area Project and included neighborhood cleanup projects, a push for better city services, and a drive to keep juveniles from adult facilities such as bars. The Project also provided "curbstone counseling" to gang members and youths at risk of delinquency, offering them advice on various problems such as truancy, unemployment, and involvement in the juvenile justice system.

A critical aspect of the Chicago Area Project was the involvement of community volunteers, community organizations, local churches, and other institutions in the process of program development and implementation. The basic idea was to develop a self-regulating, competent community that perceived a sense of ownership over the definition of the problem as well as the solution. In contrast with the vast majority of anticrime initiatives today, delinquents and gang members were viewed as *members of the community* who needed direction and social support from other community members, not as outside predators who should be imprisoned by law enforcement personnel.

Limited evaluations of the Chicago Area Project indicate that the program had some positive results, although a comprehensive evaluation was never performed. Shaw reported a reduction in the number of police contacts with juveniles over a 10-year period (1932–1942), but reductions also occurred in other neighborhoods (Schlossman & Sedlak, 1983). Stronger evidence of success comes from data indicating that parolees in the target neighborhood experienced less recidivism and were formally arrested less often than a comparison group of parolees from a comparable neighborhood (Schlossman

& Sedlak, 1983). Looking at more recent activity in the Chicago Area Project, Schlossman, Zellman, and Shavelson (1984) concluded that actual levels of delinquency were lower than predicted in the African-American and Hispanic neighborhoods. Again, these causal inferences are weak.

Regardless of evaluation data, the Chicago Area Project has been the model for a wide range of community-based youth-oriented programs in subsequent years. The Boston Mid-City project in the 1950s and the Mobilization for Youth program in Manhattan in the 1960s were attempts to replicate the basic idea of the Chicago Area Project, but evaluations of these initiatives showed they had little affect on delinquency prevention (Hope, 1995; Marris & Rein, 1972; Miller, 1962).

Youth Service Bureaus and Diversion

A more recent version of a coordinated youth-focused program is the youth service bureau, developed to help delinquent youth. The Justice Department funded hundreds of these programs in the 1970s to achieve five basic goals (Roberts, 1989, p.49): "Divert juveniles from the juvenile justice system; fill gaps in service by advocating for and developing services for youths and their families; provide case coordination and program coordinating; provide modification of systems of youth services; and involve youth in the decision-making process." Early process studies were conducted on these youth service bureaus and found that they were being grossly underused by the criminal justice system (see Underwood, 1972). Most referrals were self-referrals rather than diversions from the justice system, and program success was often determined by the location and accessibility of the program.

A fundamental question about youth service bureaus and diversion programs in general is whether the primary goal of diversion, if successfully implemented, would have had beneficial effects for the youths involved. A substantial body of research has been conducted on this subject (see Lab, 1988, Lab & Whitehead, 1988, for reviews), but the evaluations of diversion initiatives have produced mixed results. Several studies have shown positive effects on recidivism rates; however, the bulk of the literature suggests that diversion programs yield recidivism rates similar to what would be expected if these youth were processed through the juvenile justice system. Although the effects on delinquency remain uncertain, one thing is clear: Such programs have a "net-widening" effect of serving youth with minor offending problems who would have otherwise been excluded from contact with the criminal justice system. This is problematic because diversion does not entirely avoid the "labeling" criticism directed at the justice system and because the benefits of diversion (to offset this cost) remain ambiguous. Also, civil libertarians are concerned that diversion involves treatment with the presumption of guilt (rather than of innocence). Without a trial, the suspect, his or her family, and the defense attorney must put their faith in the benevolence (and skill) of this alternative service delivery system.

Despite these concerns, by the early 1990s diversion programs had reemerged as part of a restorative justice movement in the United States. This reemergence reflected the public's discontent with an ineffective criminal justice system and the public's desire to see the community more involved in rehabilitating young offenders and obtaining restitution for victims. Hence, a wide range of community-based and agency-based initiatives have emerged. The United States has moved beyond police-based youth bureaus and special programs (for example, Scared Straight) to community-run, neighborhood-based alternatives for delinquent youth. It is too early to know if this new round of programs will be more effective than the last, but the popularity of these efforts is unquestioned (see Comprehensive Partnerships later in this chapter).

Community Youth Programs

Similar to diversion efforts, the concept of community-based youth-oriented programming experienced a rebirth in the United States during the 1980s. With recent studies indicating that Neighborhood Watch and other opportunity or situational approaches to crime prevention are difficult to sustain in poorer communities because they do not address the deeper social problems of the neighborhoods (see Rosenbaum, 1987; 1988b), the social prevention model has taken on new meaning and a new set of advocates. Currie (1988) and Curtis (1987) have argued that the time has come for the United States to prevent crime by investing more in America's disadvantaged youth and families.

In 1982, the Eisenhower Foundation initiated a four-year demonstration program called the "Neighborhood Anti-Crime Self-Help Program" to demonstrate that community organizations, given adequate technical assistance, could develop and implement a range of crime prevention programs that were tailored to the problems of particular neighborhoods and effective at empowering local residents. The Neighborhood Program combined both opportunity reduction strategies (for example, Neighborhood Watch, citizen patrols) with community-based youth empowerment strategies in 10 inner-city neighborhoods. The program emphasized a "bubble-up" planning process by community groups, financial self-sufficiency, and a focus on neighborhood, family, and employment. A multiyear process and impact evaluation was conducted by researchers at Northwestern University (Bennett & Lavrakas, 1989; Lavrakas & Bennett, 1988).

In addition to watches and patrols, the Neighborhood Program resulted in numerous community-based youth-oriented programs, including athletic leagues, youth crime prevention clubs and drop-in centers, and youth employment opportunities. In addition, the community organizations raised considerable funds to continue their anticrime activity after the grant period. The impact evaluation, however, showed little affect on the neighborhood as a whole (Lavrakas & Bennett, 1988). Using a pretest-posttest control group design with community survey data, and a time-series design with police crime data, the researchers found few positive program effects. The local programs did not affect official crime rates and in some cases, were associated with an adverse change in survey-based victimization rates. One interesting finding was that fear of crime seemed to decline in neighborhoods that focused most on opportunity reduction strategies. Also, Fischer (1988) reanalyzed the Lavrakas and Bennett data, comparing residents who participated intensively and directly in block-level meetings and those who did not (ignoring their status as members of either the program or comparison neighborhood). She found that participation was associated with a stronger sense of community, less fear of crime, stronger feelings of efficacy about crime prevention activities, and other differences. Although Fischer controlled for self-selection biases in her analysis, these effects cannot be entirely removed by statistical controls.

This initial impact evaluation of the Neighborhood Program was not designed to measure the effects of prevention activities on youths, but rather focused on communitywide effects evident in the adult population. The Eisenhower Foundation has since supported small-scale local evaluations of promising youth-oriented programs in the Neighborhood Program (see Chavis, Kopacsi, & Tatum, 1989; Chavis & Tatum, 1989). In the Washington, D.C., neighborhood of Adams-Morgan, the Around the Corner to the World (ACW) program started several businesses to employ high-risk youths and ex-offenders. A weatherization and home repair business hired 11 neighborhood youths between the ages of 18 and 26 in the summer of 1985. In addition to employment, ACW workers held regular meetings in the ACW offices to discuss work and personal problems. A pre-post evaluation found that the number of arrests and contacts with the police declined during the 18 months of employment and continued at this lower level for 12 months after the program. Employees who were interviewed reported that their lives had improved in a variety of ways as a result of participation in ACW. (The evaluation did not include a control group and the sample size was only 11.) Financially, ACW was a success, generating more than one million dollars in local contracts between 1985 and 1988.

In Boston, the Dorchester Youth Collaborative (DYC) created Youth Crime Prevention Clubs for at-risk youths. The purpose of these clubs was to keep at-risk young people off the streets and involved in structured activities that would help them build self-esteem, stay in school, or find other educational opportunities. Two boys' clubs participated in a basketball league, and a girls' club created a performing dance group. An evaluation of 22 participants from 1983 to 1987 showed declines in rates of arrest, dropping out of school, and drug use. The manner in which the statistics were calculated and the absence of any control group, however, makes the findings very difficult to interpret.

The social prevention component of the Eisenhower Neighborhood Program was strongly influenced by several established, comprehensive community-based programs that are worth noting (see Eisenhower, 1990). The Argus

Community, Inc., in the South Bronx (Sturz & Taylor, 1987), and the House of Umoja in Philadelphia (Fattah, 1987) provide extended-family environments to high-risk youths. In one assessment, graduates of the Argus program had lower rates of recidivism than did members of other high-risk offender programs in New York City. Participants in the Umoja program also had lower rates of recidivism than youths released from juvenile correctional facilities (Curtis, 1987). Again, the true impact of these programs remains unknown without more thorough, controlled evaluations.

Though Argus and Umoja focus their attention on specific high-risk youth, other programs have taken a more comprehensive approach that includes attempts to improve the surrounding neighborhood. The Centro Sister Isolina Ferre (also known as "Centro") in Ponce, Puerto Rico, is a good example of a full-service community program in a very tough neighborhood (Ferre, 1987; Silberman, 1978). Working with several full-time "advocates," the Center has organized the neighborhood to improve local health services, provide extended-family activities, and extensive job training. The Eisenhower Foundation (1990, p. 14) notes, "Over the period of initial operations of Centro, from 1968 to 1977, the rate of reported juvenile offenses was fairly constant in Ponce, while it showed a two-thirds decline in LaPlaya." Again, without a formal evaluation, the effects of this program cannot be estimated with any degree of precision. Possible changes in the population, in police reporting practices, and in other variables could explain this decline.

Youth initiatives were included as part of the Community Responses to Drug Abuse (CRDA) national demonstration program, funded by the Bureau of Justice Assistance. Local grassroots community organizations, with technical assistance from the National Crime Prevention Council and the National Training and Information Center, developed the CRDA program in 10 communities spread across 9 U.S. cities. Similar to the Eisenhower programs, this initiative used the "bubble-up" approach to program development and sustainment. Youth initiatives developed under CRDA included drug prevention education at school, recreation and social activities, tutoring programs, and training and employment efforts.

The National Institute of Justice funded the University of Illinois at Chicago to perform both process and impact evaluations of the CRDA program. The process evaluation documented a wide variety of antidrug strategies, but also learned that the program emphasized removing drug dealers from the neighborhood more than helping at-risk youth (Rosenbaum, Bennett, Lindsay, & Wilkinson, 1994). The impact evaluation used a pretest-multiple posttest control group design in three intensive ("best case") sites, using telephone survey data from random samples of community residents. Rosenbaum and his colleagues (1997) reached the following conclusion:

> These findings offer mixed support for community mobilization and the implant hypothesis. In the "best case" test, the data suggest that community organizations were effective at increasing levels of citizen awareness

and participation in antidrug activities. In addition, there was some evidence that these community interventions were followed by more informal social interactions, more favorable attitudes about the police, and more positive perceptions about their neighborhood as a place to live. However, the program did not change attitudes about citizen empowerment, fear of crime or actual use of neighborhood parks and stores." (Rosenbaum, Lavrakas, Wilkinson, & Faggiani, 1997, Executive summary, p. x)[2]

Overall, the evaluation results suggest that community organizations, with limited federal funding and good technical assistance, *can* make a difference in the lives of neighborhood residents *if* they involve a well-planned, intensive, and persistent effort. The research design did not allow the researchers to draw any conclusions about the impact of CRDA on individual high-risk youth in the target communities.

In summary, community-based social prevention programs for youth hold considerable promise, but they suffer from several constraints. Historically, they have been poorly funded and have lacked adequate technical assistance from professionals (also see Eisenhower Foundation, 1990). As a result, these programs have been ripe for failure and have suffered from weak implementation. Because of resource limitations, they have generally focused on a small number of youths in a particular area of the neighborhood. A small drop-in center or training program in a high-crime neighborhood, for example, is not likely to succeed without the support of local schools, churches, police, social service agencies, parents, and other community residents. To focus on services for a handful of high-risk youths, without empowering the local community or reaching a large portion of the youths at risk, is not likely to have a sizable impact at the community level. Nevertheless, the efforts are often laudable. A final constraint is that community-based youth initiatives are rarely the primary focus of large-scale evaluations; hence, our knowledge of the effectiveness of this component is limited.

COMPREHENSIVE PARTNERSHIPS

In the arena of community crime and violence prevention, the 1990s can be defined by increasing attention to initiatives that involve the formation of interagency and intergroup partnerships and by the public's desire to "reinvent government" at the neighborhood level so that it will be responsive to local community problems. Across the nation, progressive municipal governments are looking beyond the conventional police-citizen link to solve the crime

---

2. The "implant hypothesis" (Rosenbaum, 1987) states that informal social control processes can be "implanted" through social interventions in neighborhoods where such processes are presently weak, that is, neighborhoods characterized by crime, drugs, disorder, and weak preventative social behaviors.

problem and are calling on other agencies and organizations to accept key roles in strategic, long-term plans to solve neighborhood problems. In this context, the federal government has taken a leadership role in funding innovative demonstration programs that help build and strengthen local partnerships and coalitions. We will briefly discuss three of the most prominent initiatives supported by the Office of Justice Programs, U.S. Department of Justice (also see Chapter 9 on community policing for a discussion of partnerships and their importance).[3]

Operation Weed and Seed

Using an agricultural analogy, the Weed and Seed initiative was conceived as a multi-agency strategy to "weed out" violent criminals and drug activity, then "seed" the target neighborhood with social and economic interventions that would restore and stabilize the area. Dozens of cities received funding from the Justice Department to develop better linkages between various criminal justice agencies (at the federal, state, and local level) and social service agencies, schools, businesses, and other segments of government. The Weed and Seed program is described as having four components: (1) suppression—coordinated law enforcement efforts to weed out violent offenders; (2) community-oriented policing—police working with residents to solve neighborhood problems; (3) prevention, intervention, and treatment—a variety of efforts that involve partnerships among police, social services, and the private sector; and (4) neighborhood restoration—public-private partnership efforts to restore distressed neighborhoods through economic opportunities. Roehl and her colleagues conducted a national process evaluation of the Weed and Seed initiative (Roehl, Huitt, Wycoff, Pate, Rebovich, & Coyle, 1995; 1996). They found that levels of implementation success varied by city, but in general, the Weed and Seed initiative built new bridges between agencies and helped redefine our national response to the crime problem. The majority of the Weed and Seed funds were earmarked for "weeding" (via law enforcement strategies) rather than "seeding" (via social services). Nevertheless, by bringing other nonlaw enforcement groups to the table, the Weed and Seed program brought renewed attention to the importance of *preventing* crime and addressing the root causes of violence in the community. Field observations indicate that the broad representation of community partners who sat on the seeding committees grappled with strategies for helping at-risk youth and their families. On several occasions, these partners expressed resentment that virtually all the attention and resources in the community were focused on delinquent youths who were already in trouble

---

3. We should note that the Department of Justice is not the only branch of the federal government that has invested in community-based initiatives to fight crime and drugs. The Departments of Housing and Urban Development, Health and Human Services, Education, and Labor have also been involved. Also, the private sector, especially the foundations, has contributed significantly to a wide range of community-based efforts to prevent violence and rebuild communities (see Office of Juvenile Justice and Delinquency Prevention, 1995, for a list of examples).

with the law rather than on the younger at-risk kids. Hence, these committees sought to expand the number and quality of interventions for at-risk kids. These groups also debated the question of whether "weeding" activities must, by necessity, precede "seeding" activities, and often they reached the conclusion that both strategies are important and can be introduced concurrently. Hence, the Weed and Seed initiative helped elevate further the concepts of prevention and early intervention in the national debate about crime control. The Weed and Seed initiative also taught us that restoring a neighborhood through economic investment and job opportunities is a macrolevel process that requires more than two or three years to see any results.

Comprehensive Communities Program

Beginning in 1994, the Justice Department funded the Comprehensive Communities Program (CCP) in 16 cities "to demonstrate an innovative, comprehensive and integrated multi-agency approach to a comprehensive violent crime control/community mobilization program" (Bureau of Justice Assistance, 1996, p. 1). The CCP initiative is based on the idea that the best way to fight violent crime is to leverage and coordinate the resources of communities, the private sector, and government at all levels (federal, state, and local). Cities were given planning funds and were encouraged to build comprehensive initiatives around two key strategies: community policing and community mobilization. Cities were also encouraged to pursue other strategies, including drug courts, alternatives to prosecution, gang prevention and intervention, dispute and conflict resolution, and alternatives to incarceration. A process evaluation, conducted by a team of researchers from across the country (Kelling, Rocheleau, Rosenbaum, Roth, Skogan, & Walsh, 1997), found that many CCP sites created new, or strengthened existing, interagency partnerships. In some cases, CCP flourished because of partnerships created under previous initiatives, such as Weed and Seed. Although a substantial portion of the funds were earmarked for the police departments, CCP sites emphasized community-based prevention and youth-oriented initiatives. The Boys and Girls Club, for example, played a significant role in many sites, providing youth and family counseling, mentoring, job training, and other services. In the cross-site analysis, the research team identified some common variables that were present in cities with successful implementation, including supportive leadership in the police administration and city government, a superordinate vision for the city's neighborhoods that would be facilitated further by CCP funding, a history of securing federal grants to support this vision, and a strong CCP manager. CCP has resulted in some impressive efforts to "reinvent" government at the neighborhood level. Anecdotal evidence indicates that the target communities were pleased with these interventions and that some creative youth services were introduced as a result of these efforts. Citizens frequently reported that they now had a voice in government decision making and were learning how to solve neighborhood problems. Furthermore, the "street-level bureaucrats" such as police officers, probation officers, social workers, and city officials from various agencies were learning how to work together (on a regular, interpersonal basis) to determine the most appropriate response to particular families and youths, hot spots, and larger neighborhood problems. On the downside, partnerships can be extremely challenging for everyone involved because of political, bureaucratic, and philosophical differences.[4] Not unlike marriage, maintaining strong relationships across these barriers requires continuous attention and open communication. Investing the time and energy in collaborative ventures, however, can yield valuable dividends in creative problem solving and empowering both community volunteers and professionals.

We should note that the Justice Department is not the only federal agency interested in building partnerships to reduce youth violence and drug abuse. For example, the Center for Substance Abuse Prevention launched a massive effort in 250 cities—the Community Partnership program—to build citywide coalitions against drugs. A process evaluation, with many valuable lessons, is available for review (Center for Substance Abuse Prevention, 1994; Cook & Roehl, 1993), and an impact evaluation is underway. Finally, a half dozen federal agencies have worked together to support the Pulling America's Communities Together (PACT) program, which attempts to build local coalitions against violence.[5] In each of these federal initiatives, the community is expected to take the lead role, with support from federal, state, and local government.

Communities That Care

Partnerships and coalitions are essential vehicles for identifying problems and mobilizing both community and government resources. Without careful planning and research, however, communities can get sidetracked on peripheral issues or invest resources in youth and family strategies that are unlikely to significantly affect the problems of crime and delinquency. One initiative that has systematically avoided this mistake is the Communities That Care program. Developed by researchers at the University of Washington (Hawkins & Catalano, 1992), this program can be described as a community-based risk-focused approach to preventing youth crime, drug abuse, and other adolescent problems.

From our perspective, the Communities That Care model has several important process features: (1) a decision-making community board comprising representatives of all key agencies and groups in the community; (2) a needs assessment by the community board that focuses on risk factors associated with

---

4. As one example, law enforcement personnel and social service providers generally hold different views of how best to respond to delinquent youth. Not surprisingly, the former group is generally more inclined to favor strong punitive sanctions, whereas the latter is more interested in providing preventative and rehabilitative services.

5. One of the outgrowths of PACT was the Partnerships Against Violence Network (PAVNET), an Internet system that provides information about violence prevention and technical assistance to local communities.

youth violence—risk factors uncovered through decades of research on delinquency; and (3) a prevention plan, guided by the needs assessment, that emphasizes protective factors, that is, factors that shield the individual against risk factors and help prevent the onset of undesirable target behaviors. Examples of protective factors that can reduce the likelihood of delinquent behavior include healthy beliefs and clear standards of behavior, bonding (that is, attachment and commitment to persons who can influence their thinking and behavior), and individual characteristics such as a resilient temperament (Hawkins & Catalano, 1992). Bonding is believed to occur when youths have opportunities for success, develop the necessary skills, and receive recognition for their performance.

The Communities That Care model has received widespread attention. The Office of Juvenile Justice and Delinquency Prevention (OJJDP) is using it as a blueprint for its nationwide comprehensive strategy to prevent and control serious juvenile offending (Howell, 1995; Wilson & Howell, 1993) and has funded several local programs based on this approach. In addition, Farrington (1997) has recommended this model for large-scale implementation in the United Kingdom.

The Communities That Care approach recognizes that risk factors occur at the individual, family, school, peer, and community levels. The OJJDP plan is a comprehensive strategy with programs in three categories: (1) prevention programs from conception to age 6; (2) prevention programs from age 6 through adolescence; and (3) graduated sanctions programs for known juvenile offenders. For example, at the first stage, if the list of risk factors includes perinatal difficulties and infant brain damage, the protective factors might include prenatal and perinatal medical care, and health education for pregnant or young mothers. At the next stage (after 6 years) if the risk factor is persistent antisocial behavior, a wide range of school and family interventions might be appropriate, ranging from classroom behavior management to parent training. At the stage of chronic juvenile offending, OJJDP recommends graduated sanctions but emphasizes the youth's strengths rather than his or her deficiencies.

Based on a review of the literature, OJJDP (1995) notes that successful programs for serious or chronic offenders (1) are comprehensive and intensive; (2) are delivered by energetic and committed staff; (3) incorporate a case management approach that follows the youth from intake to discharge; (4) are linked to the specific needs and problems of individuals; (5) address issues related to community, peers, school, and work; and (6) provide treatment while the youth is living at home or in the community, and always in the "least restrictive environment possible."

Even though literally hundreds of research studies have identified *risk* factors that help us predict juvenile delinquency and violence, our knowledge of *protective* factors (and their effectiveness) is considerably more limited, as we have suggested throughout this book. Evaluations of community-based efforts to protect at-risk youth from the factors that encourage criminality are few in number and not always scientifically defensible. Most crime prevention evaluations focus on communitywide efforts to prevent crime through social and situational strategies, whereas this model focuses primarily on changing the behavior of potential offenders. Clearly, the promise of this comprehensive model begs for scientific evaluations at all levels.

EMPLOYMENT AND TRAINING

In the public policy arena, employment and training are frequently proposed as a solution to the problem of delinquency and youth violence. Although the relationship between unemployment and crime is complex (see Fagan, 1995, for a review), the problem of youth unemployment is a growing concern in the United States. Millions of America's youth are unemployed and do not have sufficient education or vocational training to obtain a "good job at good wages." Aside from the business sector's concern about finding a skilled work force in the decades ahead, the students who drop out of school are at risk of chronic unemployment, employment in the illegal drug economy, violent victimization, and a criminal history. To illustrate the magnitude of the problem, one study found that 63 percent of the African-American and Hispanic students enrolled in nonselective Chicago high schools did not graduate, and, of those who did graduate, only 1 in 5 could read at or above the national average (cited in Wilson, 1987).

To compensate, several employment and training programs have been developed over the years with the goal of improving labor market experience and preventing criminal activity among at-risk youth (see Bright, 1992; Children's Defense Fund, 1990; Graham, 1990; Heckman, 1994; McGahey, 1986; U.S. Department of Labor, 1995). Reviews of the evaluation literature suggest that youth-focused employment and training programs have produced mixed results at best on these outcome measures. To avoid overgeneralizing, however, we should distinguish between summer work programs and more intensive training and employment initiatives. The available evidence suggests that summer programs, although providing short-term minimum wage jobs for disadvantaged youth, have not been able to increase the odds of long-term employment, increase school enrollment, or lower the probability of arrest.

A variety of more intensive programs are available to youth and have been evaluated. The Job Training and Partnership Act (JTPA) provides a program for approximately 125,000 disadvantaged youths ages 16 to 21, including classroom training, on-the-job training, and job search assistance. After tracking a sample of JTPA youth participants for two and a half years in a randomized field experiment, researchers found no evidence that the program yielded improvements in earnings or a favorable impact on crime relative to the control group. However, the evaluation literature offers some evidence of success with more intensive and residential programs (Orr, Bloom, Bell, Doolittle, Lin, & Cave, 1996).

One of the few success stories (in terms of preventing delinquency and drug abuse) has been the Job Corps. This national program provides educational courses (leading to the Graduate Equivalent Degree [GED]), counseling services, and job training for delinquent and high-risk youth. As Gross (1991) notes, the Job Corps, which focuses on some of the hardest to reach kids, is "a mix of vocational training, boarding school, and boot camp." Given that 8 out of 10 participants are high school dropouts from low-income families, the success of the program is surprising. According to the Labor Department statistics, participants in Job Corps are less likely to be arrested, tend to retain jobs longer, and earn more money than comparable nonparticipants (see Eisenhower, 1990). The Job Corps reports that after 6 months, 67 percent of its graduates have jobs and 17 percent have gone on to higher education (Gross, 1991). The success of these programs has been attributed to the fact that Job Corps participants have been isolated from their high-crime neighborhoods and delinquent peers and placed in structured residential settings or extended families (McGahey, 1986; Taggart, 1981). They learn the values of hard work, self-respect, and respect for others in a setting where they have curfews, dress codes, and positive role models. The potential problem is that many of these youths will eventually return to their "old neighborhoods" where the negative influences (risk factors) continue to operate. This underscores the importance of community-based initiatives that build *community* competence as well as *individual* competence.

Perhaps the most encouraging and compelling evidence of program success comes from the Conservation and Youth Service Corps, which has been evaluated recently by researchers at Abt Associates (Jastrzab, Blomquist, Masker, & Orr, 1997). The Youth Corps includes approximately 120 programs nationwide, enrolling 26,000 participants. These programs, which typically last four to five months, serve disadvantaged persons between the ages of 17 and 26. Participation is full-time, but most programs are nonresidential. The participants typically work in teams of 8 to 15 on service projects in their communities. During their enrollment, youths are paid a stipend (often equivalent to minimum wage), but the three most common reasons for joining are to get training, a GED, or a job. Abt's national evaluation of the Youth Corps included a randomized experiment with a 15-month follow-up. The results were surprising. Participants in Corps were significantly more likely than nonparticipants to be employed during the follow-up period and to have worked more hours. Most germane to our discussion here, participants were less likely to be arrested than nonparticipants.

Additional positive results were obtained from subgroups within the Youth Corps. Positive employment gains were found for African Americans and Hispanics as a whole, as well as Caucasian women. African-American males reported the most substantial changes, including increased social and personal responsibility, higher educational aspirations, and a greater likelihood of voting. For unwed African-American women, a significant reduction in pregnancy rates is noteworthy. The only group to experience negative results was white males, who reported reductions in employment outcomes. The

researchers attribute this result to their relatively greater employment opportunities outside the Corps (that is, the white male control group averaged
$1,300 in earnings versus $650 for the entire control group). Another negative
finding was that Corps participants were less likely to have earned a technical
certificate or diploma by the follow-up evaluation (8 percent in the program
versus 13 percent in the control group), suggesting that participation might
have replaced enrollment in additional education in the short term.

The Youth Corps is a costly program at nearly $10,000 per participant. The
question policy makers should ask is this: Is it worth it? A cost-benefit analysis
by the Abt researchers suggests that the answer is "yes." Although the monetary
benefits outweighed the costs by only $600 per person, this analysis looks at
only short-term benefits. As a society, we need to consider the potential long-
term gains, including the possibility of improved employment prospects and
improved quality of life. More longitudinal research is needed in this field, with
more attention to criminality, arrest rates, and other relevant outcomes.

CONCLUSIONS

This chapter has only scratched the surface of innovative programs that fit
within the general framework of social crime prevention. A wide variety of
demonstrations or model initiatives have been developed and implemented
over the past four decades, ranging from prenatal and early childhood services
to employment opportunities for high-risk adolescents. In theory, programs
that are responsive to known risk factors should be the most effective at preventing violence and related community problems. As a society, we need to
understand that children face different risk factors at different points in their
development, thus dictating the need for different interventions as the child
grows. Furthermore, research suggests that risk factors are cumulative and that
youths exposed to a larger number of risk factors are more likely to experience problems later on, including criminality (Tremblay & Craig, 1995). The
implication is that comprehensive programs that attack multiple risk factors
should have a greater preventive effect.

Social prevention programs show considerable promise, yet most programs
are poorly funded and poorly evaluated, if at all. Unfortunately, only a few
have been implemented on a large scale (such as Head Start and the Job
Corps), which brings us to the heart of the problem. A patchwork of small
(albeit promising) programs can only take us so far down the road of social
prevention. For people with the highest risk of delinquency, gross discontinu-
ities in service exist at all levels of social, psychological, and physical development. Programs and policies are needed at the state and national levels that
address these gaps in the areas of health, education, housing, employment, and
community empowerment.

One major reason that policy makers and taxpayers are afraid to invest in
social prevention programs is the high cost in money and time. We believe

that a longitudinal cost-benefit analysis will indicate that intensive, comprehensive, early-intervention programs will pay for themselves many times over. The available evidence strongly suggests, for example, that home visits and preschool education to support parents and children at risk, if properly implemented, can significantly reduce the likelihood of delinquency, criminality, and other problems later in life. In the long run, good prenatal care, family support programs, preschools, and a host of other intensive services for high-risk populations will result in massive savings in medical expenses, foster or institutional care, public assistance, drug treatment, criminal justice services, and many other reactive public responses. The earlier the intervention, the greater the impact. Our country needs the economic sensibility, if not the moral fortitude, to pursue this course of action.

We are now a deeply divided and neurotic nation regarding the treatment of delinquent adolescents. At the same time that politicians are demanding stiffer penalties and long-term imprisonment for young offenders, communities across the country are beginning to take back their wayward children through diversion, restorative justice, and rehabilitation. These community-based efforts hold promise for achieving their goals (and empowering the community in the process), but the results are uncertain. We should keep a watchful eye on these interventions because they operate outside the due process of the criminal justice system, thus the rights of the juvenile are uncertain. Also, with the expansion of computerized records on juveniles and the increased sharing of databases among agencies, these net-widening programs have the potential for violating civil liberties and privacy rights. The public might determine that this is an unavoidable risk given the current movement toward a more communitarian society that seeks to balance individual rights with responsibilities to society.

Beyond the individual level, our nation is learning how to address neighborhood and community level problems through comprehensive and integrated partnerships. Partnerships are blossoming at all levels—between police and community groups, between city departments, between law enforcement agencies, between government and the private sector, and so forth. This activity, in turn, is forcing community and civic leaders to ask new questions, to think about community problems differently and to develop solutions that are "outside the box." But this change is not simply about government and other professional agencies becoming more efficient and effective at solving community problems. To achieve long-term success, these efforts to reinvent government must establish clear roles for volunteers in the community to ensure that the goal of creating self-regulating neighborhoods (as opposed to government-dependent neighborhoods) is not compromised.

REFERENCES

Bartollas, C. (1993). *Juvenile delinquency* (3rd ed.). New York: Macmillan.

Bennett, S. F. & Lavrakas, P. J. (1988). *Evaluation of the planning and implementation of the neighborhood program.* Final process report to the Eisenhower Foundation. Evanston, IL: Northwestern University, Center for Urban Affairs and Policy Research.

Bennett, S. F., & Lavrakas, P. J. (1989). Community-based crime prevention: An assessment of the Eisenhower Foundation's Neighborhood Program. *Crime and Delinquency* 35, 345–364

Berrueta-Clement, J. R., Schweinhart, L. J., Barnett, W. S., Epstein, A. S., & Weikart, D. P. (1984). *Changed lives: The effects of the Perry Preschool Programs on youths through age 19.* Ypsilanti, MI: High/Scope.

Bright, J. (1992) *Crime prevention in America: A British perspective.* Chicago: Office of International Criminal Justice, University of Illinois at Chicago.

Bureau of Justice Assistance (1996). *Comprehensive Communities Program: Update.* Washington, DC: Bureau of Justice Assistance, U.S. Department of Justice. February 15.

Bursik, R. J. (1986). Ecological stability and the dynamics of delinquency. In Reiss, A. J. & Tonry, M. (eds.) *Communities and crime.* (Vol. 8 of *Crime and justice*). Chicago: University of Chicago Press.

Bursik, R. J. Jr., & Grasmick, H. G. (1993). *Neighborhoods and crime: The dimensions of effective community control.* New York: Lexington.

Byrne, J. & Sampson, R. (eds.) (1986). *The social ecology of crime.* New York: Springer-Verlag.

Center for Substance Abuse Prevention (1994). *National evaluation of the Community Partnership Demonstration Program, third annual report.* Bethesda, MD: Center for Substance Abuse Prevention, U.S. Department of Health and Human Services.

Chavis, D. M., Kopacsi, R. & Tatum, W. (1989). *A retrospective examination of Around the Corner to the World.* Newark, NJ: Center for Community Education, School of Social Work, Rutgers University.

Chavis, D. M., & Tatum, W. (1989). *A retrospective examination of Dorchester youth collaborative prevention clubs.* Newark, NJ: Center for Community Education, School of Social Work, Rutgers University.

Children's Defense Fund (1990). *A vision for America's future.* Washington, DC.

Cook, R. F., & Roehl, J. A. (1993). National evaluation of the Community Partnership Demonstration evaluation: Preliminary findings. In R. Davis, A. Lurigio, & D. P. Rosenbaum (eds.) *Drugs and the community.* Springfield, IL: Charles C. Thomas.

Currie, E. (1988). Two visions of community crime prevention. In T. Hope & M. Shaw (eds.) *Communities and crime reduction.* London: Her Majesty's Stationery Office.

Curtis, L. (1987). The retreat of folly: Some modest replications of inner-city success. *The annals of the American Academy of Political and Social Sciences* 494:, 71–89.

Dryfoos, J. (1990) *Adolescents at risk.* New York: Oxford University Press.

Eisenhower Foundation (1990). *Youth investment and community reconstruction: Street lessons on drugs and crime for the nineties.* Washington DC: Library of Congress.

Fagan, J. (1995). Legal work and illegal work: Crime, work, and unemployment. In B. Weisburd & J. Worthy (eds.) *Dealing with urban crisis: Linking research to action.* Evanston, IL: Northwestern University Press.

Farrington, D. P. (1987). Early precursors to frequent offending. In J. Q. Wilson & G. C. Loury (eds.) *Families, schools, and delinquency prevention.* (Vol. 3 of *From children to citizens*). New York: Springer-Verlag.

Farrington, D. P. (1997). Evaluating a community crime prevention program. *Evaluation* 3, 157–173.

Fattah, D. (1987). The House of Umoja as a case study for social justice. *The annals of the American Academy of Political and Social Sciences* 494, 37–41.

Ferre, M. I. (1987). Prevention and control of violence through community revitalization, individual dignity, and personal self-confidence. *The Annals of the American Academy of Political and Social Sciences* 494, 27–36

Fischer, B. S. (1988*). Participatory democracy in action: Crime prevention activities.* Unpublished Ph.D. dissertation, Northwestern University, Department of Political Science.

Furstenberg, F. F., Jr., Brooks-Gunn, J., & Morgan, S. P. (1987) *Adolescent mothers in later life.* New York: Cambridge University Press.

Gottfredson, M., & Hirschi, T. (1990). *A general theory of crime.* Stanford, CA: Stanford University Press.

Graham, J. (1990). *Crime prevention strategies in Europe and North America.* Helsinki, Finland: Helsinki Institute for Crime Prevention and Control.

Gross, J. (1991). A remnant of the war on poverty, the Job Corps is a quiet success. *New York Times,* February 17, p. A1.

Hawkins, J. D., & Catalano, R. F. (1992). *Communities that care.* San Francisco: Jossey-Bass.

Heckman, J. J. (1994). Is job training oversold? *The Public Interest* (Spring), 91–115.

Hirschi, T. (1969). *Causes of delinquency.* Berkeley: University of California Press.

Hope, T. (1995). Community crime prevention. In M. Tonry & D. Farrington (eds.) *Building a safer society* (Vol. 19 of M. Tonry & N. Morris, eds., *Crime and justice: A review of research.*) Chicago: University of Chicago Press.

Howell, J. C. (ed.) (1995). *Guide for implementing the comprehensive strategy for serious, violent, and chronic juvenile offenders.* Washington, DC: Office of Juvenile Justice and Delinquency Prevention, U.S. Department of Justice.

Jastrzab, J., Blomquist, J., Masker, J., & Orr, L. (1997). *Youth Corps: Promising strategies for young people and their communities.* Cambridge, MA: Abt Associates.

Jones, E. F., Forrest, J. D., Goldman, N., Henshaw, S. K., Lincoln, R., Rosoff, J. I., Westoff, C. F., & Wulf, D. (1987). *Teenage pregnancy in developed countries.* New Haven, CT: Yale University Press.

Kagan, J. (1984). *The nature of the child.* New York: Basic Books.

Kelling, G. L., Rocheleau, A. M., Rosenbaum, D. P., Roth, J. A., Skogan, W. G., & Walsh, N. (1997). *Preliminary cross-site analysis of the Bureau of Justice Assistance Comprehensive Communities Program. Final report to the National Institute of Justice.* Cambridge, MA: BOTEC Analysis Corporation.

Kinney, J. M., Madsen, B., Fleming, T., & Haapala, D. A. (1977). Homebuilders: Keeping families together. *Journal of Consulting and Clinical Psychology* 45, 667–673.

Klein, M. (1995). *The American street gang: Its nature, prevalence and control.* New York: Oxford University Press.

Lab, S. P. (1988). *Crime prevention: Approaches, practices and evaluations.* Cincinnati: Anderson.

Lab, S. P. & Whitehead, J. T. (1988). An analysis of juvenile correctional treatment. *Crime and Delinquency* 34, 60–85.

Lavrakas, P. J. & Bennett, S. F. (1988). Thinking about the implementation of citizen and community anticrime measures. In T. Hope & M. Shaw (eds.) *Communities and crime reduction.* London: Her Majesty's Stationery Office.

Lazar, I., & Darlington, R. (1982). Lasting effects of early education: A report from the Consortium of Longitudinal

Studies. *Monographs of the Society for Research in Child Development* 47(2), Serial No. 195.

Loeber, R., & LeBlanc, M. (1990). Toward a developmental criminology. In M. Tonry & N. Morris (eds.). *Crime and justice: A review of research* (Vol. 12, pp. 375–473). Chicago: University of Chicago Press.

Loeber, R., & Stouthamer-Loeber, M. (1986). Family factors as correlates and predictors of juvenile conduct problems and delinquency. In M. Tonry & N. Morris (eds.) *Crime and justice: An annual review of research* (Vol. 7). Chicago: University of Chicago Press.

Loeber, R. & Stouthamer-Loeber, M. (1987). Prediction. In H. C. Quay (ed.), *Handbook of juvenile delinquency.* New York: Wiley.

Ludman, R. J. (1993). *Prevention and control of juvenile delinquency.* (2nd ed.) New York: Oxford University Press.

Marris, P., & Rein, M. (1972). *Dilemmas of social reform.* Harmondsworth: Penguin.

McElroy, S. W., & Moore, K. A. (1997). Trends: National and international trends in early pregnancy and childbearing. In R. Maynard (ed.). *Kids having kids.* Washington, DC: Urban Institute Press.

McGahey, R. M. (1986). Economic conditions, neighborhood organization and urban crime. In M. Tonry & N. Morris (eds.), *Crime and justice* (Vol. 9). Chicago: University of Chicago Press.

Miller, W. B. (1962). The impact of a "total community" delinquency control project. *Social Problems* 10, 168–191.

Nagin, D. S., Farrington, D. P., & Moffitt, T. E. (1995). Life-course trajectories of different types of offenders. *Criminology* 33, 111–139.

Nagin, D. S., & Land, K. C. (1993). Age, criminal careers, and population heterogeneity: Specification and estimation of a nonparametric, mixed

Poisson model. *Criminology* 31, 327–362.

Nagin, D. S., Pogarsky, G., & Farrington, D. P. (1997). Adolescent mothers and the criminal behavior of their children. *Law & Society Review* 31, 137–162.

National Research Council (1993). *Understanding child abuse and neglect.* Washington, DC: National Academy of Sciences.

Office of Juvenile Justice and Delinquency Prevention (1997). *Matrix of community-based initiatives, program summary.* Washington, DC: Office of Juvenile Justice and Delinquency Prevention, U.S. Department of Justice. September.

Office of Juvenile Justice and Delinquency Prevention (1995). *Guide for implementing the comprehensive strategy for serious, violent, and chronic juvenile offenders.* Washington, DC: Office of Juvenile Justice and Delinquency Prevention, U.S. Department of Justice. June.

Ontario Ministry of Community and Social Services (1990). *Better beginnings, better futures.* Ontario, Canada.

Orr, L. L., Bloom, H. S., Bell, S. H., Doolittle, F., Lin, W., & Cave, G. (1986). *Does job training for the disadvantaged work? Evidence from the National JTPA Study.* Washington, DC: Urban Institute Press.

Patterson, G. R., Chamberlain, P., & Reid, J. B. (1982). A comparative evaluation of a parent training program. *Behavior Therapy* 13, 638–650.

Reid, S. T. (1988). *Crime and criminology* (5th edition). New York: Holt, Rinehart, & Winston.

Reiss, A. J., Jr., & Roth, J. A. (eds.) (1993). *Understanding and preventing violence.* Washington, DC: National Academy of Sciences.

Richmond, J. B., Stipek, D. J., & Zigler, E. (1979). A decade of Head Start. In E. Zigler & J. Valentine (eds.), *Project Head Start.* New York: Free Press.

Roberts, A. R. (1989) *Juvenile justice: Policies, programs, and services.* Chicago: Dorsey.

Roehl, J. A., Huitt, R., Wycoff, M. A., Pate, A. M., Rebovich, D. J., & Coyle, K. R. (1995). *National process evaluation of the Weed and Seed Initiative, cross-site summary report*. Pacific Grove, CA: Institute for Social Analysis.

Roehl, J. A., Huitt, R., Wycoff, M. A., Pate, A. M., Rebovich, D. J., & Coyle, K. R. (1996). National process evaluation of the Weed and Seed Initiative. *Research in Brief* series, Washington, DC: U.S. Department of Justice, National Institute of Justice.

Rosenbaum, D. P. (1987). The theory and research beyond Neighborhood Watch: Is it a sound fear and crime reduction strategy? *Crime and Delinquency* 33, 103-134.

Rosenbaum, D. P. (1988a). Community crime prevention: A review and synthesis of the literature. *Justice Quarterly* 5, 323–395.

Rosenbaum, D. P. (1988b). A critical eye on Neighborhood Watch: A theoretical and empirical critique. In T. Hope & M. Shaw (eds.) *Communities and crime reduction* (pp. 126–145). London: Her Majesty's Stationery Office.

Rosenbaum, D. P., Bennett, S., Lindsay, B., Wilkinson, D. (1994). *Community responses to drug abuse: A program evaluation*. Washington, DC: U. S. Department of Justice, National Institute of Justice.

Rosenbaum, D. P., Lavrakas, P. J., Wilkinson, D., & Faggiani, D. (1997). *Estimating the effects of community responses to drugs: Final impact evaluation report*. Chicago, IL: Center for Research in Law and Justice, University of Illinois at Chicago.

Rutter, M. (1979) Maternal deprivation, 1972–1978: New findings, new concepts, new approaches. *Child Development* 50, 283–305.

Rutter, M. & Giller, H. (1983). *Juvenile delinquency: Trends and perspectives*. London: Penguin.

Sampson, R. J. (1986). Crime in cities: The effects of formal and informal social control. In A. J. Reiss, Jr. and

M. Tonry (eds.) *Communities and crime* (Vol. 8 of M. Tonry & N. Morris, eds., *Crime and justice: A review of research*). Chicago: University of Chicago Press.

Schlossman, S. & Sedlak, M. (1983). *The Chicago Area Project revisited*. Santa Monica, CA: Rand.

Schlossman, S., Zellman, G., and Shavelson, R. (1984). *Delinquency prevention in South Chicago: A fifty-year assessment of the Chicago Area Project*. Santa Monica, CA: Rand.

Schorr, L. B. (1988). *Within our reach: Breaking the cycle of disadvantage*. New York: Doubleday.

Schuerman, L. & Kobrin, S. (1986). Community careers in crime. In A. J. Reiss, Jr., & M. Tony (eds.) *Communities and crime* (Vol. 8 of *Crime and Justice: An annual review of research*). Chicago: University of Chicago Press.

Schweinhart, L. J. (1987). Can preschool programs help prevent delinquency? In J. Q. Wilson & G. C. Loury (eds.), *Families, schools, and delinquency prevention* (Vol. 3 of *From children to citizens*.) New York: Springer-Verlag.

Schweinhart, L. J., & Weikart, D. P. (1983). The effects of the Perry Preschool Program on youths through age 15. In Consortium for Longitudinal Studies (ed.). *As the twig is bent…Lasting effects of preschool programs* (pp. 71–101). Hillsdale, NJ: Lawrence Erlbaum.

Seitz, V., Rosenbaum, L. K., & Apfel, N. H. (1985). Effects of family support intervention: A ten-year follow-up. *Child Development* 53, 376–391.

Shaw, C. R. & McKay, H. D. (1931). *Social factors in juvenile delinquency* (Vol. 2, No. 13). Washington, DC: U.S. Government Printing Office.

Shaw, C. R. & McKay, H. D. (1942). *Juvenile delinquency and urban areas*. Chicago: University of Chicago Press.

Silberman, C. E. (1978). *Criminal violence, criminal justice*. New York: Random House.

Spergel, I. A. (1995). *The youth gang problem: A community approach*. New York: Oxford University Press.

Sturz, E. L. & Taylor, M. (1987). Inventing and reinventing Argus: What makes one community organization. *Annals of the American Academy of Political and Social Sciences*, 494, 19–26.

Swarns, R. L. (1997). In a policy shift, more parents are arrested for child neglect. *New York Times*, October 25, p. A1.

Taggart, R. (1981). *A fisherman's guide: An assessment of training and remediation strategies*. Kalamazoo, MI: W. E. Upjohn Institute for Employment Research.

Tonry, M., Ohlin, L. E., & Farrington, D. P. (1991). *Human development and criminal behavior: New ways of advancing knowledge*. New York: Springer-Verlag.

Tremblay, R. E., & Craig, W. (1995). Developmental crime prevention, In M. Tonry & D. Farrington (special editors), *Building a safer society* (Vol. 19 in *Crime and justice*). Chicago, IL: University of Chicago Press.

Trickett, P. K., Apfel, N. H., Rosenbaum, L. K., and Zigler, E. F. (1981). A five-year follow-up of participants in the Yale child welfare research program. In E. F. Zigler & E. W. Gordon (eds.) *Day care: Scientific and social policy issues* (pp. 200–222). Boston: Auburn House.

Underwood, W. (1972). *The national study of youth service bureaus*. Washington, DC: U. S. Department of Health, Education, and Welfare, Youth Development and Delinquency Prevention Administration.

Unger, D. G. & Wandersman, L. P. (1985). Social support and adolescent mothers: Action research contributions to theory and application. *Journal of Social Issues* 41, 29–45.

U.S. Department of Labor (1995). *What's working (and what's not)*. Washington, DC: The author.

Waller, I. (1988). *Current trends in European crime prevention: Implications for Canada*. Canada: Department of Justice.

Widom, C. S. (1992). The cycle of violence. *Research in Brief* series, Washington, DC: U.S. Department of Justice, National Institute of Justice. October.

Widom, C. S. (1995). Victims of childhood sexual abuse—Later consequences. *Research in Brief* series, Washington, DC: U.S. Department of Justice, National Institute of Justice. March.

Wilson, J. J., & Howell, J. C. (1993). *A comprehensive strategy for serious, violent, and chronic juvenile offenders*. Washington, DC: Office of Juvenile Justice and Delinquency Prevention, U.S. Department of Justice.

Wilson, J. Q. (1983). Raising kids. *Atlantic Monthly* (October), 45–56.

Wilson, W. J. (1987). *The truly disadvantaged*. Chicago: University of Chicago Press.

Wilson, J. Q. & Hernstein, R. J. (1985). *Crime and human nature*. New York: Simon & Schuster.

Yoshikawa, H. (1994). Prevention as cumulative protection: Effects of early family support and education on chronic delinquency and its risks. *Psychological Bulletin* 115, 28–54.

Zabin, L. S., Hirsch, M. B., Smith, E. A., Streett, R., & Hardy, J. B. (1986). Evaluation of a pregnancy prevention program for urban teenagers. *Family Planning Perspectives* 18, 119–126.

Zabin, L. S., Streett, R., Hardy, J. B., & King, T. M. (1984). A school-, hospital-, and university-based adolescent pregnancy prevention program. *Journal of Reproductive Medicine* 29, 421–426.

PART VI

Conclusions and Policy Implications

p.232 = blank

11

❂

Some Concluding Thoughts on Crime Prevention

The United States has been fighting a "war" on crime for more than 30 years, and from the beginning policymakers have talked of expanding the role of ordinary citizens in this battle and giving more attention to crime prevention strategies. In this book, we have examined the nature, extent, and effectiveness of a wide range of crime prevention behaviors, programs, and policies. To date, the picture remains incomplete because of the absence of funding for full-scale implementation and evaluation of promising initiatives. Nevertheless, our knowledge of program effectiveness and of issues raised by specific crime prevention strategies has grown substantially during the past three decades. This book provides a summary of that knowledge, with particular emphasis on the contribution of community and situational strategies for preventing crime, disorder, and drug activity.

As a nation, we can be pleased that the crime rate, including the rate of violent crime, has continued to show steady and significant declines since 1992. Whether this is due to the collective strength of preventive strategies, the result of "get tough" criminal justice policies, or other factors remains uncertain. However, we have been able, throughout this book, to comment on the benefits and costs of specific crime prevention strategies in specific communities from which evaluation data are available. Throughout our review of the literature, we have suggested that crime prevention practices are more complex than meets the eye, and that often the effectiveness of these actions is achieved at a cost to society.

INDIVIDUAL
SELF-PROTECTIVE BEHAVIORS

Individuals can, indeed, reduce their chances of becoming crime victims by restricting their behavior and avoiding high-risk persons and environments. The price tag on these avoidance behaviors can be substantial, however, including (1) a loss of freedom or mobility, (2) elevated levels of fear, and (3) possibly an increase in neighborhood crime rates by reducing the number of available guardians who can protect public places. We have learned, for example, that crime prevention programs that sensitize citizens to the risk of crime can increase their fear of crime. Similarly, some precautionary behaviors, such as avoiding going out after dark, can reinforce perceptions that one's neighborhood is a dangerous place. In fact, if everyone thinks this way, the neighborhood might, indeed, become a dangerous place to live.

When risky environments cannot be avoided, considerable evidence indicates that self-defense measures and carrying a weapon can reduce one's chances of victimization by an attacker. For example, contrary to conventional police wisdom, women who physically resist a rapist will generally find this approach effective, with the exception of nonforceful verbal resistance (that is, crying, pleading, and attempting to reason with the rapist is often counterproductive). Surprisingly, armed resistance is one of the most effective responses to attack, but raises an important dilemma for crime prevention policy. By deciding to own a handgun, the individual might experience short-term gains in personal safety, but the long-term safety of the public might be jeopardized. As the number of guns in circulation continues to escalate, there are at least two negative outcomes: (1) the opportunities increase for these weapons to reach the "wrong hands" of juveniles, adult criminals, children, and persons at risk of suicide, and (2) the minimum threshold of acceptable self-protection in public places increases, that is, carrying a gun might be seen as a necessity for self-protection. Given these findings about avoidance, resistance, and weapons, the importance of enrolling in good self-defense training has never been more apparent.

Finally, we know that individuals can purchase and install a wide variety of devices, including locks, safes, cameras, and alarms, to protect their property from crime. These crime prevention efforts, on the whole, appear to be very effective at reducing one's risk of victimization, but the potential side effects for society should not be dismissed out of hand. Given that such protection is limited to persons of upper-income levels who can afford to purchase these crime prevention devices and services, there is the possibility that (1) crime will be displaced to lower-income neighborhoods and households where these defenses are not affordable; and that (2) investment in private crime prevention will reduce the public's interest in paying more taxes for public crime prevention. The privatization of security is a rapidly growing trend, the implications of which have not been fully examined by policy makers or researchers.

Getting the average citizen to participate in individual or collective crime prevention measures has always been a problem, but media campaigns have become a sophisticated means of reaching large audiences. The long-running national McGruff campaign appears to be an effective tool for changing public awareness, attitudes, and behaviors relative to crime prevention, although more controlled studies are needed. We have learned over the years that media anticrime public service announcements are more likely to succeed if the spots focus on specific attitudinal or behavioral change, and if they effectively respond to the known barriers to change. Crime stoppers and other "most wanted" television programs are designed to enhance citizen crime reporting and, indeed, have been credited with clearing at least a small proportion of outstanding felonies, including some of the most notorious. Cash rewards, anonymous callers, and dramatic reenactments have, however, aroused criticism from defense attorneys and civil rights groups that question whether the benefits of such programs outweigh the long-term costs to society. Whether these programs encourage "snitching" and distrust of neighbors or friends and whether they jeopardize the defendant's right to a fair jury trial are unanswered questions.

COMMUNITY MOBILIZATION
AND COLLECTIVE ACTION

At the heart of community crime prevention activity in the United States is the attempt by police and community groups to organize neighborhood residents as participants in Neighborhood Watch or citizen patrol programs. Despite the popularity of these initiatives, controlled evaluations have been unable to find consistent evidence of effectiveness in crime reduction or quality of life measures. Achieving and maintaining strong levels of citizen participation has also been problematic, especially in low-income, high-crime neighborhoods where prevention programs are most needed. A exception to this general conclusion can be found in the community antidrug efforts that emerged in the late 1980s, in which citizens began to "take back the streets" from drug dealers. Surprisingly, these initiatives have emerged disproportionately in poor, inner-city communities that experts had written off as impossible to organize, and they often involved residents working cooperatively with law enforcement authorities. Not all poor inner-city neighborhoods organized against drugs, but those that did often made a real difference in reducing the local drug trade.

Although active patrols, watches, and other collective citizen efforts have yielded considerable anecdotal evidence of increased arrests, drug house closures, and reduced drug activity at specific locations, researchers have yet to establish that such activity can successfully "implant" social order, social control, and social support processes in neighborhoods where they are naturally lacking. Furthermore, these anticrime efforts are often short-lived unless organizers focus on factors that contribute to their longevity, including strong leadership, group structure, links to outside resources, a full agenda, decentralized planning, good communication channels, and a system to reward volunteers for their participation and success. Unless these mobilization efforts remain strong, community leaders are at greater risk of retaliation from drug dealers and gangs in the community, and we have learned about many such incidents in recent years.

As average citizens get more involved in the intense, inner-city "wars" against drugs and gangs, we must continue to be vigilant that the community will does not violate the rights and freedoms of individuals guaranteed by the Constitution. During times of rampant fear of crime, research indicates that citizens are more willing to surrender some rights to restore order and security. Residents living in neighborhoods where drugs and gangs rule are often willing to wink at illegal stop-and-frisk practices by local police and often expect the police to go further than the law will allow them. Most patrols have worked responsibly in coordination with police to prevent crime and apprehend criminals, but at times citizens patrols have resulted in vigilantism, and suspects have been assaulted or threatened.

BURDENING A DYSFUNCTIONAL SYSTEM

Perhaps the most troublesome aspect of community crime prevention activities during the past 25 years is the concentrated focus on removing offenders from the community rather than strengthening the community's capacity to prevent crime. Ironically, citizen participation in anticrime and antidrug initiatives has not solved the problem of an ineffective criminal justice system (our starting point for this book) but, rather, has often exacerbated the problem. The *primary* goal of most community crime prevention programs is to *increase* (not decrease) the number of persons who have contact with the criminal justice system. From Court Watch to Neighborhood Watch, these strategies typically involve citizens working with police and other law enforcement agents to prosecute more offenders with stiffer sanctions in the hope that this will clean up their neighborhoods. The public's fear of violent criminals, fueled by the media's portrayals of young offenders as predators, has led to a mean-spirited response by community residents and lawmakers nationwide, and to strong support for punitive crime control policies.

This strategy of beefing up law enforcement is problematic for several reasons. There is the widespread practice of arresting citizens for minor disorder and drug offenses (zero-tolerance policing). In the short run, these actions can be effective at reducing the levels of visible disorder and drug transactions in particular neighborhoods, but in the long-run, they are likely to be counterproductive. These arrest practices, combined with unchecked police authority, can destroy any hope for the police to develop trusting and cooperative relations with residents in high-crime target areas. Moreover, creating arrest records for young adults will lower their chances of finding legitimate employment in the labor market (see Bushway, 1996). Hence, the stigmatization of a criminal history only increases the odds of these individuals resorting to illegal activities for economic gain, thus contributing to the vicious cycle that fuels the criminal justice system. Finally, there is the staggering cost of expanding the criminal justice system to meet the demands of drug enforcement policies.

As a consequence of these national and local policies, the U.S. prison population has swelled far beyond the capacity of our correctional institutions (Maghan, 1998). During the 10-year period from 1985 to 1995, the number of inmates in U.S. jails and prisons increased 113 percent from 744,208 to 1,585,401 (Gilliard & Beck, 1996). Over this decade, the prison population showed an average increase of 7.9 percent annually, adding about 1,618 inmates per week. At the end of 1985, 1 in every 320 United States residents were incarcerated, but by the end of 1995, this figure had changed to 1 in every 167 residents. Despite building new prisons, officials report that, in 1995, federal facilities are operating at 126 percent of their capacity, and state facilities are operating at between 114 percent and 125 percent capacity.

In essence, citizen participation in anticrime efforts is often little more than a new arm of the criminal justice system—a system that appears to be headed in a disturbing direction. These trends include a preference for punishment (over rehabilitation), determinant sentencing, and incapacitation. The enormous cost of building and maintaining new prisons has become a substantial burden to the taxpayers, and, unfortunately, little evidence can be found to support the underlying premise that incarceration is an effective crime prevention strategy (see Reiss & Roth, 1993). Above all, the growing cost of, and preoccupation with, law enforcement strategies has reduced the opportunities to fund more promising alternatives to incarceration. The cost of enforcement programs could go a long way toward funding prevention programs that promise to lower specific opportunities for crime or alter the individual's predisposition toward criminality.

The community policing movement, despite being partially trapped within the enforcement paradigm, holds considerable promise for helping communities look at problems differently and reforming the police role in this process. By focusing on the creation of interagency partnerships and problem solving strategies, some communities have been able to step "outside the box" and explore new approaches to crime prevention. The formation of diverse partnerships and coalitions helps distribute the responsibility for crime prevention among a wide range of agencies and institutions, and the problem solving model can help produce creative solutions for neighborhood problems (see Kelling, Rocheleau, Rosenbaum, Roth, Skogan, & Walsh, 1997). None of these outcomes is guaranteed and, in fact, success requires strong leadership at the highest levels of city government, multiyear funding, and exceptional program managers.

SITUATIONAL AND ENVIRONMENTAL
CRIME PREVENTION

If communities are struggling to find effective ways to change the behavior of local residents (either their willingness to engage in crime prevention activities or their predisposition to offend), there remains the option of making crime more difficult to commit in specific situations. Situational crime prevention has been instrumental in elaborating a theory of crime prevention and encouraging the development of detailed technologies for preventing specific crimes. It has been notably successful in controlling theft from public and commercial places, although the evaluation research in this field has been weak. Certainly adopting exact fare policies on buses and using video cameras to surveil potential vandals, robbers, or thieves have become widespread. But, in many ways, the most interesting and unique work to develop from the situational crime prevention perspective is the realization that persons once victimized are at far higher risk than others of future victimization. The emerging methods being used to reduce repeat victimization are likely to become important tools for law enforcement and community leaders in their efforts to bring down area crime rates.

The principles of crime prevention through environmental design (CPTED) have been incorporated into our daily lives through the work of architects, urban planners, and law enforcement agencies. Across the country, notorious high-rise public housing projects are being torn down in favor of low-rise structures with more defensible spaces. Urban design and redesign projects are assembled to ensure greater use and surveillance of public spaces, as well as increased territoriality and social cohesion. The evaluation evidence has been mixed and controlled studies have been rare, but practitioners have shown a renewed enthusiasm for the application of this approach. Researchers have learned that changes to the physical environment require a multiyear time frame, strong political support, and cooperation from all groups involved. We have also learned that changes in the physical environment, although time-consuming, are easier to achieve than changes in the social environment. Physical design features that enhance "defensible space" have been less effective in socially fragmented environments. Also, using CPTED techniques in residential neighborhoods—such as barricades, gates, and security guards on public streets—has led to some concerns about discrimination against minorities. Furthermore, although evidence suggests that cul-de-sacs, one-way streets, and other access strategies are effective crime prevention measures, they are also inconvenient for local residents. In essence, there is a price to be paid for nearly every crime prevention measure.

Situational crime prevention, despite considerable promise, also carries a potentially large price tag in a free society. Efforts to prevent crime can sometimes result in outcomes that we do not intend, and as crime prevention technologies become more sophisticated, these risks increase. We certainly have not succeeded as a civilization if we achieve low crime rates at the expense of other social conditions that we value. The thoughtless application of crime prevention programs can, for example, erode our feelings of community and security—conditions that such anticrime measures were designed, in part, to protect. Barbed wire fences, guard dogs, and security cameras are effective deterrents to criminals, but they create urban spaces that are foreboding rather than welcoming to citizens. These measures communicate the message that a place is not safe, and such perceptions are not conducive to the social cohesion of communities. In fact, they encourage suspicion of others and withdrawal from public spaces. As another example, placing bank tellers and liquor store owners behind bullet-proof glass discourages robberies, but also makes impossible informal conversation and vitiates the role that local retail establishments can play in knitting communities together. The rapidly growing use of visible cameras and recording devices by government, private industry, and even private citizens is a concern to many Americans, as it suggests that "big brother" is watching.

Finally, situational crime prevention measures applied without regard to their consequences can make everyday life just that much more complicated. Several decades ago, bus robberies were a common occurrence in many cities. Now, thanks to exact fare policies, they are virtually nonexistent. But how much time does the public spend seeking change to ride the bus? How many appointments have been missed because people forgot to carry exact change? How much has the inconvenience of remembering to carry exact change contributed to the loss of ridership on public conveyances? When we can answer these kinds of questions, we will be better able to judge the social costs as well as the known benefits of crime prevention programs.

SOCIAL CRIME PREVENTION INITIATIVES

The criminal justice system would not be the focus of our discussion about crime prevention policies if we, as a society, were doing a better job of raising healthy children and protecting them from the forces that contribute to delinquency, drug abuse, and criminality. The social prevention model redirects our attention to these risk factors and offers a variety of interventions to improve the health, family life, education, housing, work opportunities, and neighborhood activities of at-risk and youthful offenders. This model deserves more attention in the national crime prevention debate because of the potential gains and cost savings that can result from early intervention in the developmental process.

Programs that are responsive to known risk factors at different stages of human development should be the most effective at preventing violence and other problem behaviors. We have considerable research knowledge regarding the risk factors for delinquency and drug abuse, but less knowledge regarding the effectiveness of protective factors. Nevertheless, experiments in early child-hood and family support programs show encouraging results. We have learned, for example, that home visits by professionals can make a significant difference in the lives of children and their parents. Preschool programs can also be ef-fective, but only under the right conditions. Some of these include a profes-sional staff that is knowledgeable about early childhood development; a curriculum based on child development principles that is adequately sup-ported, managed, and evaluated; high teacher-pupil ratios; small classes; close collaboration between teachers and parents; and integration with local re-sources and services. Unfortunately, our society has been unwilling to invest fully in flexible, individualized, intensive and professional services because of the cost and time implications. In the long run, however, effective prevention programs are likely to be much cheaper than what we have today, namely, ex-pensive criminal justice and welfare bureaucracies that are overburdened, inef-ficient, ineffective, and discriminatory.

When it comes to handling known juvenile offenders, the solutions are less clear, and our society is conflicted about the proper course of action. The available evidence and common sense tells us what *not* to do—do not incapacitate young adolescents for extended periods (unless they are repeat violent offenders), and do not wait for delinquent youth to commit multiple offenses before taking action. The literature suggests that successful programs for serious or chronic offenders (1) are comprehensive and intensive; (2) are delivered by energetic and committed staff; (3) incorporate a case manage-ment approach that follows the youth from intake to discharge; (4) are linked to the specific needs and problems of the individual; (5) address issues related to community, peers, school, and work; and (6) provide treatment while the youth is living at home or in the community, but always in the "least restric-tive environment possible."

Thus, the successful treatment of delinquent youth will require that com-munities step up and play a major role. Community volunteers, community policing officers, probation officers, teachers, social service providers, and family members must work together to restore justice for the community and to rehabilitate and reintegrate delinquent youth. One major goal should be to minimize (rather than to increase) youths' contact with the court sys-tem. National studies suggest that coordinated partnerships between law en-forcement, schools, government, and community leaders can lead to a network of services for juveniles. Whether these coalitions will be effective has yet to be determined.

MACROLEVEL FORCES

In this book, we have suggested that a variety of community, situational, and social crime prevention programs show promise as effective responses to crime—at least in the short run—despite some serious concerns about their possible untoward effects on society. Although these crime prevention programs may make a difference under specific conditions, we feel compelled to temper our conclusion by highlighting the role of macrolevel forces in shaping the quality of life in urban neighborhoods. The problems of inner-city neighborhoods run deeper than the difficulties of organizing a march against gangs or locating mentors for at-risk kids. We must be honest with ourselves and the residents of these communities: The reality is that community members do not have complete control over the events that occur in their neighborhoods. Therefore, effective interventions must look outside the neighborhood for help. Community crime prevention strategies must reach beyond teaching residents how to be the "eyes and ears" of the police to showing them how to leverage resources at city hall and in key state and federal agencies. Empowerment must extend beyond conventional door-to-door organizing to what Hope (1995) calls "vertical" strategies for community crime prevention. All agencies and institutions that provide services to the community will need to be involved in a comprehensive effort to improve the neighborhood.

But the problems are even deeper than leveraging resources from the outside and empowerment issues. We must admit that market forces and government polices have a substantial influence on the level of public safety and quality of life in the inner city. Historically, there is reason to believe that local and federal policies have contributed to crime by producing segregating housing and labor markets, which have only intensified the negative effects of poverty (Hirsch, 1983; Massey & Denton, 1993; Sampson & Lauritsen, 1993; Skogan, 1986; Wilson, 1987). Efforts to correct these problems in the 1990s and beyond are likely to make matters worse, at least in the short run. For example, the current reform of public housing policies, including the widespread demolition of high-rise public housing, and the reduction in federal housing supports for the poor, will undoubtedly increase the number of homeless persons (see Allen, 1997), which in turn, is likely to intensify a wide range of criminal justice and health problems. Similarly, the current welfare reform process will cut benefits and remove the income safety net for millions of American families. Finally, the growing exodus of middle-class blacks and whites from public to private schools, fueled by government vouchers, will leave inner-city public school systems as little more than warehouses for America's poor, thus exacerbating the vicious cycle of neighborhood decline and poverty.

In the absence of intensive efforts to provide better education, jobs, and industry apprenticeships to those who are trapped in these pockets of concentrated poverty, we can expect these neighborhoods to suffer increases in violence and other forms of criminality in the years ahead. Efforts to create self-sufficiency among the underclass via welfare and housing reform can yield long-term benefits if properly designed and managed, but in the next decade, we can expect a period of "darkness before the dawn."

Beyond government policies, a wide variety of changes in the labor force are expected to widen even further the well-documented income gap between the rich and the poor. These factors include continued technological developments that give the advantage to skilled workers, increased immigration and women in the labor force, and growing international trade. Collectively, these changes place a damper on the short-term success of community crime prevention measures and remind us that the long-term vitality of urban neighborhoods will be determined more by our ability to forecast, prepare for, and control some external factors that affect urban neighborhoods. Clearly, there is an urgent need to establish close working partnerships among government, the private sector, and educational institutions to prepare a new labor force and create opportunities for legitimate employment of inner city residents.

Some portion of the dilemma we face with the prevention of urban violence relates to our nation's ideological and political orientation. In a nutshell, a free capitalist economy, driven by individualist (rather than collective or communal) motives does not bode well for the disadvantaged. In the absence of a strong "community" motive, crime prevention policy experts will need to appeal to self-interest. Short-term solutions to deep and complex inner-city problems will only cost the tax payers more in the long haul. In a nutshell, the prevention of crime is everyone's business, and to achieve dramatic success, we must begin to think about variables that are not fully explored in this book. We have reason to believe that levels of crime and delinquency in our society are influenced by macrolevel social policies regarding public housing, welfare, public education, health benefits, and other major interventions in the lives of those for whom the American dream has yet to be fulfilled. The United States is currently at the cross-roads on many of these watershed issues. We will soon learn whether our nation can develop humane and effective policies on health, welfare, housing, and education—policies that strengthen individual self-sufficiency, work habits, commitment to marriage, good parenting, and community values, while discouraging government dependency, drug abuse, criminality, poor health, and a host of other costly social problems.

Researchers and policy analysts will continue to question what works and what does not, but lawmakers must remember that the lack of scientific evidence regarding program effectiveness is not an excuse to walk away from our urban problems. The challenge before America is to develop cost-effective preventative solutions for the ills that increasingly characterize metropolitan areas. We cannot escape the costs associated with these problems, no matter how far we move away or how much money we spend to isolate ourselves from the visible pain and suffering of violence, ignorance, unemployment, and poverty. The future is promising *only* if we demonstrate the courage and will to improve the plight of all Americans in all communities.

REFERENCES

Allen, J. L. (1997). "Housing crunch looms for the poor." *Chicago Tribune*, September 29, Section 4, p. 1.

Bushway, S. (1996). *The impact of a criminal history record on access to legitimate employment*. Unpublished doctoral dissertation. H. John Heinz School of Public Policy and Management, Carnegie Mellon University.

Gilliard, D. K., & Beck, A. J. (1996). Prison and jail inmates, 1995. *Bureau of Justice Statistics Bulletin*, August, NCJ-161132. Bureau of Justice Statistics. Washington, DC: U.S. Government Printing Office.

Hirsch, A. R. (1983). *Making the second ghetto: Race and housing in Chicago, 1940– 1960*. Chicago: University of Chicago Press.

Kelling, G. L., Rocheleau, A. M., Rosenbaum, D. P., Roth, J. A., Skogan, W. G., & Walsh, N. (1997). *Preliminary cross-site analysis of the Bureau of Justice Assistance comprehensive communities program*. Final report to the National Institute of Justice. Cambridge, MA: BOTEC Analysis Corporation.

Maghan, J. (1998). Corrections countdown: Today's inmates. In P. Carlson & J. S. Garrett (eds.). *Prisons and jail administration: Organization, principles, and practices*. Gaithersburg, MD: Aspen.

Massey, D. S., & Denton, N. A. (1993). *American apartheid: Segregation and the making of the underclass*. Cambridge, MA: Harvard University Press.

Reiss, A. J., Jr., & Roth, J. A. (eds.) (1993). *Understanding and preventing violence*. Washington, DC: National Academy of Sciences.

Sampson, R. J., & Lauritsen, J. L. (1993). Violent victimization and offending: Individual-, situational-, and community-level risk factors. In A. J. Reiss, Jr., & J. A. Roth (eds.) *Understanding and preventing violence* (Vol. 3, *Social influences*). Washington, DC: National Academy of Sciences.

Skogan, W. G. (1986). Fear of crime and neighborhood change. In A. J. Reiss, Jr., & M. Tonry (eds.), *Communities and crime* (Vol. 8 in M. Tonry & N. Morris [eds.] *Crime and justice: An annual review of research*). Chicago: University of Chicago Press.

Wilson, W. J. (1987). *The truly disadvantaged*. Chicago: University of Chicago Press.

p.244 = blank

Author Index

Subject Index